An Appetizing State

This book is dedicated to the great state of North Carolina; to its rich soil and agricultural traditions; to its fertile coastal fisheries, lakes, and rivers; and to its people, for continuing the customs and traditions that make North Carolina An Appetizing State.

NORTH CAROLINA

An *Appetizing* State

menus | recipes | traditions

The North Carolina Museum of History Associates is a statewide support and membership group that provides awareness of and funding for the North Carolina Museum of History in Raleigh and its branch and regional museums.

This copper kettle (ca. 1775-1777) was used by General Francis Nash during the American Revolution. Nash, a native of Hillsborough, was given command of the North Carolina brigade of the Continental Army under George Washington and was one of only ten Revolutionary generals to die from wounds received during the war. The city of Nashville, and Nash County, are named in his honor.

SPONSORS

Sponsors

Butterball Turkey

Neese's Country Sausage

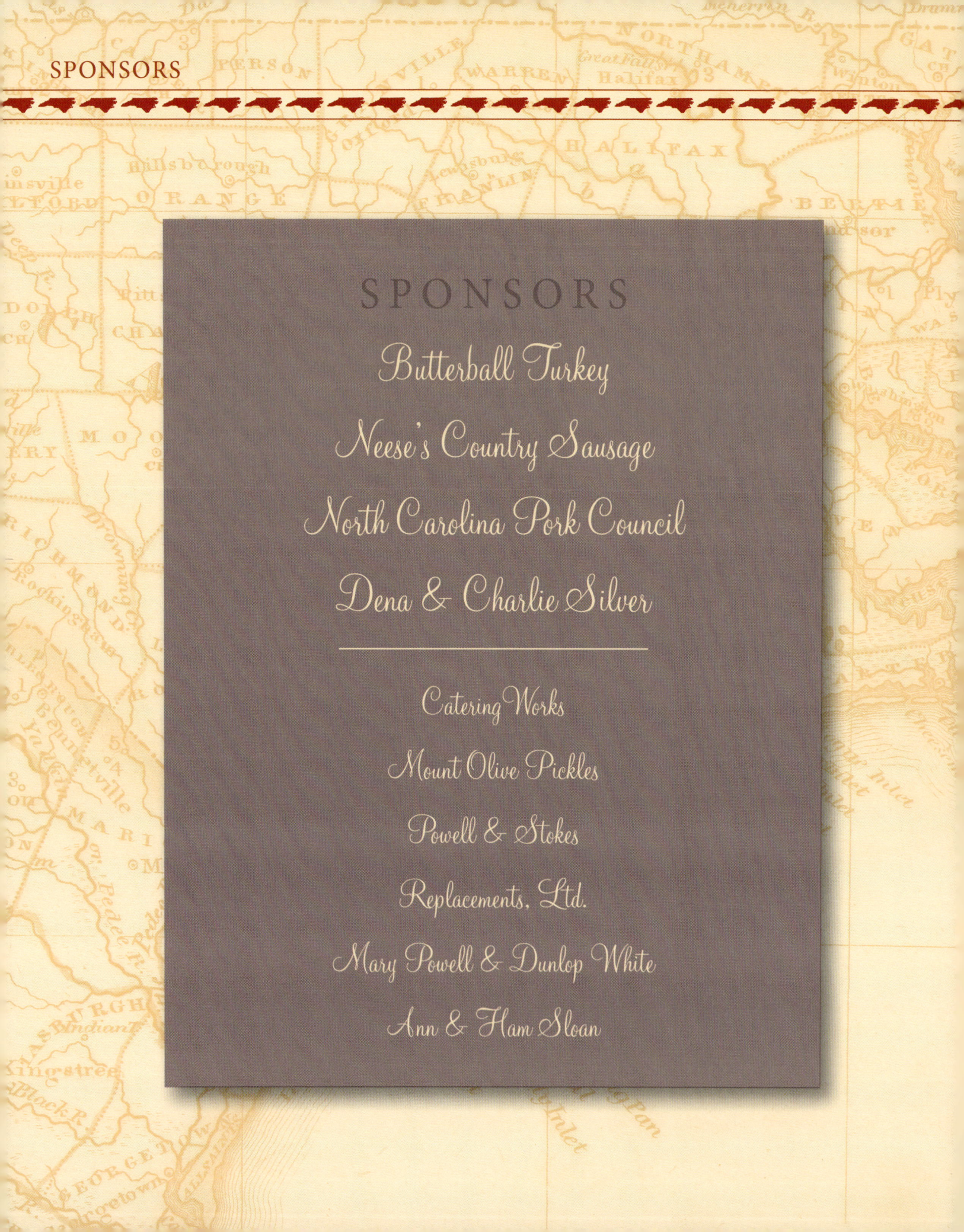

North Carolina Pork Council

Dena & Charlie Silver

Catering Works

Mount Olive Pickles

Powell & Stokes

Replacements, Ltd.

Mary Powell & Dunlop White

Ann & Ham Sloan

COOKBOOK COMMITTEE

Cookbook Co-Chairs

Betty Anne Lennon
Charlie Silver

Producing a cookbook is no small undertaking, especially when it is a volunteer-driven effort that aims to reflect an entire state's culinary history. Those volunteers, and their leadership and dedication, are the reason this project, three years in the making, has been successful and become a reality. The North Carolina Museum of History Associates is tremendously grateful for their extraordinary efforts and for the support of its many friends who shared special recipes and stories.

Recipe and Tasting Committee Chairs

Edwina Shaw
Flo Winston

This cookbook is full of special recipes and family stories submitted from folks across North Carolina and from out-of-state friends, as well. The response was so plentiful that we, unfortunately, were not able to share all that we received. Of the recipes we were able to include, each one has been verified from preparation to taste by the remarkable members of our tasting committee.

Recipe and Tasting Committee

Liz Crute
Ginny Kirkland
Sydney Langford
Jill Moye
Ann Peden
Tricia Phoenix
Kay Schoellhorn
Beth Steed
Margaret Steed
Lianda Taylor
Cathy Ward
Robin Zevenhuizen

These dedicated "foodies" gave their time and culinary talents to assure that this cookbook includes the best-of-the-best recipes for your table. After careful food preparation, committee members spent countless hours selecting the right recipes for our new taste of North Carolina. Without them, and their discerning palates, none of this work would have been possible.

Freeman Woods, a noted silversmith and skilled engraver, was a New Jersey native who relocated to New Bern, North Carolina, to open a silver- and gold-smithing shop. This teapot (ca. 1766–1834) is typical of his work, which was noted for its simplicity, graceful lines, perfect proportion, and artful embellishment. Woods advertised in the North Carolina Gazette *that he offered a large number of service pieces "made in the newest fashion and at short notice."*

FOREWORD

*N*othing is more sacred than a meal around a table... a place where people come together to enjoy the blessings of life, food, and fellowship... and a time when cherished memories—some that become our most valuable treasures—are made.

Some of my treasured memories were made around my grandparents' table, enjoying the meal that we begged our grandmother to make for us again and again. It was during those Sunday meals that my grandfather would mesmerize us with stories of North Carolina. I dare anyone to find another soul on this Earth more proud of North Carolina than my grandfather—Thad Eure Sr., Secretary of State for 52 years. Sitting around that table of food and memories and tales, he made North Carolina history come alive for us. Which is why I am most pleased to introduce this book.

The North Carolina Museum of History's first cookbook, *A Taste of History*, came out 30 years ago. That collection of recipes, which was published by the museum support group, the Museum of History Associates, was so popular that this second cookbook had to be created. More than simply a cookbook, *North Carolina, An Appetizing State* combines delicious recipes with the rich history of North Carolina and provides a fascinating look at the diverse regions of our state. The chosen recipes reflect countless hours by professional chefs and home cooks who toiled over each recipe. Historians and experts on our state's history have added some special ingredients of their own: pieces of the culture and tradition that make this state authentically unique. These storied recipes will renew your love of North Carolina as they transport you back into the kitchens of the Old North State.

In the words of Leonora Martin and Mary Burke Kerr:

Here's to the land of the longleaf pine,
The summer land where the sun doth shine,
Where the weak grow strong and the strong grow great,
Here's to "down home," the Old North State!

Our favorite recipes are the ones we ask our parents and grandparents to make over and over. I believe some of the recipes in this book will be added to the request list your children and friends have for you. Think of the carefully selected menus here as a foundation for creating your own blend of Tar Heel hospitality.

And remember—everything's better when it's prepared with love.

Van Eure
Owner of The Angus Barn

TABLE OF CONTENTS

Introduction 10

NORTHEASTERN REGION 12
Eastern Shore Hunt & Gather Menu 14
Late-Afternoon Tea Party Menu 20

COASTAL REGION 26
Coastal Bounty Seafood Dinner Menu 28
Al Fresco Seaside Menu 34

AGRICULTURAL REGION 40
Down East Supper Menu 42
Farm-to-Table Vegetarian Menu 48

CENTRAL REGION 54
Tobacco Road Tailgate Menu 56
'Tis the Season Holiday Menu 62

SANDHILLS REGION 70
Laissez-faire Brunch Menu 72
Steeplechase Picnic Menu 78

PIEDMONT REGION 84
Continental Breakfast Menu 86
From the Hearth Simple Menu 92

This silver ladle (ca. 1898–1900) is from the Museum of History's vast silver collection and could be representative of a kitchen tool or other item that is passed down through generations—much like many of the recipes in our new cookbook.

The North Carolina Museum of History is part of the North Carolina Department of Cultural Resources. It is the flagship museum of the Division of State History Museums, which collects and preserves artifacts and other historical materials relating to the history and heritage of North Carolina—in a local, regional, national, and international context—to assist people in understanding how the past influences the present.

TABLE OF CONTENTS

The meat and vegetable chopper (ca. 1870–1900), invented one hundred years before the food processor, would have been considered one of the most useful and labor-saving inventions of its time.

FOOTHILLS REGION 98
Uptown Power Lunch Menu 100
Cosmopolitan Cocktail Party Menu 106

MOUNTAIN REGION 112
Down Home Family-Style Menu 114
Horn of Plenty Thanksgiving Menu 120

BEVERAGES & APPETIZERS 128

SOUPS & SALADS 140

ENTRÉES & MAIN DISHES 148

VEGETABLES & SIDE DISHES 164

SWEETS & DESSERTS 174

Index 188
Recipe Contributors 191
Acknowledgments 192

INTRODUCTION

North Carolina is blessed with many natural attributes favorable to agriculture and food production. Good soil, a moderate climate, and a long growing season, along with abundant seafood, have been central to keeping North Carolina's cupboards full throughout colonial and state history.

When it comes to preparing food, historian John Beck of Elon University cites four primary influences on North Carolina's cuisine: Native Americans; English settlers; Scots-Irish settlers; and West Africans. Native Americans brought a focus on corn, squash, pumpkins, beans, and sweet potatoes—and they barbecued meat.

The English introduced milk, cheese, roasted meats, soup, and beer, while the Scots-Irish added kale, turnips, collards, and distilled beverages to the table. West African fare conditioned palates to highly spiced soups, stews, okra, and sugar.

The past informs us. Long ago many North Carolinians cooked on open pits, a tradition carried on today in the preparation of barbecue. Because early settlers had to preserve food for their very survival, they perfected ways of curing hams, an art still practiced today. In a sense we can actually taste our history.

Corn, which has always been prominent in North Carolina, was the state's leading crop into the eighteenth century. Corn sustained people and their livestock—and corn bread and grits were staples for the dinner table.

These foods are still part of Tar Heel diets today, but not as regularly as they used to be. In our age of luxury and convenience, when you find yourself complaining about a crowded grocery store or the stress of preparing a big meal, just remember the Moravians of the mid-1700s during their first year at Wachovia Tract near present-day Winston-Salem. In 1900, John H. Clewell, the principal of Salem Female Academy, wrote of the challenges of his forebears: "During the days following their arrival, the Brethren had chiefly pumpkins and cornmeal. When the first stag was killed in November, we were glad of it as corn alone is not good eating. In December, the Moravians went sixty miles for salt. In January, they made maple syrup. In July, they made vinegar from blackberries, and in July the first butter was churned."

Whether you're guided by family customs, ethnic or religious heritage, or other influences, we hope you'll find something to whet your appetite within these pages. Meanwhile, you and your family's recipes and culinary traditions continue to add to the rich heritage of food and cooking in North Carolina, our appetizing state.

INTRODUCTION

This rare, blue transfer-printed pearlware platter (ca. 1826–1838) features a floral border surrounding an oval reserve inscribed "NORTH CAROLINA." The central scene represents North Carolina's state seal, and the reverse of the rim bears a transfer-printed representation of the Great Seal of the United States above the mark of Staffordshire potter T. [Thomas] Mayer. Mayer, an English potter, had an extensive trade with America and is known for creating many printed wares with Romantic American themes for export trade.

NORTHEASTERN REGION

Northeastern North Carolina is a region of farms and charming small towns featuring soil as rich as its considerable history. Flat and ancient, elevations in this section range from sea level to two hundred feet, and the low-lying land lays claim to many historical firsts and superlatives. Since World War II, peanuts have been a leading crop of the region, making North Carolina a national leader in production of this versatile little legume.

On Roanoke Island in the 1580s, the first English settlements in the New World were established; there in 1587 Virginia Dare was born—the first child in America born to English parents. The state's first established town, Bath, is also the site of the state's oldest church, St. Thomas. Nathaniel Batts, a rugged fur-trader, is thought to be the first independent European settler in North Carolina. In the mid-1600s, Batts and his family settled between the Chowan and Roanoke Rivers.

Lake Mattamuskeet is the largest natural lake in North Carolina. Largely known for its wildfowl, the lake bed made some of the most productive farmland in the state during the 19-teens into the 1930s, when it was regularly pumped dry in an effort emulating drainage techniques of Holland. The lake bottom produced bountiful crops of rice, wheat, and soybeans, but the challenge to pump it was overwhelming.

The Dismal Swamp is considerably smaller than it once was, but this still vast place that was daunting to early travelers is now bisected by a four-lane U.S. 17 and the Intracoastal Waterway, and tourists are welcomed at Dismal Swamp State Park.

The Wright Brothers first went airborne at Kitty Hawk and today in mainland Dare County, the U.S. Navy takes aerial bombing practice in an exceedingly remote section, where, too, sometimes U.S. Navy Seals train. The town of Washington, the first community named to honor George Washington, is in Beaufort County, and nearby Washington County is the first president's namesake, too.

Edenton has been around nearly three hundred years and has long been prominent in North Carolina; in and near it are the oldest buildings in the state. Today it attracts tourists and retirees and is a leading community in historic preservation.

The women of Edenton demonstrated courageous leadership in 1774 when they staged the Edenton Tea Party. Fifty-one patriotic ladies led by Penelope Barker gathered over tea and signed an agreement to do everything they could to support the American cause for independence. Even the London newspapers took note. Gatherings in the Northeast aren't always so serious, but for one reason or another, folks in the region still come together over food and beverage, though now it's more likely a shrimparoo instead of a tea party.

NORTHEASTERN REGION

EASTERN SHORE HUNT & GATHER MENU

Duck Appetizer with Asian Sauce

Duck Breast Salad

Salmon in Ginger Sauce

Cold Curried Rice with English Peas

Roasted Asparagus

Sour Cream Muffins

Lemon Chess Pie

EASTERN SHORE HUNT & GATHER

Duck Appetizer with Asian Sauce

2½ pounds pintail or mallard duck breasts
1 (24-ounce) bottle Italian salad dressing
¾ cup soy sauce
Dipping Sauce

Dipping Sauce
¾ to 1 cup apricot preserves
2½ cups sweet Asian chili sauce
2½ tablespoons Sriracha sauce or
½ teaspoon red pepper flakes
2 tablespoons minced fresh ginger
1 tablespoon red wine vinegar

Rinse the duck and pat dry. Place the duck in a sealable plastic bag. Mix the salad dressing and soy sauce in a bowl and pour over the duck. Seal the bag and turn to coat. Marinate in the refrigerator overnight. Remove the duck and discard the marinade. Grill the duck over a medium-hot fire until cooked through. Remove the duck to a cutting board and let rest for 10 minutes. Cut into strips and serve with the Dipping Sauce.

Dipping Sauce
Stir the preserves, chili sauce, Sriracha sauce, ginger and vinegar in a saucepan. Bring to a slow boil over low heat, stirring frequently. Serve warm.
Serves 14 to 16
Note: The sauce can be kept in the refrigerator for up to 4 weeks.

Duck Breast Salad

6 cups chopped romaine
6 cups baby spinach
3 cups orange segments
2 cups blueberries
12 cooked duck breasts, sliced
¼ cup white balsamic vinegar
¾ cup extra-virgin olive oil
1 teaspoon Dijon mustard
1 teaspoon salt
1 teaspoon pepper
½ cup teriyaki sauce
1½ cups toasted salted walnut pieces

This can also be made as individual salads, using equal portions of the salad, duck, dressing, and walnuts.

Combine the romaine, spinach, oranges and blueberries in a large bowl and toss to mix. Remove to a large serving platter and arrange the duck over the salad. Whisk the vinegar, olive oil, Dijon mustard, salt and pepper in a bowl until emulsified. Whisk in the teriyaki sauce. Drizzle over the duck and salad and sprinkle with the walnuts.
Serves 12

As hunting in the Old World was largely restricted to aristocrats with access to fields and pastures, many colonists learned the art of hunting from Native Americans who frequently used decoys to attract live birds. Decoys, such as this canvasback drake duck decoy (ca. 1920) made by James Best and drake redhead duck decoy (ca. 1995) made by Homer Fulcher, would have been used by commercial hunters and sportsmen to lure their prey.

EASTERN SHORE HUNT & GATHER

Salmon in Ginger Sauce

1/4 cup (1/2 stick) butter
1 teaspoon curry powder
1/2 teaspoon crushed saffron
2 1/2 to 3 pounds (1-inch) salmon fillets, pin bones removed
2 tablespoons lime juice
2 tablespoons minced fresh ginger
1/2 cup sliced green onions
1/4 cup white wine
1 teaspoon salt
1 teaspoon freshly ground pepper

Heat the butter in a small saucepan over low heat until foamy. Remove from the heat and stir in the curry powder and saffron. Let stand for 15 minutes. Arrange the fillets in the center of a large piece of baking parchment paper, allowing 6 to 7 inches of paper to extend beyond the fish on all sides. Drizzle the butter mixture evenly over the fish and sprinkle with the lime juice, ginger and green onions. Drizzle the wine over the top and sprinkle with the salt and pepper. Bring opposite sides of the parchment paper together over the fish. Pinch together and fold down to the fish. Tuck the remaining sides of the parchment paper under the fish to seal the fish inside the parchment. Set the parchment packet in a shallow baking dish. Bake at 375 degrees for 16 to 20 minutes. Open the parchment packet carefully. Remove the fish and sauce to serve.

Serves 6 to 8

CURRIED SALMON SALAD

Make Curried Salmon Salad with leftover salmon. Combine 3/4 cup mayonnaise, 6 tablespoons each lemon juice and chopped chutney, 1/2 to 1 teaspoon curry powder and salt and pepper to taste in a small bowl. Mix 2 cups poached fresh salmon, and 1 chopped medium cucumber and green onion in a bowl. Add 1/3 of the mayonnaise mixture or to taste and toss lightly. Serve stuffed in 4 to 6 large tomatoes or on lettuce leaves.

ANNE'S BAKED SHAD EXQUISITE

I acquired this recipe from a nutritionist and graduate of The University of North Carolina at Greensboro. She authored North Carolina Home Cooking From the Highlands to The Lowlands.

Sprinkle the inside and outside of a 1 1/2- to 5-pound shad with salt, pepper and paprika. Prepare enough Pepperidge Farm Stuffing mix according to the package directions to fill the fish cavity. Sprinkle the inside of the fish with lemon juice; fill with the stuffing. Place the fish on the greased top layer of 3 layers of foil; fold and seal the foil to enclose the fish. Place on a baking sheet. Bake at 250 degrees for 5 to 5 1/2 hours for a 2-pound fish or 5 1/2 to 6 1/2 hours for a 2 1/2-pound fish or until the fish flakes easily. Open the foil; cut the fish into slices, including stuffing with each slice.

NORTHEASTERN REGION

Cold Curried Rice with English Peas

Cook the rice mix according to the package directions and let cool. Mix the rice, 1/4 teaspoon curry powder, 1 cup peas and onion in a bowl. Whisk the oil, soy sauce, vinegar, 1 teaspoon curry powder, sugar and salt in a small bowl. Add to the rice mixture and toss to coat. Chill, covered, for 2 to 24 hours. Garnish with additional peas and red bell pepper strips and serve.

Serves 8

Note: English peas are the same as green peas.

1 cup long grain and wild rice mix
1/4 teaspoon curry powder
1 cup frozen English peas, thawed
1/4 cup diced onion
1/2 cup vegetable oil
3 tablespoons soy sauce
2 tablespoons cider vinegar
1 teaspoon curry powder
1 teaspoon sugar
1/4 teaspoon salt
Additional peas and red bell pepper strips

Ann's Roasted Asparagus

Break off and discard the tough ends of the asparagus. Arrange the asparagus in a shallow baking pan. Drizzle with the olive oil and roll the asparagus spears to coat with oil. Sprinkle with the salt. Roast at 450 degrees for 8 to 15 minutes or until tender-crisp. Drizzle with the lemon juice and remove to a serving platter. Sprinkle with almonds and garnish with small lemon slices.

Serves 8

1 pound asparagus
1 tablespoon olive oil
1/2 teaspoon sea salt
2 tablespoons lemon juice
Thinly sliced almonds (optional)
Lemon slices

Sour Cream Muffins

Combine the flour, melted butter and sour cream in a bowl and mix just until blended. Fill ungreased miniature muffin cups two-thirds full. Bake at 350 degrees for 20 to 30 minutes or until the muffins test done. Remove the muffins from the pan to a wire rack to cool.

Makes 2 dozen

Variations: Add 1/3 cup finely chopped, dried cranberries or 3 tablespoons chopped chives to the batter.

2 cups self-rising flour, sifted
3/4 cup (1 1/2 sticks) butter, melted
1 cup sour cream

EASTERN SHORE HUNT & GATHER

Anne's Lemon Chess Pie

2 cups sugar
1 tablespoon all-purpose flour
1 tablespoon cornmeal
¼ teaspoon salt
¼ cup (½ stick) butter, melted
2 teaspoons grated lemon zest
¼ cup fresh lemon juice
¼ cup milk
4 medium eggs, beaten
1 unbaked (9-inch) pie shell
Whipped cream and fresh raspberries

Mix the sugar, flour, cornmeal and salt in a bowl. Add the melted butter, lemon zest, lemon juice, milk and eggs and mix well. Pour into the pie shell. Bake at 350 degrees for 50 minutes. Remove to a wire rack to cool. Garnish with whipped cream and raspberries and serve.
Serves 6

BEST PIE CRUST

Mix 2 cups all purpose flour and 1 teaspoon salt in a bowl. Cut in ⅔ cup Crisco vegetable shortening until crumbly. Sprinkle with 7 tablespoons ice water, mixing with a fork until mixture forms a ball. Shape into 2 portions and roll out on a lightly floured surface to fit the pie plates.

LEMONY ICE CREAM PIE

Combine one quart of vanilla ice cream and a 6-ounce can of partially thawed lemonade concentrate in a bowl and stir until blended. Spoon into a 9-inch graham cracker crust. Freeze until firm. Garnish with fresh raspberries, lemon slices and sprigs of mint. Serves 6 to 8.

The Sharrock china press (ca. 1790–1800) is attributed to the Sharrock family of Northeastern North Carolina. Thomas Sharrock learned the cabinetmaking trade in Virginia and settled in North Carolina in 1776. His son George was also a cabinetmaker and it is difficult to determine the precise maker of any individual pieces as they used similar construction technique and design. Fewer than 25 examples of furniture made by the Sharrock family are known to exist.

NORTHEASTERN REGION

LATE AFTERNOON TEA PARTY MENU

Coffee Punch or Milk Punch

Parched Peanuts

Tea Sandwiches:
Tomato Basil,
Egg Salad & Chicken Salad

Cream Cheese & Olive Spread
on Date Nut Bread

Brown Edge Cookies

Fig Cake with Buttermilk Glaze

LATE AFTERNOON TEA PARTY

Coffee Punch

4 cups heavy whipping cream
5 tablespoons sugar
5 teaspoons vanilla extract
1/2 gallon vanilla ice cream
16 cups strong brewed coffee, chilled

Beat the whipping cream, sugar and vanilla in a mixing bowl until firm peaks form. Scoop the ice cream into a large punch bowl and add the whipped cream. Pour the cold coffee into the punch bowl and mix well.
Serves 50 to 60

Jean's Old Fashioned Milk Punch

2 1/2 gallons of milk
1 fifth bourbon
1/2 gallon vanilla ice cream
Few drops of almond extract

Milk was adopted as the official state beverage by the North Carolina General Assembly in 1987.

Combine all ingredients in a large container and mix until the consistency of thick eggnog. Mix no more than 30 minutes before serving.

Jon's Parched Peanuts

Redskin peanuts
Cooking oil
Salt to taste

Spread enough redskin peanuts to cover a shallow cookie sheet 1 peanut deep. Roast the peanuts at 350 degrees for 7 to 8 minutes. Shake the pan gently to rotate the peanuts. Roast for 5 minutes longer. Drizzle with oil and sprinkle with salt to taste. Roast for 7 to 8 minutes longer. Remove from the oven and let cool. Wait a while before tasting as peanuts will continue roasting for several minutes longer.
Important: Peanuts should cook for a total of 20 minutes.

This blue and white Chinese export tea caddy (ca. 1780–1784) is reported to have been owned by Penelope Barker, who presided over the signing of the 1774 Edenton Resolves. The canister-shaped tea caddy (ca. 1774) with cobalt blue decoration with floral accents descended in the family of Mary Bonner and daughter Lydia Bonner, both signers of the Resolves. The punch bowl (ca. 1765–1775) belonged to Winifred Hoskins, who acted as secretary for the group.

LATE AFTERNOON TEA PARTY

Tomato Basil Tea Sandwiches

2 cups mayonnaise
¼ teaspoon salt
¾ cup chopped basil
Thinly sliced white bread
Thinly sliced Roma tomatoes
Salt to taste

Combine the mayonnaise, ¼ teaspoon salt and basil in a bowl and mix well. Chill, covered, for 24 hours. Cut rounds from the bread with a biscuit cutter. Spread the basil mayonnaise over the bread rounds and top each with a tomato slice. Sprinkle lightly with salt. *Serves 36*

Note: You may add another bread round over the tomato or serve open-face.

Egg Salad Tea Sandwiches

8 hard-cooked eggs, chopped
⅔ cup mayonnaise
½ teaspoon salt
½ teaspoon pepper
1 tablespoon Dijon mustard
½ cup finely chopped celery
1 tablespoon chopped chives (optional)
Sliced bread, crusts removed

Combine the eggs, mayonnaise, salt, pepper, Dijon mustard, celery and chives in a bowl and mix well. Chill until cold. Spread the egg salad over one-half of the bread slices and top each with another bread slice. Cut diagonally into quarters. *Serves 36*

Chicken Salad Tea Sandwiches

4 cups diced cooked chicken breasts
1 cup finely chopped celery
⅓ cup drained sweet pickle cubes
⅔ cup mayonnaise
1 tablespoon fresh lemon juice
½ teaspoon salt
½ teaspoon pepper
Sliced bread, crusts removed

Combine the chicken, celery, pickles, mayonnaise, lemon juice, salt and pepper in a bowl and mix well. Chill overnight. Spread the chicken salad over one-half of the bread slices and top with another bread slice. Cut diagonally into quarters.

Variation: Omit the pickle cubes from the chicken salad and add ½ teaspoon curry powder and 2 tablespoons chopped mango chutney.

Governor Daniel Gould Fowle (1831–1891) of Beaufort County was the first governor to occupy the Executive Mansion. He moved into the unfinished mansion in January 1891. Since he was a widower, his oldest daughter, Helen, assumed the role of hostess. Fowle only enjoyed the new residence three months before his death on April 8, 1891. A bequest to the mansion was his 109-piece set of rose medallion Chinese export porcelain.

NORTHEASTERN REGION

Cream Cheese and Olive Spread

Reserve 3 tablespoons of brine from the olives. Drain the remaining olive brine and discard. Chop the olives. Beat the cream cheese, salt, Worcestershire sauce and reserved olive brine in a mixing bowl at low speed until smooth. Stir in the olives. Spread over one-half of the bread slices and top with another bread slice. Cut sandwiches into quarters and serve.

Serves 36

1 (8-ounce) jar pimento-stuffed green olives
20 ounces cream cheese, softened
1 teaspoon salt
1 tablespoon Worcestershire sauce
Jill's Date Nut Bread, sliced

Jill's Date Nut Bread

Combine the dates, walnuts, baking soda, salt and shortening in a bowl. Pour the boiling water over the mixture and stir to mix. Let stand for 15 minutes. Beat the eggs and sugar together in a bowl with a fork. Stir in the flours. Add the date mixture and mix until blended. Spoon into a greased $4^{1}/_{2} \times 8^{1}/_{2} \times 3$-inch loaf pan. Bake at 350 degrees for 40 to 50 minutes or until a few moist crumbs cling to a straw inserted into the center. Do not overbake. Run a knife around the edge of the pan and turn the loaf onto a wire rack to cool completely.

Makes 1 loaf
Note: This bread freezes well.

1 cup pitted chopped dates
1 cup coarsely chopped walnuts
$1^{1}/_{2}$ teaspoons baking soda
$^{1}/_{2}$ teaspoon salt
3 tablespoons vegetable shortening
$^{3}/_{4}$ cup boiling water
2 eggs
$^{3}/_{4}$ cup sugar
$^{1}/_{2}$ cup whole wheat flour
1 cup all-purpose flour

Marguerite's Brown Edge Cookies

Beat the butter, shortening and granulated sugar in a mixing bowl until light and fluffy. Beat in the eggs. Beat in the flour and salt. Beat in the vanilla. Drop by rounded teaspoonfuls onto an ungreased cookie sheet. Bake at 350 degrees in the center of the oven for 15 to 17 minutes or until the edges are browned. Cool on the cookie sheet for 1 minute. Loosen the cookies with a spatula and leave on the cookie sheet for 5 minutes. Remove the warm cookies and coat in confectioners' sugar, shaking off any excess sugar. Cool the cookies completely on a wire rack. Store the cookies in an airtight container, placing waxed paper between the layers of cookies. These cookies will keep for 3 weeks at room temperature or can be frozen for up to 6 months.

Makes 5 dozen

$^{1}/_{4}$ cup ($^{1}/_{2}$ stick) butter, softened
$^{1}/_{2}$ cup shortening
1 cup granulated sugar
2 eggs
$1^{1}/_{2}$ cups all-purpose flour
$^{1}/_{2}$ teaspoon salt
1 teaspoon vanilla extract
Confectioners' sugar

LATE AFTERNOON TEA PARTY

Ocracoke Fig Cake with Buttermilk Glaze

I first encountered this cake on Ocracoke Island and years later got the recipe when it was published in the N&O. Figs are one of the only fruits that grow in the island's salty coastal climate. Multiple versions of this recipe have been created by residents.

Ocracoke Fig Cake
- 3 eggs
- 1 1/2 cups sugar
- 1 cup oil
- 2 cups all-purpose flour
- 1 teaspoon ground nutmeg
- 1 teaspoon ground allspice
- 1 teaspoon ground cinnamon
- 1 teaspoon salt
- 1/2 cup buttermilk (see Note)
- 1 teaspoon baking soda, dissolved in a little hot water
- 1 teaspoon vanilla extract
- 1 cup (or more) coarsely chopped fig preserves (best with homemade fig preserves)
- 1 cup coarsely chopped pecans or walnuts, optional

Buttermilk Glaze
- 1/2 cup buttermilk
- 1/2 cup sugar
- 1/4 cup (1/2 stick) butter
- 1 1/2 teaspoons cornstarch or flour
- 1/4 teaspoon baking soda
- 1 teaspoon vanilla extract

Grease and flour a 10-inch tube pan and set aside. Beat the eggs until light yellow and smooth. Add the sugar and oil and continue beating well to make a thick smooth batter.

Combine the flour with nutmeg, allspice, cinnamon and salt in a small bowl and stir with a fork to mix well. Add half the flour mixture to the batter and stir with a wooden spoon to blend well. Add the buttermilk and mix well. Add the remaining flour along with the baking soda mixture and the vanilla. Stir everything together into a fairly smooth batter. Gently stir in the fig preserves and the pecans, mixing just until they are evenly distributed throughout the batter.

Quickly scrape the batter into the prepared pan. Bake at 350 degrees for 40 to 50 minutes or until the cake is handsomely brown and firm on top and a wooden skewer inserted in the center comes out clean. While the cake bakes, prepare the buttermilk glaze and set aside until the cake is done.

Cool the cake in the pan on a wire rack or folded kitchen towel for about 15 minutes. Loosen the cake from the pan gently, running a table knife around the side of the pan, and then gently turn it out onto the wire rack. Turn the cake top side up and carefully place it on a serving plate or cake stand. Spoon the buttermilk glaze over the warm cake. Cool completely before serving.

Note: If you don't have buttermilk, stir 1 tablespoon of vinegar or lemon juice into 1 cup of milk and let stand for 10 minutes.

For the glaze: Combine the buttermilk, sugar, butter, cornstarch and baking soda in a medium saucepan. Bring to a gentle boil. Remove from heat at once and mix. Cool to room temperature. Add the vanilla. Spread the glaze over the warm cake.

Note: This moist spice cake will keep for at least a week, which makes it an ideal choice when you have houseguests. The cake also will keep in the freezer for six months.

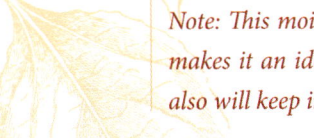

COASTAL REGION

The Coastal Region has always been rich in natural resources. Much of the region was once covered by longleaf pine forests, which were central to North Carolina's original leading industry, naval stores. The stores provided lumber, tar, pitch, and turpentine, which were used mostly in the construction and maintenance of sailing ships. Today vegetable and fruit farms have replaced some of the forest land. Blueberries, blackberries, and strawberries flourish in the sandy, organic coastal soil. And just offshore shrimp, crab, and a variety of seafood thrive.

The first settlers were in Wilmington by the 1730s, and that port city on the Cape Fear River has generally been bustling ever since. Always one of the largest communities in eastern North Carolina, Wilmington is known for its mix of charm and vitality, along with its waterfront, nearby beaches, restaurants, historic homes, the Battleship USS *North Carolina* memorial, and the Azalea Festival.

The Coastal Region is true low country, featuring tidal creeks, rivers, and numerous swamps. The southernmost portions of Brunswick and New Hanover Counties are semitropical places where the flora and fauna are truly different. The Venus flytrap, palmetto trees, alligators, and the coral snake can be found here. In the eighteenth and early nineteenth centuries Boundary House, an early version of a visitors' center and rest stop, straddled the border of the Carolinas not too far from present-day Calabash, which is known for its fried seafood.

Back in 1795 Hinton James walked all the way from what is now Pender County to Chapel Hill to enroll as the first student at the University of North Carolina. Pender is known for farming and swamps, as well as oysters, which are important to the culture of its oceanfront communities of Topsail and Hampstead. The Battle of Moore's Creek Bridge, an important conflict of the American Revolution, was fought in Pender.

Onslow County is home to bustling Jacksonville and Camp Lejeune Marine Base. Carteret County, which features an extensive waterfront, includes the communities of Beaufort and Morehead City. If traveling by land, one can follow U.S. Highway 70 for 2,400 miles, from Arizona to its eastern terminus at Atlantic, NC. The ocean by the same name is just ahead.

New Bern is one of the oldest towns in the state, and Oriental is popular for its sailing. Tryon's Palace in New Bern hosted George Washington during his 1791 presidential visit; however, a lesser-known spot now long gone, Shine's Tavern near Trenton in the wilds of Jones County, was recognized as a surprisingly nice stop for eighteenth-century travelers. There is no documentation of what Shine's served; but it is reasonable to assume that guests were offered some form of pork and corn, along with a little imported tea or coffee, not to mention some American or Caribbean rum. Cheers!

COASTAL REGION

COASTAL BOUNTY SEAFOOD DINNER MENU

Southern Sweet Tea

Watermelon Gazpacho

Pickled Shrimp or Crab Cakes

Baked Fish with Parmesan Crust

Marinated Asparagus

Corn Pudding

Vinegar Pie

Rum Raisin Cheesecake with Rum Sauce

COASTAL BOUNTY SEAFOOD DINNER

Margaret's Perfect Southern Sweet Tea

3 cups water
6 tea bags
1 cup sugar
6 cups cold water

Bring 3 cups water to a boil in a saucepan. Remove from the heat and add the tea bags. Cover and let steep for 5 minutes. Remove and discard the tea bags. Add the sugar and stir until the sugar is dissolved. Stir in 6 cups cold water. Pour into a pitcher and chill.

Serves 8 to 10

Watermelon Gazpacho

6 cups cubed seedless watermelon
1/2 cup chopped red bell pepper
1/2 cup chopped red onion
1 1/2 cups chopped seeded cucumber
3 cups chopped fresh red tomatoes
2 1/2 tablespoons chopped seeded green chiles
1/4 cup sliced scallions
3 garlic cloves, chopped
3 tablespoons chopped fresh cilantro
1/2 cup fresh lime juice
Salt and freshly ground white pepper to taste
2 cups seedless watermelon, cut into small dice
1 fresh yellow tomato, cut into fine dice

Combine 6 cups watermelon, bell pepper, onion, cucumber, tomatoes, chiles, scallions, garlic and cilantro in a large bowl. Add the lime juice, salt and white pepper; toss to mix. Marinate in the refrigerator for 4 hours. Process in a food processor fitted with the steel blade until smooth. Adjust the seasonings. Chill overnight. Ladle into soup bowls. Garnish with the remaining watermelon and yellow tomato.

Serves 6

Watermelon still-life (ca. 1890–1910) was painted by Mary Lyde Hicks Williams, a North Carolina born artist renowned for work with portraits. She studied art and portrait painting in Washington, D.C., and New York. During her lifetime she painted more than five hundred portraits, many of them portraying political and military leaders.

COASTAL BOUNTY SEAFOOD DINNER

Martha's Pickled Shrimp

2 pounds shrimp
1/2 cup celery leaves
3 1/2 teaspoons salt
1/4 cup pickling spice
2 cups sliced onions
7 or 8 bay leaves
1 1/4 cups vegetable oil
1 1/4 cups white vinegar
1 1/2 teaspoons salt
2 1/2 teaspoons celery seeds
2 1/2 tablespoons capers with juice
Dash of Tabasco sauce

Cover the shrimp with water in a saucepan. Add the celery leaves, 3 1/2 salt and pickling spice. Cook for 10 minutes or until the shrimp turn pink. Drain and add cold water to cool the shrimp. Peel and devein the shrimp under cold running water. Alternate layers of the shrimp and onions in a shallow dish and sprinkle with the bay leaves. Whisk the oil, vinegar, 1 1/2 teaspoons salt, celery seeds, capers and Tabasco sauce in a bowl. Pour over the shrimp and onions. Chill, covered for 24 hours to 3 days. Remove and discard the bay leaves before serving.

Serves 8 to 10

Classic Crab Cakes

1 pound crab meat, drained and flaked
1/2 teaspoon salt
1/2 teaspoon pepper
1 teaspoon dry mustard
1/2 cup mayonnaise
1 egg yolk
2 teaspoons Worcestershire sauce
1 teaspoon chopped parsley
1 tablespoon butter, melted
1 to 2 tablespoons bread crumbs

Combine the crab meat, salt, pepper, mustard, mayonnaise, egg yolk, Worcestershire sauce, parsley and melted butter in a bowl and mix well. Mix in the bread crumbs until the mixture holds together. Shape into 8 patties and arrange in a shallow baking pan. Bake at 450 degrees for 15 to 20 minutes.

Serves 8

Café Atlantic Baked Fish with Parmesan Crust

2 cups (8 ounces) grated or shredded Parmesan cheese
3/4 cup mayonnaise
3/4 cup chopped green onions
4 teaspoons minced garlic
1 teaspoon hot red pepper sauce
1/4 cup (1/2 stick) butter, melted
4 (3/4-inch-thick) grouper, flounder or mahi mahi fillets

Combine the cheese, mayonnaise, green onions, garlic, hot sauce and melted butter in a bowl and mix well. Spread equal portions over each fish fillet. Arrange the fish in a shallow baking pan. Bake at 425 degrees for 12 minutes or until the fish begins to flake.

Serves 4

COASTAL REGION

Mama Sally's Marinated Asparagus

This is also delicious using fresh asparagus spears that have been cooked just until tender-crisp.

Arrange the asparagus spears in a 9×13-inch baking dish. Whisk the vinegar, soy sauce, sugar, oil and pepper in a small bowl and pour evenly over the asparagus. Marinate, covered, in the refrigerator for 24 hours. Sprinkle with the pecans and serve.

Serves 6

3 (15-ounce) cans asparagus spears, rinsed and drained
1/4 cup cider vinegar
1/4 cup soy sauce
1/4 cup sugar
2 tablespoons vegetable oil
Pepper to taste
3/4 cup pecans pieces, lightly toasted

Corn Pudding

Melt the butter in a saucepan. Stir in the flour, sugar and salt. Cook until bubbly, stirring constantly. Stir in the milk. Cook until thickened, stirring constantly. Stir in the corn. Remove from the heat and let cool slightly. Stir in the eggs gradually. Pour into a buttered baking dish. Place the baking dish in a larger baking pan. Add hot water to the larger pan to come halfway up the side of the baking dish. Bake at 350 degrees for 45 minutes. Remove the baking dish carefully from the hot water and serve.

Serves 6

1/4 cup (1/2 stick) butter
1/4 cup all-purpose flour
1 1/2 tablespoons sugar
2 teaspoons salt
1 3/4 cups milk
3 cups frozen corn kernels, chopped
3 eggs, well beaten

Alma's Vinegar Pie

Beat the butter and sugar in a mixing bowl until light and fluffy. Add the eggs, one at a time, beating well after each addition. Beat in the vinegar. Pour into the pie shell and place the pie on a baking sheet. Bake at 350 degrees for 20 to 25 minutes or until the filling is set and lightly browned. Remove to a wire rack to cool.

Serves 6 to 8

6 tablespoons unsalted butter, softened
1 cup sugar
2 extra-large eggs
3 to 4 tablespoons cider vinegar
1 unbaked (9-inch) pie shell

COASTAL BOUNTY SEAFOOD DINNER

Kay's Rum Raisin Cheesecake with Myers's Rum Sauce

Rum-Raisin Cheesecake
1 cup graham cracker crumbs
¼ cup (½ stick melted butter
⅓ cup Myers's rum
1 cup seedless raisins
3 pounds cream cheese, soften
2 cups sugar
2 eggs, at room temperature
1 teaspoon vanilla extract

Myers's Rum Sauce
1 cup packed brown sugar
2 tablespoons butter
½ cup corn syrup
½ cup cream
¼ cup Myers's rum
½ teaspoon vanilla extract

For the cheesecake, combine the graham cracker crumbs and melted butter in a small bowl; mix well. Press over the bottom of a 10-inch springform pan. Chill until firm.

Bring the cup rum to a boil in a saucepan; remove from the heat. Add the raisins. Steep, covered, for 10 minutes or longer. Beat the cream cheese and sugar in a mixer bowl until smooth; scrape down the side. Add the eggs one at a time, beating well after each addition. Stir in the vanilla and rum-raisin mixture. Spoon gently into the chilled crust, being careful not to puncture the crust.

Bake at 300 degrees for 1 hour. The top of the cheesecake should be golden, but the filling will still be loose and not firm. Let stand at room temperature for 1 hour. Chill overnight. Run a hot knife around the edge of the pan and remove the side of the pan. Cut into wedges to serve.

For the rum sauce, combine the brown sugar, butter, corn syrup and cream in a saucepan. Bring to a boil over medium heat, stirring constantly; remove from the heat. Stir in the rum and vanilla. Serve warm over servings of the cheesecake.

Serves 12 to 16

This castor set (ca. 1780–1820) was associated with the family of John London, one of the directors of the Bank of Cape Fear from 1805 until his death in 1816. Castor sets of four to seven bottles were commonly used to contain salt and pepper, sugar, spices, vinegars, and oils.

COASTAL REGION

AL FRESCO SEASIDE MENU

Rum Punch

Easy Guacamole

Bleu Cheese Coleslaw

Grilled Corn with Bacon & Vidalia Onion

Barbequed Shrimp or Shrimp Creole

Strawberry Pie

Farm House Pie

AL FRESCO SEASIDE

Rum Punch

¾ **pound white sugar**	Dissolve the sugar in the water in a large container. Add the lemon juice, rum and brandy. Chill in the refrigerator for 24 hours or longer before serving.
2 quarts (8 cups) water	
4 cups freshly squeezed lemon juice	
1 fifth light rum	*Makes 30 punch-cup servings*
1 cup peach brandy	

Charlie's Easy Guacamole

5 avocados	Combine the avocados, salsa, lime juice, onion, cilantro, garlic powder, salt, pepper and chile powder in a bowl. Mash with a potato masher to mix well but leave some small avocado chunks. Cover with plastic wrap, pressing the plastic wrap onto the surface of the guacamole to prevent discoloration. Chill for at least 1 hour. Serve at room temperature with tortilla chips.
2 cups salsa	
Juice of 1 lime	
1 small red onion, finely chopped	
2 tablespoons dried cilantro or chopped fresh cilantro to taste	
2 teaspoons garlic powder or minced fresh garlic to taste	*Serves 8 to 12*
1 teaspoon salt	*Note: You may use cayenne pepper instead of chipotle chile powder. Use a spicy salsa if you prefer a lot of heat in your guacamole.*
1 teaspoon pepper	
¼ teaspoon chipotle chile powder	

This pitcher (ca. 1805–1810) is decorated with the inscription "A North View Of Govr. Wallaces Shell Castle & Harbour North Carolina." Shell Castle was built by merchants John Gray Blount and John Wallace and became one of the most successful ports of the time, providing a facility where oceangoing ships could transfer cargo to barges and then smaller vessels that could manage the region's shallow sounds and rivers to New Bern, Edenton, and other ports. Shell Castle Island was home to one of North Carolina's earliest lighthouses (1798–1818).

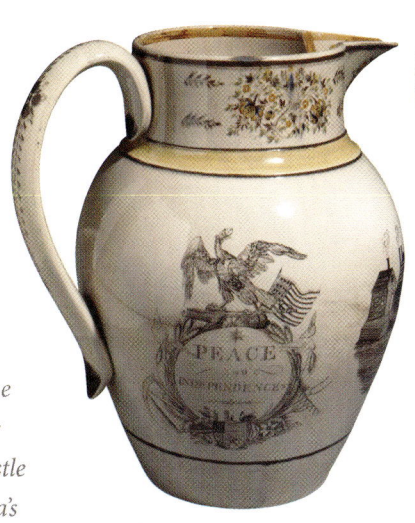

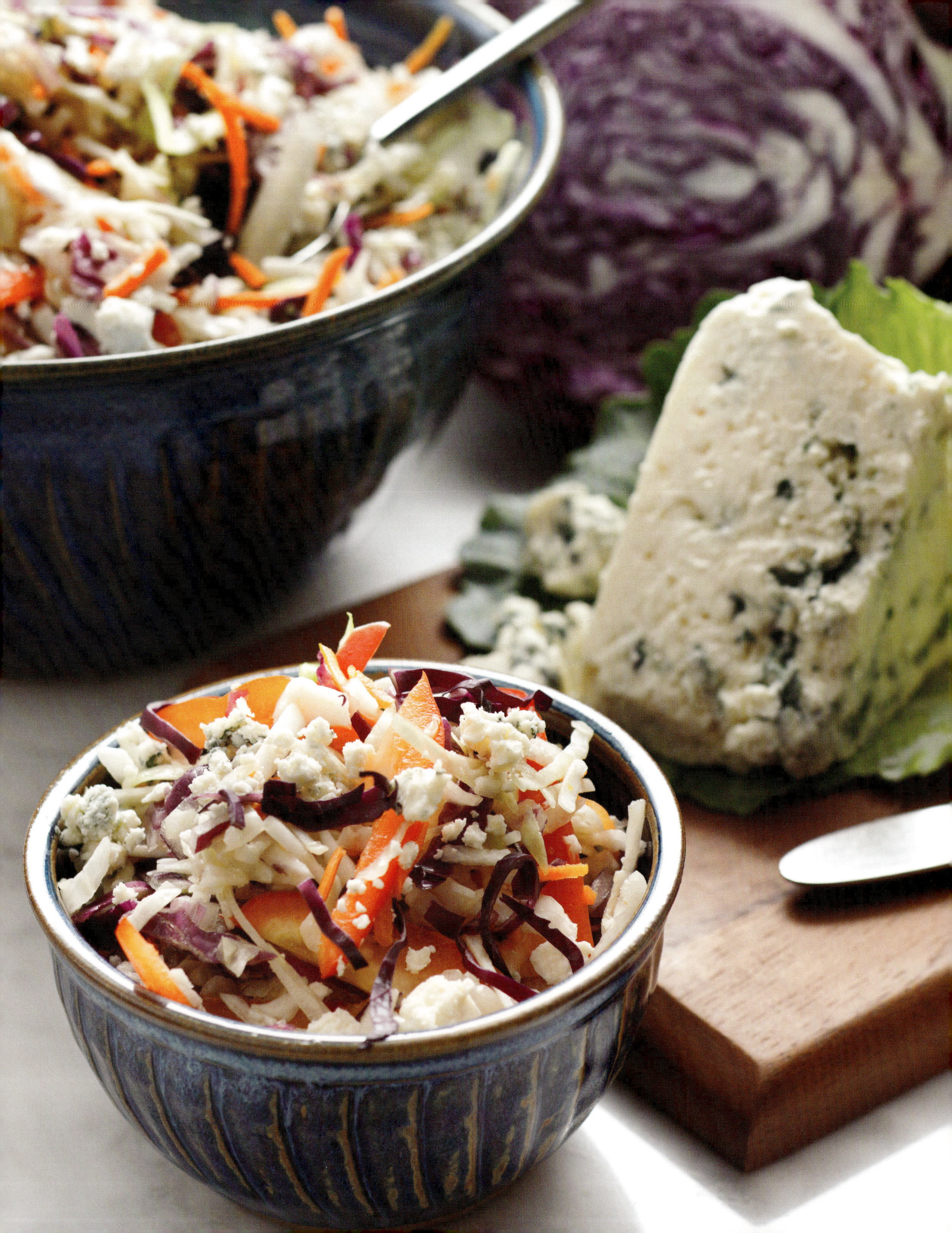

AL FRESCO SEASIDE

Bertie's Bleu Cheese Coleslaw

1 (2-pound) head cabbage, shredded
8 ounces bleu cheese, crumbled
1/4 cup finely chopped white onion
3/4 cup vegetable oil
1/3 cup cider vinegar
2 garlic cloves, minced
2 tablespoons sugar
1 teaspoon celery seeds
1/2 teaspoon salt
1/2 teaspoon white pepper
1/4 teaspoon dry mustard

Combine the cabbage, cheese and onion in a large bowl and toss to mix. Combine the oil, vinegar, garlic, sugar, celery seeds, salt, white pepper and mustard in a container with a tight-fitting lid. Seal the container and shake well. Pour over the cabbage and toss to coat. Serve immediately.

Serves 8 to 10

Grilled Corn with Bacon & Vidalia Onion

16 ears corn, shucked
1/2 cup finely chopped bacon
1 teaspoon unsalted butter
1 cup finely chopped Vidalia onion
1 cup heavy cream
1 teaspoon salt
Freshly ground pepper to taste
1 tablespoon minced chives

Cook the corn on a grill until lightly charred. Remove to a cutting board. Cut the kernels off the cob and set aside. Scrape the cobs over a bowl to remove all of the liquid. Sauté the bacon in a skillet over medium-high heat until cooked through and slightly crisp. Add the corn kernels and cook for 1 minute, stirring constantly. Remove from the heat and set aside. Melt the butter in a saucepan over medium-low heat. Add the onion and sauté for 2 to 3 minutes or until tender. Stir in the corn kernels, reserved corn liquid and cream. Reduce the heat to low and cook for 4 to 5 minutes, stirring frequently. Stir in the salt, pepper and chives. Serve with shrimp or fish.

Serves 8

COASTAL REGION

Joe's Barbecued Shrimp

Mix the Worcestershire sauce, garlic and lemon juice in a 9×13-inch baking dish. Add the shrimp and toss to coat. Sprinkle the shrimp with the Old Bay seasoning and pepper. Arrange the lemon slices and butter slices over the top. Bake at 450 degrees for 10 minutes or until the shrimp turn pink. Serve with crusty bread. Roll up your sleeves and have plenty of napkins on hand.

Serves 4

1/4 cup Worcestershire sauce
3 garlic cloves, chopped
2 tablespoons lemon juice
1 1/4 pounds unpeeled shrimp
2 tablespoons Old Bay seasoning
1 tablespoon pepper
2 lemons, sliced
1/2 cup (1 stick) butter, cut into slices

Teeny's Shrimp Creole

Heat the olive oil in a large saucepan. Add the bell pepper, onions, celery, celery leaves and parsley and sauté until the vegetables are tender. Stir in the tomatoes, chili sauce, raisins, curry powder, thyme, cayenne pepper, salt, black pepper and bay leaves. Bring to a boil, stirring frequently. Reduce the heat and simmer for 1 hour, stirring occasionally. Stir in the shrimp and cook until the shrimp turn pink. Remove and discard the bay leaves. Serve over rice and sprinkle with almonds and bacon.

Serves 6 to 8

Note: The sauce can be made ahead and freezes well. Thaw and heat to a simmer before adding the shrimp.

1/2 cup olive oil
1 cup diced green bell pepper
2 1/2 cups diced onions
1 cup diced celery
1/2 cup chopped celery leaves
1/2 cup chopped parsley
1 (16-ounce) can diced tomatoes
1/2 cup chili sauce
1/2 cup golden raisins
1 tablespoon curry powder
1/2 teaspoon thyme
1/4 teaspoon cayenne pepper
Salt and black pepper to taste
2 or 3 bay leaves
2 pounds peeled shrimp
Hot cooked rice
Toasted almonds (optional)
Crumbled cooked bacon (optional)

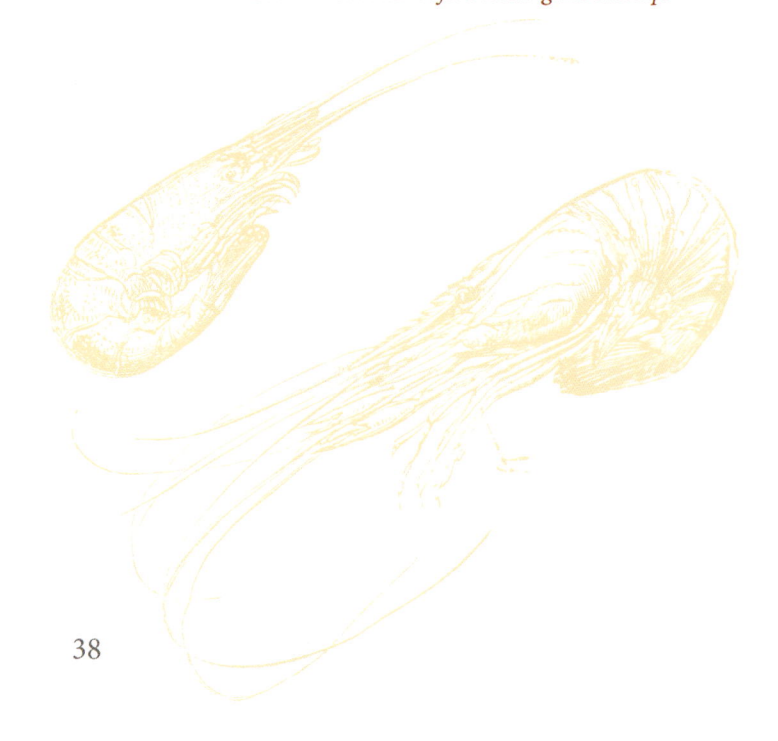

AL FRESCO SEASIDE

Sandra's Strawberry Pie

3 ounces cream cheese, softened
3 tablespoons sour cream
1 baked (9-inch) pie shell, cooled
2 to 4 cups strawberries, washed, hulled and dried well
1 cup water
1 cup sugar
3 tablespoons cornstarch
1/2 (3-ounce) package strawberry gelatin

Beat the cream cheese and sour cream in a bowl until smooth. Spread evenly over the bottom of the pie shell. Chill until cold. Fit the strawberries snugly, stem side down, over the cream cheese layer. Chill until cold. Mix the water, sugar and cornstarch in a saucepan. Cook until thickened and slightly clear, stirring constantly. Remove from the heat and let cool for 5 minutes. Add the gelatin and mix well. Pour evenly over the strawberries. Chill until firm.

Serves 6 to 8

Betsy's Farm House Pie

8 ounces cream cheese, softened
1 cup confectioners' sugar, sifted
1 tablespoon grated lemon zest
2 tablespoons lemon juice
8 ounces extra creamy whipped topping
2 baked (9-inch) deep-dish pie shells
1 to 2 cups fresh blueberries, raspberries or sliced strawberries

My mother and I adapted this recipe from the famous Farm House restaurant outside Chapel Hill. My parents, who both attended UNC-CH, always loved going to the Farm House together. Years later, I met my husband at UNC-CH, and we too enjoyed many dinners there.

Beat the cream cheese, confectioners' sugar, lemon zest and lemon juice in a mixing bowl. Add the whipped topping and beat until light and fluffy. Pour into the pie shells and arrange the berries evenly over the top. Chill for 8 hours. Slice and serve.

Serves 6 to 8 per pie

This pie safe (ca. 1820–1850) was made in Warren County and has its original lock and key. Pie safes were used in American households to protect baked goods, produce, and other perishables from pests and the elements.

Vine-Ripened
TOMATOES
2⁰⁰ lb.

CHERRY
TOMATOES
$2.⁰⁰ pt.

PEAS
lb

Small Oranges
5 for $1.⁰⁰

SUGAR
SNAPS
$3.⁰⁰ lb

AGRICULTURAL REGION

*A*n eastern swath of the Old North State that borders South Carolina and stretches nearly to Virginia, the Agricultural Region is a place of farms and small towns and cities. Rocky Mount, Wilson, Kinston, and Goldsboro were once the brightest lights; however, Greenville, a booming educational and medical center, is now the hub.

Eastern North Carolina barbecue, the vinegar-and-pepper-based style, is enjoyed throughout this area, which features several popular commercial eateries famous for serving traditional whole-hog barbecue. Mt. Olive Pickles, headquartered at Cucumber and Vine Streets in a small Wayne County town of the same name, is one of America's top pickle producers.

Corn, wheat, oats, sweet potatoes, Irish potatoes, cucumbers, melons, soybeans, peanuts, cotton, and tobacco all push their way up through this belt's rich loam. Forestry is important throughout the area, especially in Bladen County where blueberries abound, too. Pigs, hogs, and poultry are raised in the region; there's even a town named Turkey in Sampson County.

William Rufus King, the only North Carolinian elected Vice-President of the United States, was born and raised in Sampson County, graduated from the university in Chapel Hill, and began his legal and political career in Sampson. However, in spite of his North Carolina heritage, by the time King was elected vice-president in 1852 he was a popular U.S. Senator from Alabama. Ill with tuberculosis, he served as vice-president only six weeks.

Five counties in the region are named in honor of heroes of the American Revolution. Wayne, Greene, Nash, and Lenoir are named for American Revolutionary officers, while Pitt takes its name from eighteenth-century British leader William Pitt, who sided with the Americans. Going even further back in history for its name, Columbus County is named for Christopher Columbus. Sampson, Duplin, Bladen, and Columbus are among the largest counties in this area of the state, each about three-fourths the size of the state of Rhode Island.

Specialty processing is important in the Agricultural Region. A Duplin County vintner makes wine from native muscadine grapes, while a Lenoir County firm bottles non-alcoholic muscadine beverages. The charming Tarboro Town of Common, now fifteen acres, was established in 1760. Exactly two hundred years later and thirty miles away, the fast-food chain Hardee's got its start in Greenville.

41

AGRICULTURAL REGION

DOWN EAST SUPPER MENU

Minted Orange Iced Tea

Dove & Sausage Gumbo

Edamame Salad

Grilled Potato Salad

Perfect Ribs

Jim Bane Sauce

Pound Cake with Buttercream Frosting

Date Nut Bar Cookies

DOWN EAST SUPPER

Minted Orange Iced Tea

4 cups water
1/2 cup mint sprigs
5 English breakfast tea bags
1 cup freshly squeezed orange juice
1 tablespoon frozen orange juice concentrate
Fresh mint sprigs

Bring the water and 1/2 mint to a boil in a large stainless steel or enameled saucepan; remove from the heat. Add the tea bags. Let steep for 5 minutes to make a strong tea. Remove the tea bags; cool to room temperature. Stir in the orange juice and concentrate. Pour into a pitcher. Chill until serving time. Pour into ice-filled glasses. Garnish with fresh mint sprigs.

Makes 6 servings

Note: Bruise the mint sprigs to release the mint flavor before garnishing.

Dove and Sausage Gumbo

15 dove breasts
1 (10 1/2-ounce) can consommé
1 beef bouillon cube
1/2 cup vegetable oil
1/2 cup all-purpose flour
1 1/2 cups finely chopped onions
2 ribs celery, finely chopped
2 tablespoons Worcestershire sauce
2 garlic cloves, minced
1 or 2 bay leaves
1/2 teaspoon dried basil
1/4 teaspoon poultry seasoning
1/4 teaspoon freshly ground black pepper
1/8 teaspoon cayenne pepper
1/8 teaspoon ground allspice
1/8 teaspoon ground cloves
8 ounces smoked sausage, cut into 1/4-inch slices
1/4 cup dry red wine
1/8 teaspoon hot red pepper sauce
Hot cooked rice

Cover the dove breasts with water in a large heavy saucepan. Bring to a boil and cook for 10 minutes. Remove the dove with tongs to a cutting board and let cool. Remove the meat from the bones. Measure the cooking liquid and add water if needed to make 2 1/4 cups liquid. Return the cooking liquid to the saucepan. Add the consommé and bouillon cube and cook until the bouillon cube is dissolved. Remove from the heat. Heat the oil in a large skillet. Add the dove meat and sauté until browned. Remove to paper towels to drain. Remove and discard all but 1/4 cup of the oil from the skillet.

Whisk the flour into the oil. Cook over medium heat for 10 to 15 minutes or until the mixture is a copper color, stirring constantly. Whisk in 1 1/2 cups of the cooking liquid gradually. Cook until thickened and bubbly, whisking constantly. Stir in the onions and celery. Cook for 5 minutes or until the vegetables are tender, stirring frequently. Stir into the remaining cooking liquid in the saucepan. Stir in the Worcestershire sauce, garlic, bay leaves, basil, poultry seasoning, black pepper, cayenne pepper, allspice and cloves. Simmer the sausage in 1/4 inch of water in a skillet; drain. Cook the sausage in the skillet until browned; drain. Stir the sausage and dove meat into the gumbo. Simmer for 1 1/2 hours, stirring occasionally. Stir in the wine and hot sauce. Remove and discard the bay leaves. Serve the gumbo over rice.

Serves 8

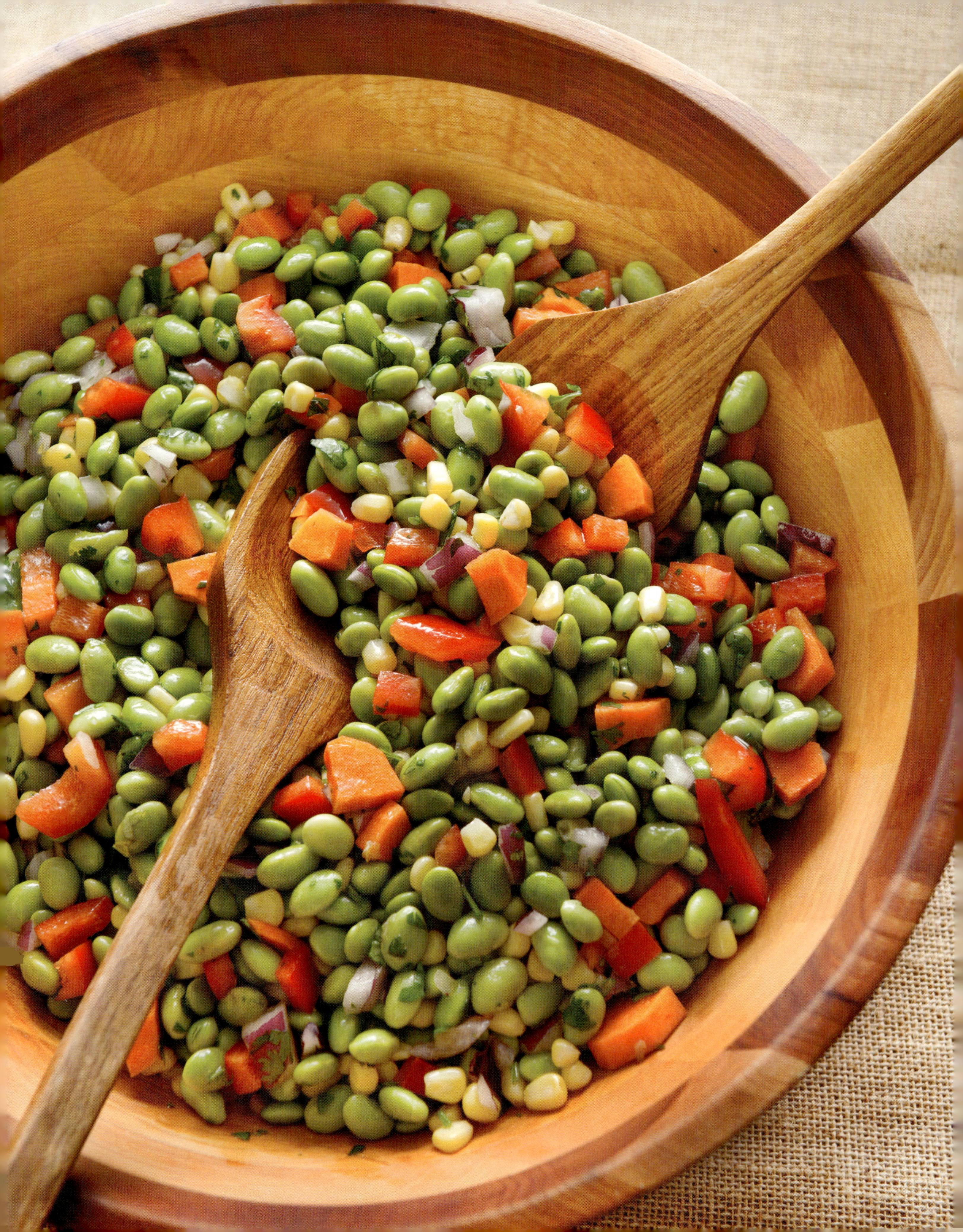

DOWN EAST SUPPER

Anne's Edamame Salad

2 pounds frozen shelled edamame, thawed
1 cup finely diced onion
1/2 cup coarsely chopped cilantro
1 cup frozen corn kernels, thawed
1 cup diced red bell pepper
1 cup diced tomato
1/4 cup half-moon sliced carrot
1/4 cup canola oil
Few drops of sesame oil (optional)
1 cup rice vinegar
1 teaspoon finely chopped garlic
1 tablespoon finely chopped fresh ginger
2 tablespoons salt
1 tablespoon pepper

Combine the edamame, onion, cilantro, corn, bell pepper, tomato and carrot in a large bowl and toss to mix. Whisk the canola oil, sesame oil, vinegar, garlic, ginger, salt and pepper in a bowl. Add to the salad and toss to mix. Serve immediately or chill for up to 4 days.

Serves 8

Note: The dressing is strong so drain the salad after 1 to 2 days if not eaten by then.

Grilled Potato Salad

2 pounds new red potatoes
Olive oil or nonstick cooking spray
Salt and pepper to taste
1 pound bacon, crisp-cooked and crumbled
3 hard-cooked eggs, sliced
2 ribs celery, diced
1 red onion, diced
1 cup mayonnaise
2 tablespoons spicy brown mustard
1/2 cup sweet pickle relish
Chopped chives

Cover the potatoes with water in a saucepan. Bring to a boil and reduce the heat. Cook for 15 minutes. Drain and let cool to room temperature. Cut small potatoes into halves and larger potatoes into quarters. Place the potatoes in a bowl. Drizzle with olive oil and toss to coat. Sprinkle with salt and pepper. Arrange the potatoes on a baking sheet and grill over high heat or under a broiler until golden brown on all sides. Remove to a serving bowl and let cool. Add the bacon, eggs, celery, onion, mayonnaise, mustard and pickle relish and toss to mix. Season with salt and pepper and garnish with chives.

Serves 6 to 8

Note: Grilled potatoes can be used in any recipe for potato salad.

AGRICULTURAL REGION

Perfect Ribs

Wipe the ribs dry. Season with salt, garlic salt and red pepper flakes, rubbing the seasonings in well. Place in a large 12×17-inch baking pan lined with heavy-duty foil. Rib racks should not touch each other. Sprinkle with vinegar and additional red pepper flakes. Combine the barbecue sauce, 3 cups vinegar and brown sugar in a saucepan. Bring to a boil. Add 1 tablespoon red pepper flakes. Simmer for 2 minutes. Drizzle the ribs with the sauce. Bring the foil over the ribs tent-fashion and fold edges to seal. Be sure the foil does not touch the ribs. Bake at 375 degrees for 3 hours. Open the foil and spoon the remaining sauce over the ribs. Reseal and bake for 1 hour longer. Let rest for 30 minutes before serving. Cut the racks into serving portions and serve with any remaining reheated sauce.
Makes 4 servings per rack
Note: Do not use Kraft's thick sauce, as the ribs may burn.

- 2 racks baby back ribs
- Salt
- Garlic salt
- Red pepper flakes
- Cider vinegar
- 1 (39-ounce) bottle Kraft Original Barbecue Sauce or 2 (17^1/$_2$-ounce) bottles
- ^{1}/$_2$ cup packed brown sugar

Jim Bane Sauce

Combine all the ingredients in a blender container. Process at low speed for 1 to 2 minutes or until the sauce is smooth and well blended. Serve as a sauce with ribs, shrimp, fish or chicken.
Makes 2 quarts
Note: This sauce ages well, improving when made in advance. The longer it sits, the better it tastes. Will keep indefinitely if refrigerated.

- 1 (14-ounce) bottle catsup
- 1 (12-ounce) bottle chili sauce
- 1 (5-ounce) bottle Worcestershire sauce
- 1 (10^1/$_2$-ounce) bottle of A.1. sauce
- 2 (8-ounce) jars chutney
- ^{1}/$_2$ cup bourbon

This green glass bottle (ca. 1680–1720) was discovered by John Harvey Jr. at the site of Nooherooka, a Tuscarora Indian fort outside Snow Hill (Greene County). The bottle's shape was common between 1660 and 1740 and could have actually contained any of a variety of liquids. It may have been made in England, but it may have come from Jamestown, Virginia, or Charles Town (present-day Charleston), South Carolina.

DOWN EAST SUPPER

Mary Elizabeth's Favorite Pound Cake with Buttercream Frosting

1 cup (2 sticks) butter, softened
3 cups sugar
6 eggs
3 cups cake flour
1 cup heavy cream
2 teaspoons vanilla extract

Buttercream Frosting
1/2 cup (1 stick) butter, softened
3 tablespoons (or more) milk
3 cups (or more) confectioners' sugar
1 teaspoon vanilla extract
Food color (optional)

Beat the butter and sugar in a mixing bowl until light and fluffy. Add the eggs, one at a time, beating well after each addition. Beat in the flour alternately with the cream, beginning and ending with the flour. Add the vanilla and beat for 4 minutes. Pour into a greased and floured tube pan. Bake at 325 degrees for 1 1/2 hours or until a wooden pick inserted in the center comes out clean. Cool in the pan. Invert onto a serving plate and frost with Buttercream Frosting.

Serves 16

Buttercream Frosting

Combine the butter and milk in a mixing bowl and sift 2 cups of the confectioners' sugar into the bowl. Beat until smooth. Sift the remaining 1 cup confectioners' sugar into the bowl and beat until smooth. Beat in the vanilla. Beat until light and fluffy, scraping the side of the bowl as needed. Beat in a few drops of food color if colored frosting is desired. Use immediately or chill for up to 3 days. This frosting may be frozen for up to one month. Thaw and stir before using.

Makes 2 cups

Imogene's Date Nut Bar Cookies

1 package chopped dates
1 cup granulated sugar
1 cup water
1 teaspoon vanilla extract
1 1/2 cups all-purpose flour
1 1/2 teaspoons baking soda
1/2 teaspoon salt
1 cup packed brown sugar
1 1/2 cups rolled oats
1 cup (2 sticks) butter, melted
1 cup chopped pecans

Combine the dates, granulated sugar and water in a saucepan. Cook until thickened, stirring frequently. Remove from the heat and stir in the vanilla. Cool to room temperature, stirring occasionally to prevent sticking. Sift the flour, baking soda and salt into a bowl. Add the brown sugar and oats and mix well. Add the melted butter and pecans and mix well. Press one-half of the oat mixture onto the bottom of a greased 8×8-inch baking pan. Spread the date filling evenly over the bottom layer. Top evenly with the remaining oat mixture and press gently. Bake at 350 degrees for 30 minutes. Remove to a wire rack to cool completely. Cut into squares when cool.

Makes 20 cookies

AGRICULTURAL REGION

FARM-TO-TABLE VEGETARIAN MENU

White Bean Croustades with Pickled Red Onions

Cream of Fresh Tomato Soup

Roasted Beet Salad

Summer Succotash

Sugar Snap Pea Salad

Cornmeal Muffins

Buttermilk Pie

Fig Nut Roll Cookies

FARM-TO-TABLE VEGETARIAN

White Bean Croustades with Pickled Red Onion

Pickled Red Onion
1 red onion
1 cup red wine vinegar
1 cup sugar
1 teaspoon salt

White Bean Croustades
4 slices bread, cut into circles
Olive oil
Salt and pepper to taste
Chopped fresh herbs (optional)
1 cup cooked white beans
Grated zest and juice of 1 lemon
1/4 cup olive oil
Dash of Worcestershire sauce
Dash of Tabasco sauce
Splash of white wine
Parsley leaves

To make the pickled onion, slice the onion very thinly and place in a metal bowl. Bring the vinegar, sugar and salt to a boil in a saucepan. Pour over the onion and let stand until it cools to room temperature. Spoon the onion and liquid into an airtight container and chill for 12 hours to 5 days.

To make the croustades, roll out the bread circles with a rolling pin until thin. Brush with olive oil and season generously with salt, pepper and herbs. Press each bread round into a muffin cup. Bake at 350 degrees until golden brown. Cool in the pan before removing the bread cups. Purée the beans, lemon zest, lemon juice, 1/4 cup olive oil, Worcestershire sauce, Tabasco sauce and wine in a food processor. Season with salt and pepper. Spoon equal portions of the bean mixture into the bread cups. Top each with a small amount of pickled onion. Garnish with a parsley leaf or other fresh herb and serve.
Serves 4

Cream of Fresh Tomato Soup

1/4 cup French olive oil
2 onions, chopped
4 garlic cloves, chopped
5 tomatoes, sliced
2 tablespoons tomato paste
2 tablespoons whole wheat flour
1 cup vegetable stock
3/4 cup half-and-half
Garlic salt to taste
Sugar to taste
Dill weed to taste
Italian seasoning to taste
Seasoned croutons

Heat the olive oil in a saucepan. Add the onions and garlic and sauté until the vegetables are tender. Add the tomatoes and sauté for 5 minutes. Purée in a food processor or blender and return to the saucepan. Mix the tomato paste and flour in a small bowl and stir into the puréed mixture. Stir in the stock, half-and-half, garlic salt, sugar, dill weed and Italian seasoning. Simmer for 15 minutes. Serve in bowls and top with croutons.
Serves 4

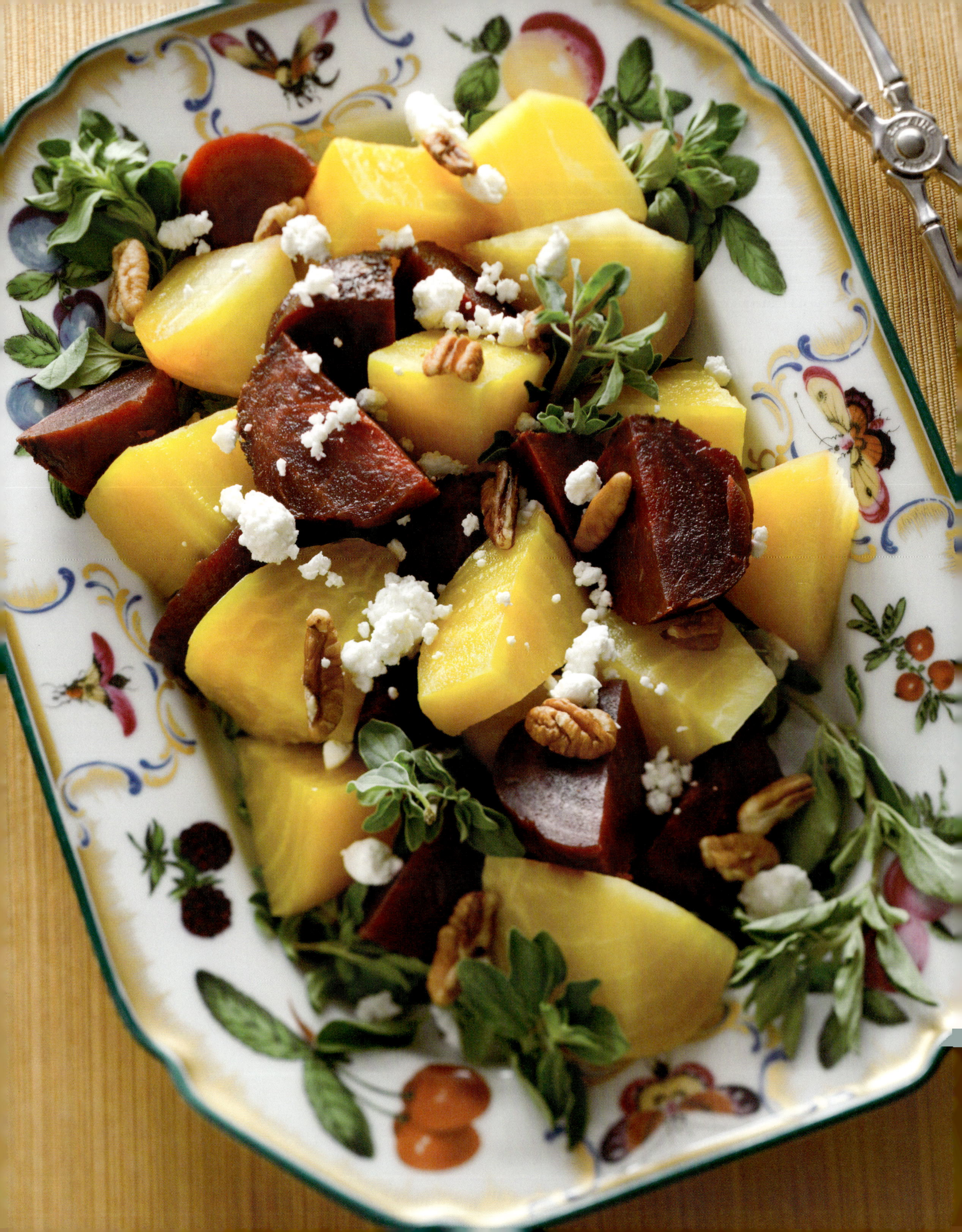

FARM-TO-TABLE VEGETARIAN

Roasted Beet Salad

8 to 10 beets (combination of red and golden variety)
3 tablespoons extra-virgin olive oil
3 tablespoons good-quality balsamic vinegar
Sea salt and freshly ground pepper
4 ounces goat cheese, crumbled
2 tablespoons chopped fresh oregano
1/2 cup chopped lightly toasted pecans

Rinse the beets and trim the leaves. Arrange the beets in a shallow roasting pan. Roast at 400 degrees for 30 to 45 minutes or until tender. Let cool until warm. Peel the beets and discard the tops and tails. Cut the beets into thick wedges and remove to a large serving bowl. Drizzle with the olive oil and vinegar. Season generously with salt and pepper. Sprinkle the cheese, oregano and pecans over the beets and serve.

Serves 8 to 12

Julie's Summer Succotash

2 cups freshly shelled butter beans (about 8 ounces)
4 cups water
1 teaspoon salt
Freshly ground pepper
2 tablespoons olive oil
1 Vidalia onion, diced
1 red bell pepper, diced
2 summer squash, cut into 1/3-inch slices
Freshly cut kernels of 4 ears of corn
2 cups cherry tomatoes, halved
2 tablespoons unsalted butter
Salt to taste
1/4 cup thinly sliced basil

Bring the beans and water to a boil in a saucepan over medium-high heat, stirring occasionally. Reduce the heat and stir in 1 teaspoon salt and a few grinds of pepper. Simmer for 15 minutes or until the beans are tender; drain. Heat the olive oil in a large skillet over medium-high heat until shimmering. Add the onion and sauté for 3 minutes or until tender. Add the bell pepper and sauté for 2 to 3 minutes. Add the squash and sauté for 5 to 6 minutes. Add the beans, corn, tomatoes and butter and season with salt and pepper. Sauté for 3 minutes or until the tomatoes and corn are tender. Stir in the basil and remove from the heat. Serve warm or at room temperature.

Serves 8 to 10

Note: You may use frozen butter beans or lima beans instead of fresh butter beans.

Reportedly transported from England between 1700 and 1750, this blue-and-white mug typifies a desire for pieces created in the style of Chinese export pottery. This piece was used by the Matthews and Williams families in Nash County.

AGRICULTURAL REGION

Garden Club Sugar Snap Pea Salad

Blanch the asparagus in boiling water in a saucepan for 2 minutes; drain and immerse in an ice water bath. Blanch the sugar snap peas in boiling salted water in a saucepan for 30 seconds; drain and immerse in an ice water bath. Drain asparagus and sugar snap peas. Combine with the spring greens in a large salad bowl. Combine the lime zest, juices, mint leaves, yogurt, olive oil and honey in a blender container. Process until emulsified. Serve over the salad. Sprinkle with the feta cheese.

Serves 4 to 6

- 1 bunch asparagus, trimmed
- 1 container sugar snap peas
- 1 container mixed young spring greens
- Grated zest and juice of 1 lime
- Juice of 1 lemon
- 1/4 cup mint leaves
- 1/2 cup plain yogurt or Greek yogurt
- 1/4 cup olive oil
- 1 teaspoon honey
- Crumbled feta cheese (optional)

June's Cornmeal Muffins

This is the recipe of my mother, who was born in Johnston County on September 22, 1914. The youngest of six daughters (there were also three brothers), she was crowned Miss Eastern North Carolina while at Selma College. After attending East Carolina Teachers College, she married in 1934. The young bride could only make fudge and sweet tea, but in time, she became an excellent cook.

- 1 cup cornmeal
- 2 teaspoons baking powder
- 1/2 teaspoon salt
- 1 egg
- 3/4 cup buttermilk
- 1/2 cup cold water

Mix the cornmeal, baking powder and salt together. Beat the egg and buttermilk in a bowl. Stir in the dry ingredients. Add the water and mix well. Spoon into hot greased muffin cups. Bake at 450 degrees for 20 minutes or until the muffins test done.

Makes 8

Highly valued by its owners, and often passed from one generation to another, cast-iron cookware was an essential tool for preparing foods of many kinds. Pieces such as this stick pan (ca. 1900) became popular after colonists learned the art of making cornmeal-based breads from American Indians who had used ground corn as a food staple for thousands of years.

FARM-TO-TABLE VEGETARIAN

Balentine's Buttermilk Pie

1 3/4 cups sugar
1/4 cup flour
1 tablespoon vanilla
3 eggs, beaten
1/3 cup melted butter
3/4 cup buttermilk
1 teaspoon freshly grated nutmeg
1 unbaked (9-inch) pie shell

Combine the sugar and flour in a bowl. Whisk until well mixed. Add the vanilla. Whisk until evenly distributed. Add the beaten eggs. Whisk until incorporated. Whisk in the butter, buttermilk and nutmeg until blended.

Pour into the pie shell. Bake at 350 degrees for 45 minutes or until the pie is a light golden color with an ever-so-slightly firm center. Cool on a wire rack.

Serves 6 to 8

Fig Nut Roll Cookies

4 cups all-purpose flour
3/4 teaspoon baking soda
1 teaspoon baking powder
1 teaspoon cinnamon
1/2 teaspoon salt
1 cup (2 sticks) margarine, softened
1 cup granulated sugar
1 cup packed brown sugar
2 eggs
1 teaspoon vanilla extract
1 pound dried figs
1/4 teaspoon salt
1 cup granulated sugar
3/4 cup water
1 cup nuts, chopped

Mix the flour, baking soda, baking powder, cinnamon and 1/2 teaspoon salt together. Beat the margarine, 1 cup granulated sugar and brown sugar in a mixing bowl until light and fluffy. Add the eggs, one at a time, beating well after each addition. Beat in the dry ingredients gradually. Beat in the vanilla. Chill for 1 hour to overnight. Combine the figs, 1/4 teaspoon salt, 1 cup granulated sugar and water in a saucepan. Cook until the water is absorbed, stirring frequently. Remove to a blender and pulse to a thick paste. Remove to a bowl and stir in the nuts. Divide the dough into 4 parts and roll each portion into a rectangle on lightly floured waxed paper. Spread one-quarter of the fig filling over each rectangle, leaving a 1/2-inch border on one side. Roll up each rectangle starting from the opposite side of the border, using the waxed paper to aid in rolling. Press the dough edge to seal and wrap in plastic wrap. Freeze until firm. Cut the rolls into 1/4- to 1/3-inch slices. Arrange on a baking parchment paper-lined cookie sheet, cut side up. Bake at 350 degrees for 15 minutes or until lightly browned. Cool on the cookie sheet for 5 minutes. Remove to a wire rack to cool completely. Store in an airtight container at room temperature, or these may be frozen.

Makes 5 dozen

Variation: You may use dates instead of figs. If using dates, you do not need to process the filling in the blender.

Tip: Work with a one-fourth portion of the dough and filling at a time, as the chilled dough will be easier to handle.

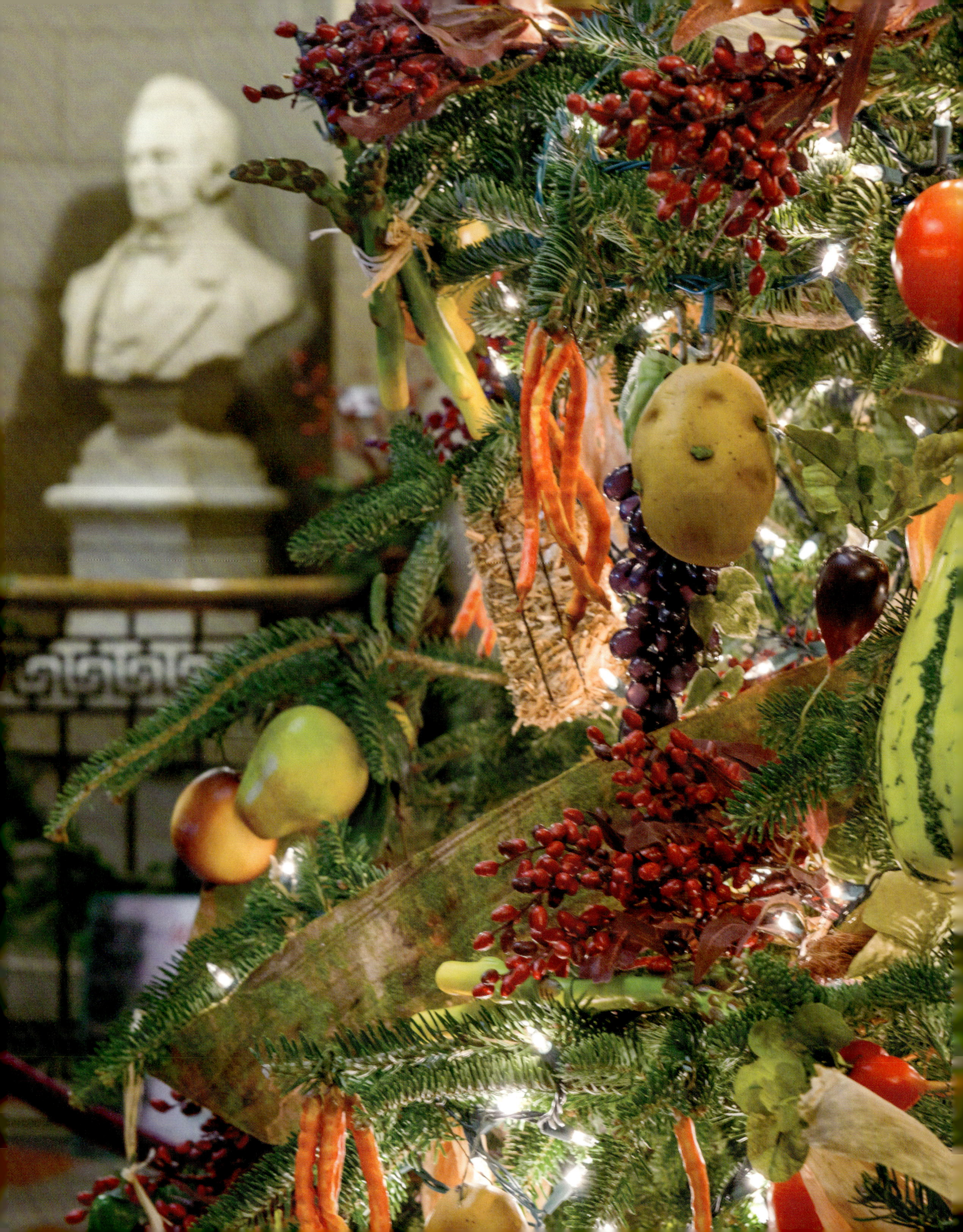

CENTRAL REGION

The Central Region has a rich history, a wide range of demographics, and a variety of weather. On winter days news reporters often remark about how it is colder and snowier in Roxboro and Person County than any place else in the region. President James Madison spent little, if any, time in North Carolina; however, snow or no snow, he may have briefly visited Person to see his wife Dolley's family.

Wake County now exceeds one million people in population, but the number swells even larger in the fall when visitors pour into Raleigh for college football and the annual North Carolina State Fair. Award-winning agricultural products and livestock are on display at the fair, and food vendors with their "fair fare" are legendary.

The rivalries between N.C. State, UNC, and Duke are long-running and well-documented. In Raleigh, Shaw and St. Augustine's Universities are cross-town rivals. In recent years Durham's N.C. Central University has stepped up to compete athletically with its big-time neighbors. At the professional level the Carolina Hurricanes take to the ice as part of the National Hockey League. In this part of North Carolina, football and hockey fans along Tobacco Road have at least one thing in common; they love to gather before games for tailgate picnics.

Johnston County features soil more like the Coastal Plain, while Person and Orange Counties have typical Piedmont red clay. Chatham County has poultry houses and processing, a large Hispanic population, and the charming courthouse town of Pittsboro. However, juxtaposed to agriculture and historic charm, booming suburbia spills over into Chatham from the Triangle.

Louisburg College in Franklin County is one of the oldest schools in the state, and Warren County is full of historic antebellum buildings. Robert E. Lee's family took refuge in Warrenton for most of the Civil War. Farming still makes a go of it in parts of the region, especially Vance, Granville, Johnston, and areas of Wake County. N.C. State University in Raleigh has done much to advance agriculture in North Carolina and beyond.

The booming Research Triangle Park (RTP) was formed by leaders and visionaries during the 1950s; and the original concept of a home for major research and development-related organizations remains strong in the twenty-first century. The RTP was laid out between Raleigh, Durham, and Chapel Hill on scrubby land. As land parcels were acquired for the park, some joked that vegetation was so sparse a rabbit would have to pack its lunch to cross the assembled tract. Today both rabbits and people are eating well in the Central Region.

CENTRAL REGION

TOBACCO ROAD TAILGATE MENU

Beer 'Garitas

Cheese Pecan Crisps

Curry Dip for Fresh Vegetables

Oven Fried Chicken

Ham & Cheese Roll

Pimento Cheese

Marinated Vegetable Salad

Sugar Cookies

Caramel Nut Fudgies

TOBACCO ROAD TAILGATE

Beer 'Garitas

1 cup frozen limeade concentrate, thawed
1 cup tequila
1/2 cup orange liqueur
Crushed ice
1/2 to 1 cup cold beer

Combine the limeade concentrate, tequila and orange liqueur in a pitcher; stir to blend well. Fill 4 medium glasses with crushed ice. Pour the limeade mixture evenly over the ice. Add beer to taste to each glass.

Serves 4

Cheese Pecan Crisps

1/2 cup (1 stick) butter, softened
8 ounces extra-sharp Cheddar cheese, shredded
1/4 teaspoon Worcestershire sauce
1 1/4 cups all-purpose flour
1/2 teaspoon salt
Dash of cayenne pepper
Dash of Tabasco sauce
1 cup pecans, finely chopped

Beat the butter and cheese together in a bowl. Add the Worcestershire sauce, flour, salt, cayenne pepper, Tabasco sauce and pecans and mix well. Chill until firm. Shape the mixture into 1 1/4-inch-diameter logs. Wrap in plastic wrap and freeze until firm. Remove from the freezer and let stand for 5 minutes. Slice the logs into thin rounds and arrange the rounds on an ungreased baking sheet. Bake at 350 degrees for 10 minutes. Cool on the baking sheet for 2 minutes. Remove to a wire rack to cool completely.

Makes 3 dozen

Curry Dip for Fresh Vegetables

1 cup mayonnaise
1 tablespoon chili sauce
1 tablespoon chutney
1 tablespoon Worcestershire sauce
2 tablespoons grated onion
1 teaspoon curry powder
1 teaspoon Tabasco sauce
Garlic salt to taste

Combine the mayonnaise, chili sauce, chutney, Worcestershire sauce, onion, curry powder, Tabasco sauce and garlic salt in a bowl and mix well. Chill until ready to serve. Serve with fresh vegetables, cold cooked shrimp or fried chicken breast nuggets for dipping.

Serves 16

The bottom of this stoneware jug (ca. 1861–1862) is embossed with the words "Morning Salute/B.F. & Co. N.Y." The bottle pays homage to soldiers of the 11th New York Volunteer Infantry Regiment of the Union Army; the unit was also known as "the Fire Zouaves," and was among the first to occupy territory within a Confederate state. The bottle was found, washed ashore, by Robert Clendenin, Company E, 13th North Carolina Troops, near Hampton Roads, Virginia, where the Zouaves were stationed for a time.

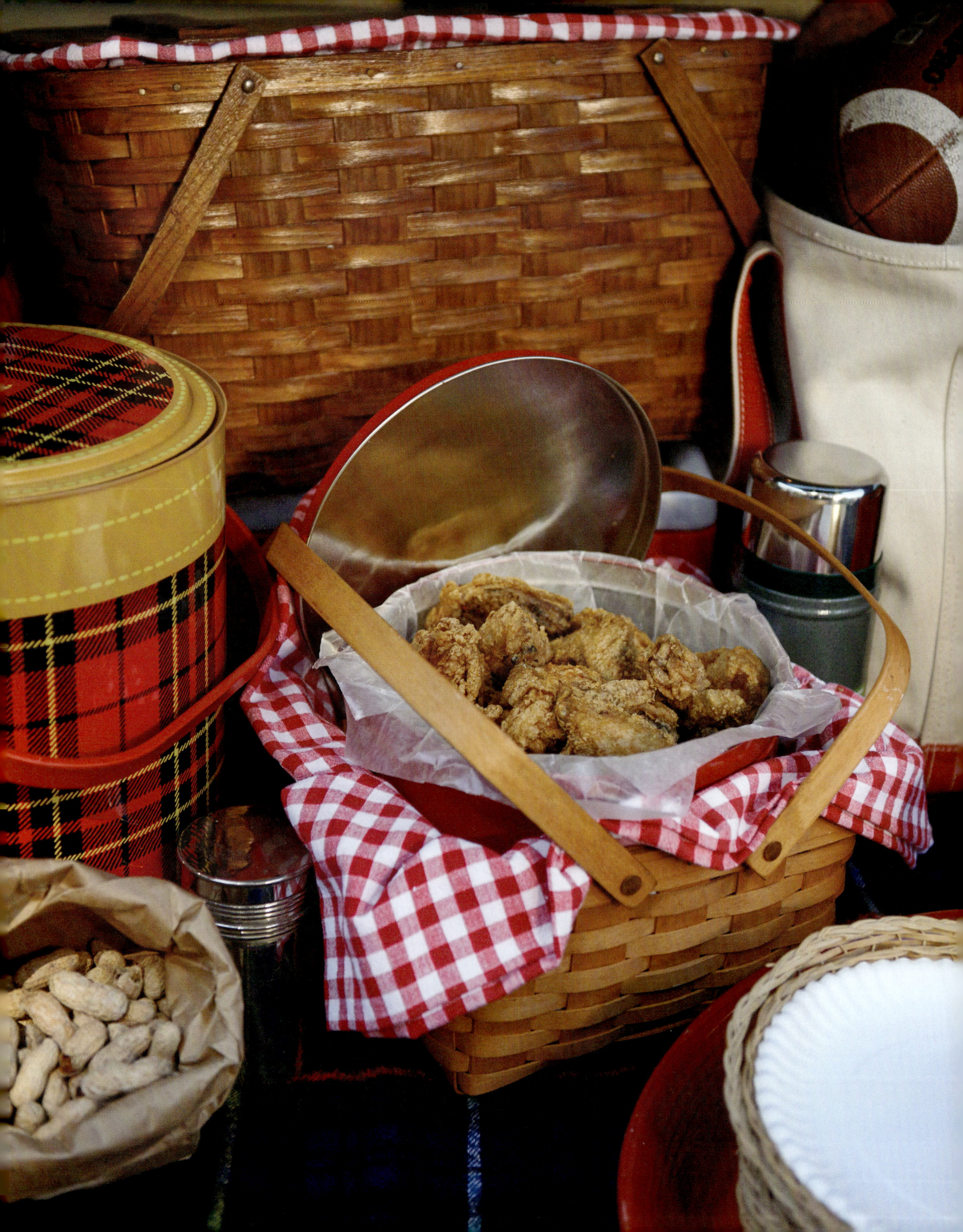

TOBACCO ROAD TAILGATE

Anne's Oven Fried Chicken

2 cups all-purpose flour
2 tablespoons smoky paprika
2 teaspoons salt
1/4 teaspoon garlic powder
1/4 to 1/2 teaspoon cayenne pepper or to taste
1 cup milk
1/4 to 1/2 cup butter or margarine
6 boneless, skinless chicken thighs, cut into halves
2 boneless, skinless chicken breasts, cut into thirds

Combine the flour, paprika, salt, garlic powder, and cayenne pepper in a shallow dish. Pour the milk into a second shallow dish. Melt 1/4 cup butter in each of one or two 9×13-inch baking dishes, depending on the size of the chicken pieces. Coat the chicken with the flour mixture; dip each piece into the milk. Dredge thoroughly in the flour mixture again. Place the chicken in the melted butter in the baking pan or pans. Bake at 425 degrees for 12 to 15 minutes. Remove from the oven; turn the chicken pieces over. Bake for 12 minutes longer or until the chicken tests done. Remove the chicken immediately to a wire rack to cool. May be made a day ahead and stored in the refrigerator.

Makes 6 servings

Ham and Cheese Rolls

2 packages frozen rolls in foil pans
8 ounces shredded Smithfield ham
8 ounces baby Swiss cheese, thinly sliced
3/4 cup (1 1/2 sticks) butter
2 tablespoons yellow mustard
2 tablespoons Worcestershire sauce
1/4 cup packed light brown sugar
1/4 cup packed dark brown sugar
Poppy seeds

Cut the frozen rolls in half crosswise and fit the bottom half of the rolls snugly back into the foil pans. Layer the ham and cheese evenly over the roll bottoms. Heat the butter, mustard, Worcestershire sauce, light brown sugar and dark brown sugar in a saucepan to boiling, stirring occasionally. Pour one-half of the butter mixture evenly over the cheese layers. Fit the roll tops into the pans and cut between the rolls with a knife to make removal easier for serving. Pour the remaining sauce evenly over the top of the rolls and sprinkle with poppy seeds. Bake at 350 degrees for 25 to 30 minutes.

Serves 12

Note: This freezes well. Thaw before reheating.

This 19th century Mulberry Transfer plate (ca. 1820-1846) depicts the Antonio Canova statue of George Washington that was commissioned by the North Carolina Legislature in 1821. The statue was placed in the rotunda of the original Capitol until the building burned in 1831 and the dome fell on the statue. The Museum still has fragments from the original statue, although a replica can be seen in the current Capitol, which was built in 1840.

CENTRAL REGION

Pimento Cheese

Combine the cheese, Worcestershire sauce, Tabasco sauce, undrained pimentos and sugar in a large bowl and toss to mix well. Stir in the drained pimentos. Add the mayonnaise and mix well. Chill, covered, for 24 hours.

Makes 3 cups

16 ounces New York extra-sharp Cheddar cheese, grated
1 1/2 teaspoons Worcestershire sauce
1/4 teaspoon Tabasco sauce
1 (4-ounce) jar diced pimentos, undrained
1 teaspoon sugar
1 (4-ounce) jar diced pimentos, drained
1 cup mayonnaise

Marinated Vegetable Salad

Makes a great summer salad with homemade fried chicken like we used to have on Sundays at my grandmother's.

Combine the sugar, vinegar, oil, pepper and salt in a saucepan. Bring to a boil. Cook until the sugar dissolves, stirring constantly. Remove from the heat; cool. Pour into a large salad bowl. Combine all of the vegetables in a bowl and mix well. Add to the cooled dressing; mix lightly. Chill, covered, until serving time.

Makes 8 to 10 servings

1 cup sugar
3/4 cup white vinegar
1/2 cup vegetable oil
1 teaspoon pepper
1/2 teaspoon salt
1 (16-ounce) can French green beans, drained
1 (17-ounce) can dark green peas, drained
1 (12-ounce) can Shoe Peg corn, drained
1 cup chopped celery
1 green bell pepper, finely chopped
1 bunch green onions, chopped
1 can red kidney beans, drained (optional)

BLACK-EYED SUSAN

Cream 2 sticks of softened butter in a bowl and stir in 1 pound of grated cheese, 12 ounces of all-purpose flour and salt and pepper to taste. Roll out thinly on a floured surface and cut out about 120 rounds with a biscuit cutter. Slice enough pecan-stuffed dates to make about 120 rounds. Place a date piece on each circle; fold the dough over to make small crescents and seal the edges. Sprinkle with sugar and bake on a baking parchment paper-lined baking sheet at 400 degrees for about 15 minutes.

TOBACCO ROAD TAILGATE

Olzie's Sugar Cookies

1 cup sugar
½ cup (1 stick) butter, melted
1 egg, beaten
1½ cups sifted all-purpose flour
1 teaspoon baking powder
½ teaspoon salt
1 tablespoon cream
½ teaspoon vanilla extract

When I was about 12, my older sister and I went to my dad's cousin Olzie's house, and she taught us how to make these delicious sugar cookies. I make them every year at Christmas.

Mix the sugar and melted butter in a bowl. Add the egg and mix well. Mix the flour, baking powder and salt together and stir into the butter mixture. Add the cream and vanilla and mix well. Chill for 20 minutes. Shape the dough into two logs. Wrap each in waxed paper and chill until firm. Slice the logs into thin rounds and arrange the rounds on an ungreased cookie sheet. Bake at 350 degrees for 8 to 10 minutes or until the edges are lightly browned. Cool on the cookie sheet for 2 minutes. Remove to a wire rack to cool completely.

Makes 3 dozen cookies

Caramel Nut Fudgies

Crust
1 cup all-purpose flour
1½ cups rolled oats
¾ cup packed brown sugar
½ teaspoon baking soda
¼ teaspoon salt
¾ cup (1½ sticks) butter, melted

Caramel
⅔ cup light corn syrup
⅔ cup packed brown sugar
6 tablespoons butter
½ teaspoon baking soda
2 cups chocolate chips
2 cups chopped walnuts

To make the crust, mix the flour, oats, brown sugar, baking soda and salt in a bowl. Add the melted butter and mix well. Press onto the bottom of a greased and floured 9×13-inch baking pan. Bake at 350 degrees for 10 minutes.

To make the caramel, combine the corn syrup, brown sugar, butter and baking soda in a saucepan. Bring to a boil, stirring constantly. Remove from the heat. Pour one-half of the caramel evenly over the baked crust. Sprinkle evenly with the chocolate chips and walnuts. Drizzle the remaining caramel over the walnuts. Bake for 10 minutes. Remove to a wire rack to cool completely. Cut into 12 squares when cool.

Serves 12

As the U.S. economy thrived after World War II, America's burgeoning middle class gained access to consumer goods like never before. Suburban housing markets exploded, along with demand for modern home appliances and furnishings, such as these steel kitchen canisters (ca. 1950).

CENTRAL REGION

'TIS THE SEASON HOLIDAY DINNER MENU

Christmas Grapefruit Starter

Oyster Stew

Butternut Squash with Pecans & Bleu Cheese

Green Bean Bundles

Holiday Mashed Potatoes

Roasted Beef Tenderloin

Rice Pudding Supreme with Cherry Sauce

Best Brownies Ever

Peppermint Stick Ice Cream

'TIS THE SEASON HOLIDAY DINNER

Lou's Christmas Grapefruit Starter

3 whole grapefruit
2 cups grapefruit juice from the fruit, plus additional grapefruit juice if needed
1 large package flavored gelatin (yellow for summer; red or green for Christmas, if desired)
¼ to ½ cup sugar
3 ounces cream cheese, softened
2 tablespoons honey
Juice of 1 large lime
1 cup whipped cream

This recipe became a holiday favorite of our family while we were living in England. It was given to me by an American friend.

Remove the grapefruit pulp and clean the shells of membrane. Reserve any juice and supplement to make 2 cups. Reserve the fruit from the shell. Heat the grapefruit juice in a saucepan. Add the gelatin and stir to dissolve. Add the sugar and stir to dissolve. Add the grapefruit. Pour into grapefruit halves, dispersing the fruit and liquid evenly. Carefully place on pans. Chill until set; cut each shell in half to make 12 "moons." Combine the cream cheese, honey and lime juice in a small bowl. Fold in the whipped cream. Serve over the grapefruit.
Serves 12

Kay's Oyster Stew

2 to 3 tablespoons butter
Chopped fresh parsley or dried parsley
1 pint oysters
2 cups milk, heated
1 teaspoon Worcestershire sauce
Salt and pepper to taste

Melt the butter in a saucepan. Stir in the parsley. Add the oysters and cook until the edges curl. Stir in the hot milk, Worcestershire sauce, salt and pepper. Cook over low heat until heated through.
Serves 4

This ceramic fish tureen (ca. 1935–1945) is part of a collection of gifts sent to North Carolina by way of the French Gratitude Train. In 1949, an ocean freighter delivered 49 small French boxcars, all filled with gifts from the citizens of France in appreciation for U.S. military involvement in World War II. The boxcar intended for North Carolina was officially received by Governor W. Kerr Scott and, following the reception ceremony and a parade, the boxcar and the gifts were moved to the state Museum of History for display.

MISS DUNCAN'S HOT APPLE TODDY

*Christmastime is here again
The brightest of the year.
So I send to you my recipe
For a bit of Christmas cheer.
To a quart of bottled apple juice
You can buy at any store,
Add a glass of apple jelly.*

*Of whole spice, a spoon or more.
Boil about five minutes well
And set aside to fuse.
Then mix with whiskey
    or brandy fine
In proportions as you choose.
Heat again and to each glass
Add a twist of lemon peel.*

*On your own mixture will
    depend
The cheer that you will feel.
But if you're generous as I think
'Twill warm your heart and body,
And now I give you Merry
    Christmas
In my own hot apple toddy.*

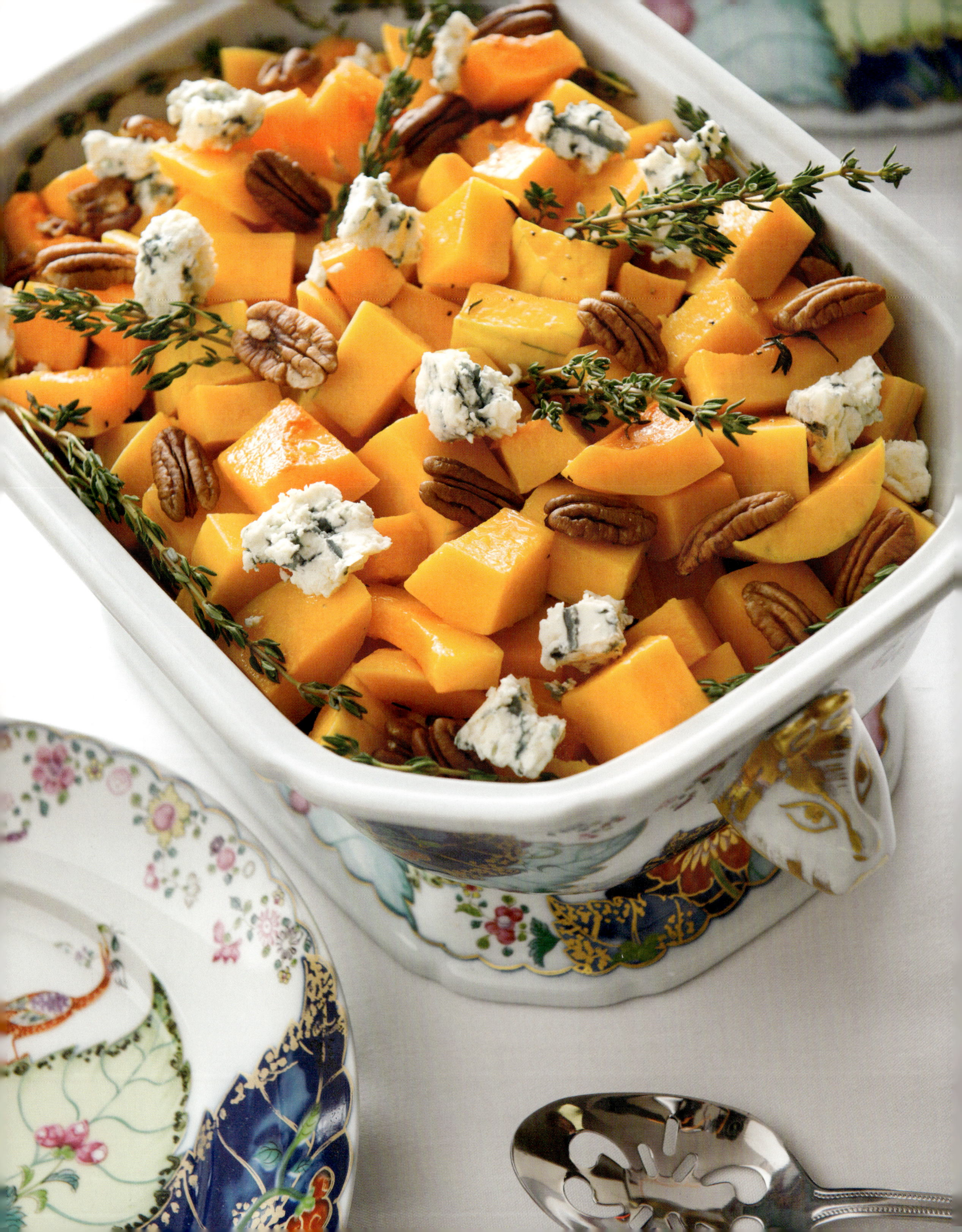

'TIS THE SEASON HOLIDAY DINNER

Jill's Butternut Squash with Pecans and Bleu Cheese

4 cups (1-inch cubes) peeled butternut squash
3 tablespoons olive oil
Leaves of 6 to 8 thyme sprigs
1/2 cup chopped salted pecans
1/2 cup (2 ounces) crumbled bleu cheese
Sea Salt and freshly ground peper
Additional thyme leaves

Arrange the squash in a single layer in a shallow baking pan. Drizzle with the olive oil and sprinkle with the thyme. Toss to coat and spread the squash in a single layer. Roast at 425 degrees for 30 to 45 minutes or until the squash is tender. Let cool slightly and remove to a serving bowl. Add the pecans and cheese and toss to mix. Sprinkle with sea salt and pepper to taste. Garnish with additional thyme leaves.
Serves 4 to 6

Green Bean Bundles

8 ounces sliced bacon, cut into halves
2 cans whole green beans, drained
3 tablespoons butter
3 tablespoons tarragon vinegar
1/2 teaspoon salt
1 teaspoon paprika
1 tablespoon chopped parsley
1 teaspoon onion juice

Wrap one half-slice of bacon around 5 beans and secure with a wooden pick. Repeat with the remaining beans and bacon. Arrange the bundles on a broiler pan. Broil until the bacon is cooked through. Remove the bean bundles to a serving platter and keep warm. Bring the butter, vinegar, salt, paprika, parsley and onion juice to a simmer in a small saucepan, stirring frequently. Drizzle over the beans and serve.
Serves 8 to 12

This Thomas Day dining table (ca. 1840–1849) is an excellent example of antebellum craftsmanship. Day, a native of Caswell County, and his work were lauded by many prominent and prosperous customers of the time. His artistic and entrepreneurial success is even more remarkable given that he was a free black man, living in the pre–Civil War South.

CENTRAL REGION

Holiday Mashed Potatoes

Cover the potatoes with water in a saucepan. Bring to a boil over high heat. Reduce the heat to low and simmer for 20 minutes or until tender; drain. Combine the potatoes, milk, cream cheese and butter in a mixing bowl. Mash with a potato masher or beat at medium speed until creamy. Stir in the garlic salt and pepper. Chill, covered, for up to 24 hours. Spoon the potatoes into a slow cooker coated with nonstick cooking spray. Cook, covered, on Low for 3 to 3 1/2 hours, stirring twice during cooking.

Serves 16

5 pounds Yukon Gold or russet potatoes, peeled and cut into 2-inch chunks
1/2 cup milk
8 ounces cream cheese, softened
1/4 cup (1/2 stick) butter
1 teaspoon garlic salt
1/4 teaspoon pepper

Roasted Beef Tenderloin

Mix the onion powder, white pepper, black pepper, garlic powder, oregano, salt and cornstarch in a bowl. Rub over all sides of the beef. Tuck under the thinner end of the beef to ensure even cooking. Place the beef in a foil-lined roasting pan and sprinkle any remaining rub over the beef. Roast at 500 degrees in the center of the oven for exactly 24 minutes for medium-rare; do not open the oven door during roasting. Remove the tenderloin and let rest for 15 minutes before carving.

Serves 16 to 18

2 tablespoons onion powder
2 tablespoons white pepper
2 tablespoons black pepper
2 tablespoons garlic powder
2 tablespoons ground oregano
2 tablespoons salt
2 tablespoons cornstarch
1 (7- to 8-pound) beef tenderloin

HORSERADISH CREAM SAUCE
Add 1 teaspoon salt to 1 cup heavy cream and whip until stiff. Fold in 1/4 cup horseradish. Serve at once with roasted beef tenderloin. Makes about 2 cups.

This [Gerhard] Henry Mahler cream pitcher, or creamer, (ca. 1852–1860) is made of North Carolina coin silver. Born in Osnabrück, in present-day Germany, Mahler became a silversmith, emigrated from Germany to the United States, and became part of a jewelry store in Raleigh. During the Civil War, Mahler supported the Confederacy by making belt buckles, buttons, sword butts, and other metal needs in partnership with other German citizens in town.

'TIS THE SEASON HOLIDAY DINNER

Susan's Rice Pudding Supreme with Cherry Sauce

Rice Pudding
6 cups water
1/2 cup rice
2 cups milk
1 tablespoon sugar
1 teaspoon salt
1 tablespoon butter
2 cups milk
1/2 cup plus 3 tablespoons sugar
3 envelopes unflavored gelatin
1/2 cup cold water
2 cups heavy whipping cream
2 tablespoons vanilla extract

Cherry Sauce
1/4 cup cornstarch
1/2 cup water
6 cups pitted sour cherries
2 cups water
2 tablespoons lemon juice
1 1/3 cups sugar
1/4 cup (1/2 stick) butter
Red food color (optional)

Years ago, when I was a young child, my mother found this recipe in an old Farm Journal *cookbook. When she served it for dessert at our Christmas Day dinner, it was an instant hit and became a family tradition, which continued after I married. My now adult children and grandchildren remind me every year to serve Rice Supreme for dessert at Christmas Day dinner.*

Bring 6 cups water to a boil in a saucepan. Add the rice and boil for 2 minutes. Drain and rinse with cold water. Drain and return to the saucepan. Stir in 2 cups milk, 1 tablespoon sugar and salt. Bring to a boil and add the butter. Reduce the heat and simmer, covered, for 20 minutes; do not stir. Remove to a bowl and stir in 2 cups milk and 1/2 cup plus 3 tablespoons sugar. Sprinkle the gelatin over 1/2 cup cold water in a small saucepan and let stand for 5 minutes. Cook over low heat until the gelatin is dissolved, stirring constantly. Stir into the rice mixture. Chill until thickened. Beat the whipping cream in a bowl until firm peaks form and add the vanilla. Fold into the rice mixture. Pour into a mold or an 8×11-inch pan and chill overnight. Serve with Cherry Sauce.

Cherry Sauce

Mix the cornstarch and 1/2 cup water in a small bowl. Combine the cherries, 2 cups water, lemon juice and sugar in a saucepan and bring to a boil. Stir in the cornstarch mixture. Cook for 2 to 3 minutes or until clear and thickened, stirring constantly. Remove from the heat and stir in the butter and food color. Pour into a bowl and chill.

Serves 8

CENTRAL REGION

GIFTS FROM THE KITCHEN

Billy's Family Fudge

A special thing at my house at Christmas is fudge-making. My great aunt passed the recipe to my grandmother who passed it down to my mom. It has a great rich and sweet taste. It is special because my family gets together before Christmas to make bunches of it to take to friends. I love it when I get to lick the fudge bowl.

Combine the sugar, margarine and milk in a saucepan. Bring to a boil and boil for 9 minutes, stirring constantly. Remove from the heat and stir in the chocolate chips, marshmallow creme and nuts. Pour into two greased 9×13-inch pans. Cool completely before cutting into squares.

Makes 5 pounds

5 cups sugar
1 cup (2 sticks) margarine
1 (12-ounce) can evaporated milk
3 cups semisweet chocolate chips
1 (7-ounce) container marshmallow creme
Chopped nuts to taste

Mary Ruth's Candied Grapefruit Strips

Combine the grapefruit peel and salt in a heavy saucepan and cover with cold water. Bring to a boil and boil for 20 minutes; drain. Repeat the boiling two more times, omitting the salt; drain well. Combine the peel and 2 cups sugar in a saucepan. Simmer until almost all of the sugar has been absorbed by the peel, stirring constantly. Spread the peel over waxed paper. Sprinkle with sugar and let dry. Store in an airtight container.

Makes 3 cups

Peel from 3 grapefruits, cut into 1/4-inch strips
1 teaspoon salt
2 cups sugar
Additional sugar for sprinkling

Jenny's Hot Fudge Sauce

Melt the butter and chocolate in the top of a double boiler over simmering water and stir to blend well. Remove from the heat. Stir in the sugar and salt. Stir in the evaporated milk gradually. Return the double boiler to the heat. Cook for 4 minutes, stirring constantly. Remove from the heat and stir in the vanilla and almond extracts. Spoon the warm sauce over peppermint ice cream. Store in the refrigerator and reheat if desired.

Makes 3 cups

3/4 cups (1 1/2 sticks) butter
9 ounces unsweetened chocolate
2 cups sugar
Pinch of salt
2 cups evaporated milk
1 tablespoon vanilla extract
1 1/2 teaspoons almond extract (optional)

'TIS THE SEASON HOLIDAY DINNER

Best Brownies Ever

4 ounces unsweetened chocolate
3/4 cup (1 1/2 sticks) butter
1 1/2 cups granulated sugar
1/2 cup packed brown sugar
3 eggs, at room temperature
1 cup all-purpose flour
1 teaspoon vanilla extract
Salt
1 cup semisweet chocolate chips (optional)

Line an 8×8-inch baking pan with foil, allowing the foil to extend 2 to 3 inches over the side of the pan. Grease the foil lightly and set aside. Microwave the chocolate and butter in a large microwave-safe bowl on High for 1 1/2 to 2 minutes or until melted and smooth, stirring every 30 seconds. Whisk in the granulated sugar and brown sugar. Add the eggs, one at a time, whisking just until blended after each addition. Whisk in the flour, vanilla and salt. Stir in the chocolate chips. Pour into the prepared pan. Bake at 350 degrees for 40 to 44 minutes or until a wooden pick inserted in the center comes out with a few moist crumbs. Remove to a wire rack and cool in the pan. Lift the brownies out of the pan to a cutting board. Remove the foil and cut the brownies into squares.

Serves 16

Peppermint Stick Ice Cream

8 ounces peppermint stick candy, crushed
2 cups whole milk
1 cup evaporated milk
1 cup whipping cream
Half-and-half
Peppermint extract to taste (optional)
4 ounces peppermint stick candy, crushed

Stir 8 ounces crushed candy into the whole milk in a bowl. Chill, covered, overnight. Stir in the evaporated milk and cream. Pour into an ice cream freezer container and add half-and-half to the fill line. Add peppermint extract. Freeze using the manufacturer's directions. Fold in 4 ounces crushed candy and freeze until firm.

Makes 1 quart

The first small-scale ice cream–making machines were patented in 1843 and, with subsequent improvements, a once rare and exotic dessert became more accessible to the public. Freezers such as this one (ca. 1915–1920) were often cranked to produce a confectionary treat on the spot, at family gatherings and reunions.

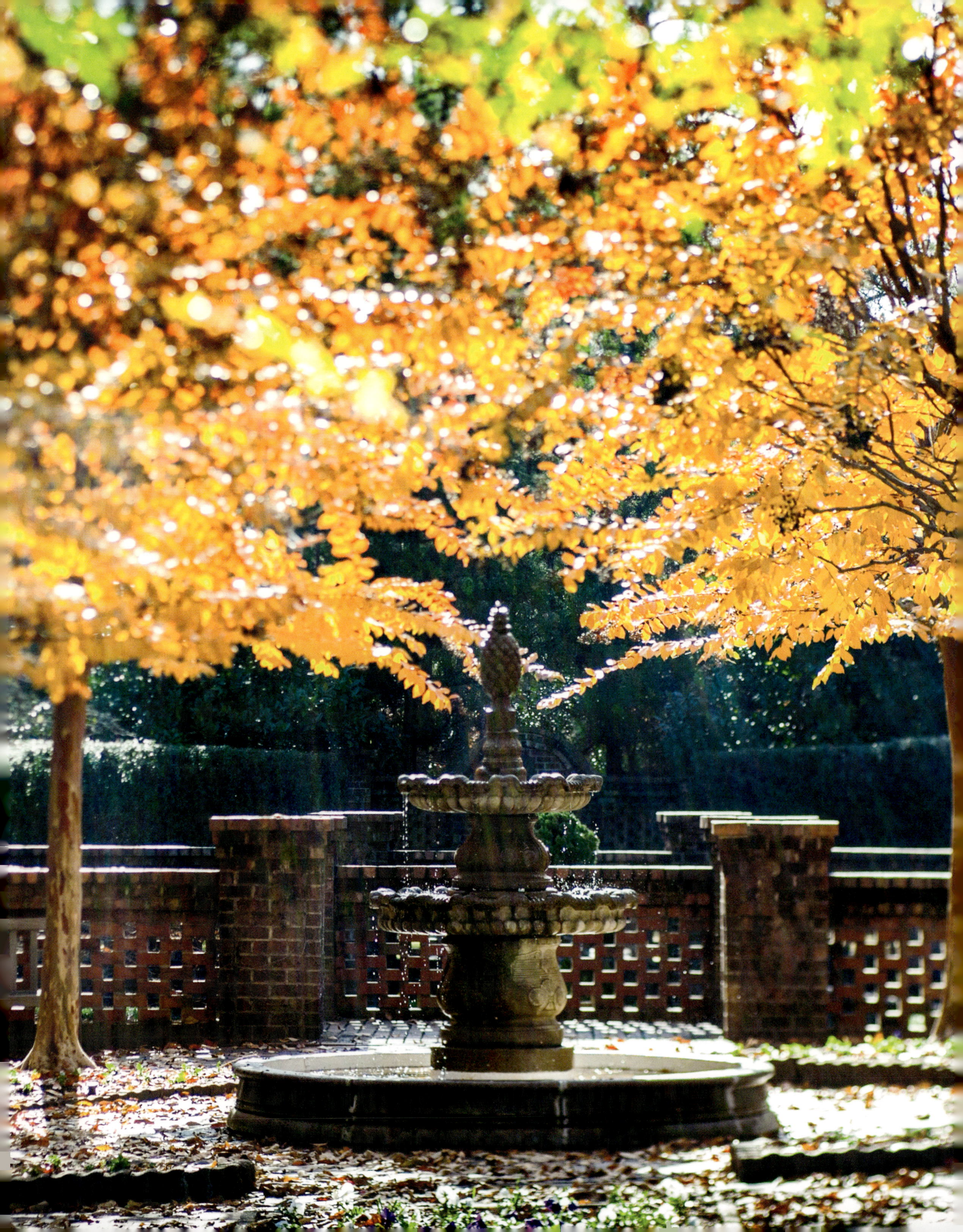

SANDHILLS REGION

The Sandhills Region covers south-central North Carolina and includes the geographical center of the state, which is near the town of Star in northern Montgomery County. This is a diverse region geographically and geologically. The western portions of the region feature clay soil and some small mountains; however, much of the region is sandy or has soil that combines sand with clay.

The Fall Line—the geological boundary between the upland and the coastal plain—occurs in the eastern portion of the Sandhills. To the west the Uwharrie Mountains lie in parts of Montgomery, Stanly, and Randolph Counties, with some elevations topping a thousand feet. Geologists reckon the Uwharries to be the oldest mountains in North Carolina.

Pinehurst and Southern Pines are synonymous with the Sandhills. Folks from around the world travel to golf resorts in Moore County to play on some of the highest-ranked courses in the world. The men's and women's U.S. Open Golf Tournaments have been staged here. Lavish tailgate meals are often spread at steeplechases where fine food and its presentation, along with festive attire, are de rigueur.

In Moore County it is not uncommon to hear and feel the rumble of artillery or the roar of airplanes because not too far to the east are Fort Bragg and Pope Air Force Base. Retired military veterans have sometimes made Moore County their home. The great George C. Marshall, a five-star general and Army Chief-of-Staff during World War II, owned a cottage in Pinehurst from 1946 until his death in 1959.

Historically, the region has relied on timber, textiles, apparel, and hosiery for industry, while also raising corn, wheat, soybeans, and tobacco. Peaches are an important crop in Moore, Montgomery, and Richmond Counties. Although many bushels of peaches are shipped out of the area, makeshift markets offering the succulent fruit crowd Sandhills roadsides every summer. Both large- and small-scale chicken and turkey producers are scattered throughout much of the region. Union County is a center of poultry production.

Lake Tillery and Badin Lake on the Pee Dee River have a number of second homeowners, retirees, and commuters living on their shores, but they also remain popular public destinations for water play and fishing. The North Carolina State Zoo is near Asheboro; and Fayetteville's Dogwood Festival celebrates music, arts, and crafts.

In 1921 the commander-in-chief of all Allied forces in World War I, France's Ferdinand Foch, toured the United States. His only stop in North Carolina was in Monroe. After Foch's speech, he and Governor Cameron Morrison adjourned to enjoy a large banquet at the Hotel Joffre in celebration of the occasion. The menu from that day hasn't been located, but perhaps something among these tasty Sandhills brunch offerings awaited the dignitaries.

SANDHILLS REGION

LAISSEZ-FAIRE BRUNCH MENU

Magnolias

Fruit Salad with Honey Citrus Dressing

Herb Cheddar Biscuits

Green Tomato Pickle Relish

Eggs Bel Mar

Eggy Muffins

Peach Cobbler

Peach Ice Cream & Shortbread

LAISSEZ-FAIRE BRUNCH

Magnolias

4 cups orange juice, chilled
1 bottle Champagne, chilled
1/2 cup Grand Marnier, chilled
Orange slices and maraschino cherries

Combine the orange juice, Champagne and Grand Marnier in a pitcher; mix lightly. Pour into glasses and garnish with orange slices and maraschino cherries.

Fruit Salad with Honey Citrus Dressing

Dressing
8 to 10 mint leaves
1/2 cup sourwood honey or other good-quality honey
1 to 2 teaspoons poppy seeds
Dash of grated orange zest
Dash of grated lemon zest
Juice of 1 orange
Juice of 1 lemon
1/4 cup dry white wine (optional)

Salad
4 bananas, sliced
4 oranges, cut into bite-size pieces
4 apples, cut into bite-size pieces
4 cups strawberries
2 cups blackberries, raspberries or blueberries
Mint leaves

My husband is always responsible for bringing the salads to a marvelous Easter afternoon potluck at the home of fellow Moravians. The secret is high-quality honey, obtained for many years from great-granddaddy in Caldwell County.

To make the dressing, process the mint, honey, poppy seeds, orange zest, lemon zest, orange juice, lemon juice and wine in a blender at high speed for a short time.

To make the salad, combine the bananas, oranges, apples, strawberries and blackberries in a large bowl and toss gently to mix. Pour the dressing evenly over the fruit and garnish with mint leaves. Chill, covered, for 1 hour.

Serves 8 to 10

Note: Try using different mints for the dressing, such as a combination of spearmint and lemon mint. Feel free to use your favorite fruits in the salad.

This stenciled fruit painting was created by Annie McIntyre, a native of Fayetteville, likely between 1815 and 1825. The style of stencil painting was known as theorem, or "formula," painting, and was often done on velvet, as this example is. Its popularity peaked from 1820 to 1840 and classes were frequently included in the curriculums of fashionable girls' boarding schools. Subjects often included seasonal foods and local scenes.

SANDHILLS REGION

Chancy's Herb Cheddar Biscuits

This was a winner in the University of Georgia's Fall 2007 "Taste of Home". The University of North Carolina Chapel Hill was chartered in 1789 and began enrolling students in 1795. The University of Georgia in Athens was chartered in 1785, making it the first state-chartered public university; however, Georgia didn't begin admitting students until 1801.

Sprinkle the baking soda over the flour in a bowl. Cut in the shortening and butter with a pastry blender or fork until crumbly. Stir in the rosemary, cheese and Tabasco sauce. Stir in the buttermilk until a thick dough forms. Pat or roll out the dough on a lightly floured surface to 1/2 to 3/4 inch thick. Cut the dough with a biscuit cutter and arrange the biscuits on a baking sheet lined with baking parchment paper. Bake at 450 degrees on the top rack in the oven for 5 to 7 minutes.
Makes 20 to 24 buscuits

1 scant teaspoon baking soda
2 cups self-rising flour
1/3 to 1/2 cup mixture of shortening and butter or all butter
1 tablespoon dried ground rosemary, ground sage or ground thyme
1/4 to 1/2 cup shredded sharp Cheddar cheese
Dash of Tabasco sauce
3/4 to 1 cup good quality full-fat buttermilk

Frances' Green Tomato Pickle Relish

My grandmother lived in Beaufort with her children during WWII, while my grandfather served in the Marine Corps. My father has shared many memories of his life there on the farm with aunts, uncles, and cousins. This is a particular family favorite, which I remember my grandmother making for us. It was served next to our eggs in the morning!

Mix the tomatoes, green bell peppers, red bell peppers, celery and salt in a very large saucepan. Add just enough water to cover the vegetables and let stand for several hours; drain. Add the vinegar, brown sugar and mustard and mix well. Add the cheesecloth bag. Bring to a boil and reduce the heat, stirring occasionally. Simmer for 25 minutes, stirring occasionally. Remove and discard the cheesecloth bag. Pack the relish into hot sterilized canning jars leaving 1/2-inch headspace. Seal with two-piece lids. Process in a boiling water bath for 10 minutes.
Makes 12 pints
Tip: Use a food processor to finely chop the vegetables.

12 pounds green tomatoes, finely chopped
12 green bell peppers, finely chopped
12 red bell peppers, finely chopped
3 ribs celery, finely chopped, or 1 tablespoon celery seeds
3/4 cup pickling salt
8 cups vinegar
6 3/4 cups packed brown sugar
1 tablespoon dry mustard
1 tablespoon whole cloves and 1 cinnamon stick, tied in a cheesecloth bag

LAISSEZ-FAIRE BRUNCH

Anne's Eggs Bel Mar

¼ cup (½ stick) margarine
¼ cup all-purpose flour
2 cups milk
3 tablespoons margarine
⅓ cup chopped green onions
⅓ cup chopped red or yellow bell pepper
1 can sliced mushrooms, drained
1 cup chopped ham (optional)
3 tablespoons margarine
18 eggs, beaten
1 teaspoon salt
½ teaspoon pepper
1 cup soft bread crumbs

Melt ¼ cup margarine in a saucepan. Whisk in the flour. Cook for 1 minute, whisking constantly. Stir in the milk gradually. Cook until thickened, stirring constantly. Remove from the heat and let cool. Melt 3 tablespoons margarine in a skillet. Add the green onions, bell pepper, mushrooms and ham and sauté until the green onions and bell pepper are tender. Remove from the heat and set aside. Melt 3 tablespoons margarine in a skillet. Add the eggs and cook until scrambled but still moist, stirring constantly. Remove to a large bowl. Add the white sauce, sautéed vegetables, salt and pepper and mix well. Spoon into a 9×13-inch baking dish coated with nonstick cooking spray. Sprinkle with the bread crumbs. Bake at 325 degrees for 45 to 50 minutes.

Serves 10 to 12

Note: This can be made ahead and chilled overnight. Adjust the baking time if chilled.

Julia's Eggy Muffins

12 hard-cooked eggs, diced
16 ounces sharp Cheddar cheese, shredded
1 small to medium onion, diced
8 ounces bacon, crisp-cooked and crumbled
1 tablespoon spicy mustard
Worcestershire sauce or soy sauce to taste
Tabasco sauce to taste
Garlic powder to taste
Freshly ground pepper to taste
Mayonnaise
8 English muffins, split
Grated Parmesan cheese

Combine the eggs, Cheddar cheese, onion and bacon in a bowl and toss to mix. Add the mustard, Worcestershire sauce, Tabasco sauce, garlic powder and pepper and toss to mix. Stir in mayonnaise until the consistency of chicken salad. Spoon equal portions over the muffin halves and sprinkle with Parmesan cheese. Arrange on a baking sheet and broil until hot and bubby. Serve with Frances' Green Tomato Pickle Relish on the side.

Serves 8

Note: The egg mixture can be made ahead and kept in an airtight container in the refrigerator for up to 3 days.

Split baskets, like this egg basket (ca. 1900–1910), were frequently made of white oak splints due to the tree's abundance in North Carolina, its relatively low chance of splintering while being worked, and its durability. Such baskets were typically made after the planting and harvesting seasons from young white oak trees with straight bark.

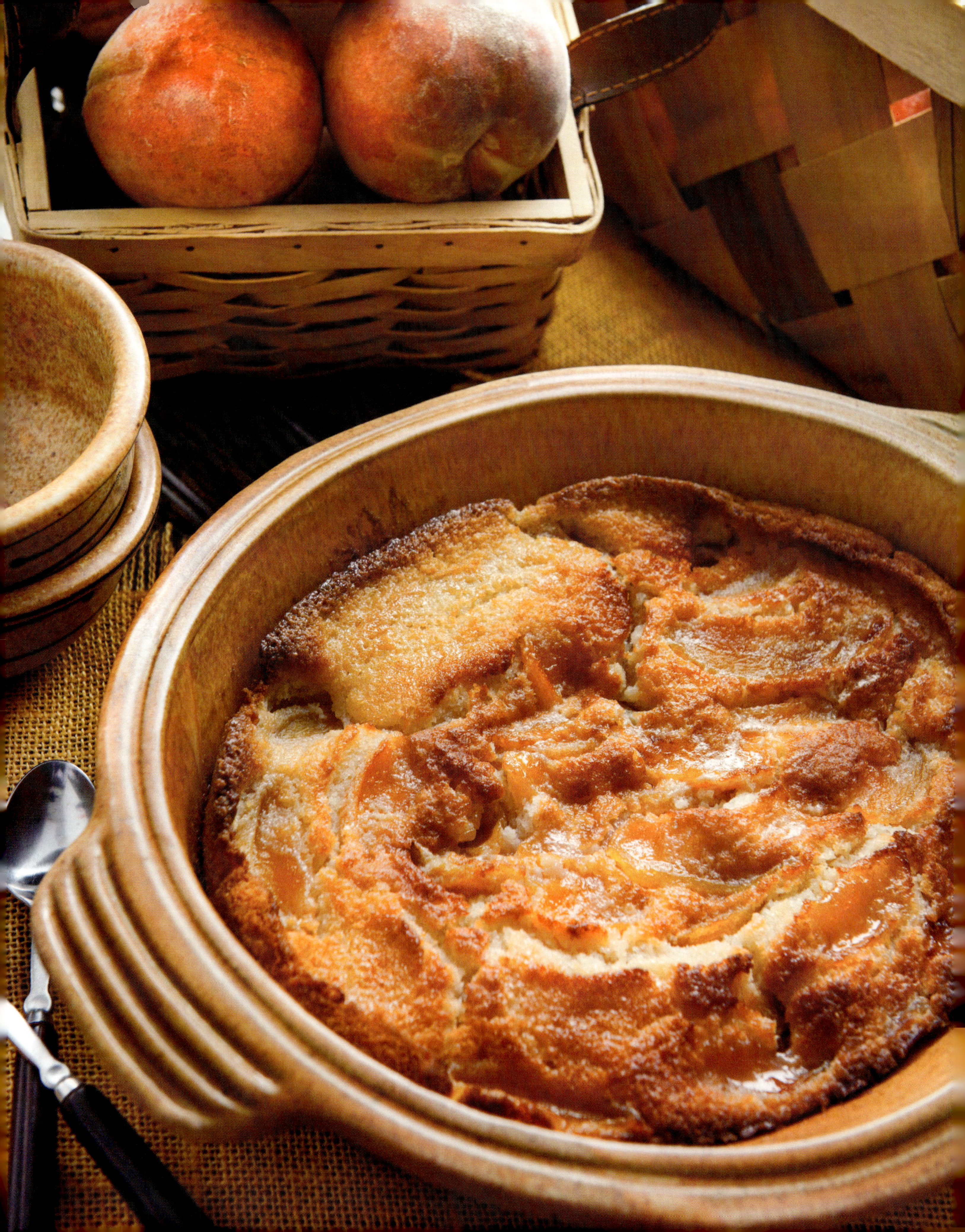

LAISSEZ-FAIRE BRUNCH

Charlie's Peach Cobbler

4 cups peeled sliced peaches
3/4 cup sugar
1/2 cup water
12 tablespoons (1 1/2 sticks) unsalted butter
1 1/4 cups sugar
1 1/2 cups all-purpose flour
2 1/2 teaspoons baking powder
3/4 teaspoon salt
1 1/2 cups whole milk
Sugar for sprinkling

Combine the peaches, 3/4 cup sugar and water in a saucepan. Bring to a boil, stirring constantly. Reduce the heat and simmer for 10 to 12 minutes or until syrupy; set aside. Melt 4 tablespoons of the butter in a 9×13-inch heatproof glass dish in a 350-degree oven. Combine the remaining 8 tablespoons butter, 1 1/4 cups sugar, flour, baking powder and salt in a mixing bowl. Stir in the milk. Spread in the buttered pan. Layer the peaches carefully over the batter. Sprinkle with additional sugar. Bake at 350 degrees until the topping is crisp. Do not overbake.
Makes 12 servings

Note: You may substitute 2 pints of blueberries mashed with 2 tablespoons sugar in place of the peaches.

Peach Ice Cream

5 pounds peaches (or more if they are very "bruised"), peeled chopped
2 1/2 cups sugar
Dash of almond extract
6 cups half-and-half

Combine the peaches and sugar in a large bowl. Let stand for 30 minutes or until very juicy. Very ripe peaches will take less time. Purée 1/2 at a time in a blender container. Pour both batches into a 4-quart ice cream freezer container. Stir in the almond extract and half-and-half. Freeze using the manufacturer's directions.
Makes 3 quarts

Scottish Shortbread

1 cup (2 sticks) butter, softened
1/4 cup sugar
2 cups all-purpose flour
1/4 cup cornstarch
Pinch of salt

Cream the butter and sugar in a mixer bowl until the mixture is the consistency of mayonnaise. Sift the flour, cornstarch and salt together. Stir into the creamed mixture gradually until well mixed. Pat or roll into a 1/2-inch-thick round on an ungreased baking sheet. Bake at 325 degrees for 30 minutes. Turn the oven off. Cut the shortbread into pieces and return to the warm oven to crisp.
Makes 30 pieces

Originally carved in Europe, this butter stamp (ca. 1770–1820) was brought to America by a Scottish immigrant family in the 1700s. Used to mark the top of a block of butter, stamps like this were typically used by wealthy families and reserved for entertaining.

SANDHILLS REGION

STEEPLECHASE PICNIC MENU

Mint Julep

*Hearts of Palm,
Artichoke & Belgian Endive Salad*

Tomato Pie

Ham & Swiss Quiche

Sweet Potato Biscuits

Country Ham with Bourbon Cream Sauce

Man Catcher Biscuits

Blueberry Tea Cakes

STEEPLECHASE PICNIC

Mint Julep

Fresh mint sprigs
1 teaspoon superfine sugar
3 ounces Kentucky bourbon

For each serving, place 5 or 6 mint leaves in a chilled 12-ounce silver julep cup or highball glass. Add the sugar and crush slightly with a muddler. Pack the glass with finely crushed ice and pour the bourbon over the ice. Stir briskly until the glass is frosty. Add additional ice and stir again just before serving. Garnish with mint sprigs. Serve with a short straw.

Makes 1 serving

Hearts of Palm, Artichoke and Belgian Endive Salad

1 (14-ounce) can artichoke hearts, drained and chopped
1 (14-ounce) can hearts of palm, drained and chopped
4 ounces bleu cheese, crumbled
8 slices bacon, crisp-cooked and crumbled
1/4 cup chopped green onions
2 tablespoons finely chopped fresh parsley
2 garlic cloves, crushed
6 tablespoons extra-virgin olive oil
2 tablespoons fresh lemon juice
Salt and pepper to taste
8 heads Belgian endive, split and sliced

Mix the artichokes and hearts of palm in a bowl. Stir in the cheese, bacon, green onions, parsley and garlic. Whisk the olive oil and lemon juice in a bowl. Add to the artichoke mixture and toss to coat. Season with salt and pepper and stir in the endive. Chill until ready to serve.

Serves 8 to 10

This stoneware tea service (ca. 1930) includes a tray, a teapot, a sugar bowl, and a creamer—all marked "Jugtown Ware." Juliana and Jacques Busbee began stamping pieces from Jugtown, their pottery near Seagrove (Moore County), in the early 1920s. Initially, the Busbees had local potters make the products, then shipped the wares to New York, where the pieces were marketed and sold at a tearoom and craft shop in Greenwich Village. As the business grew, they trained new, young potters.

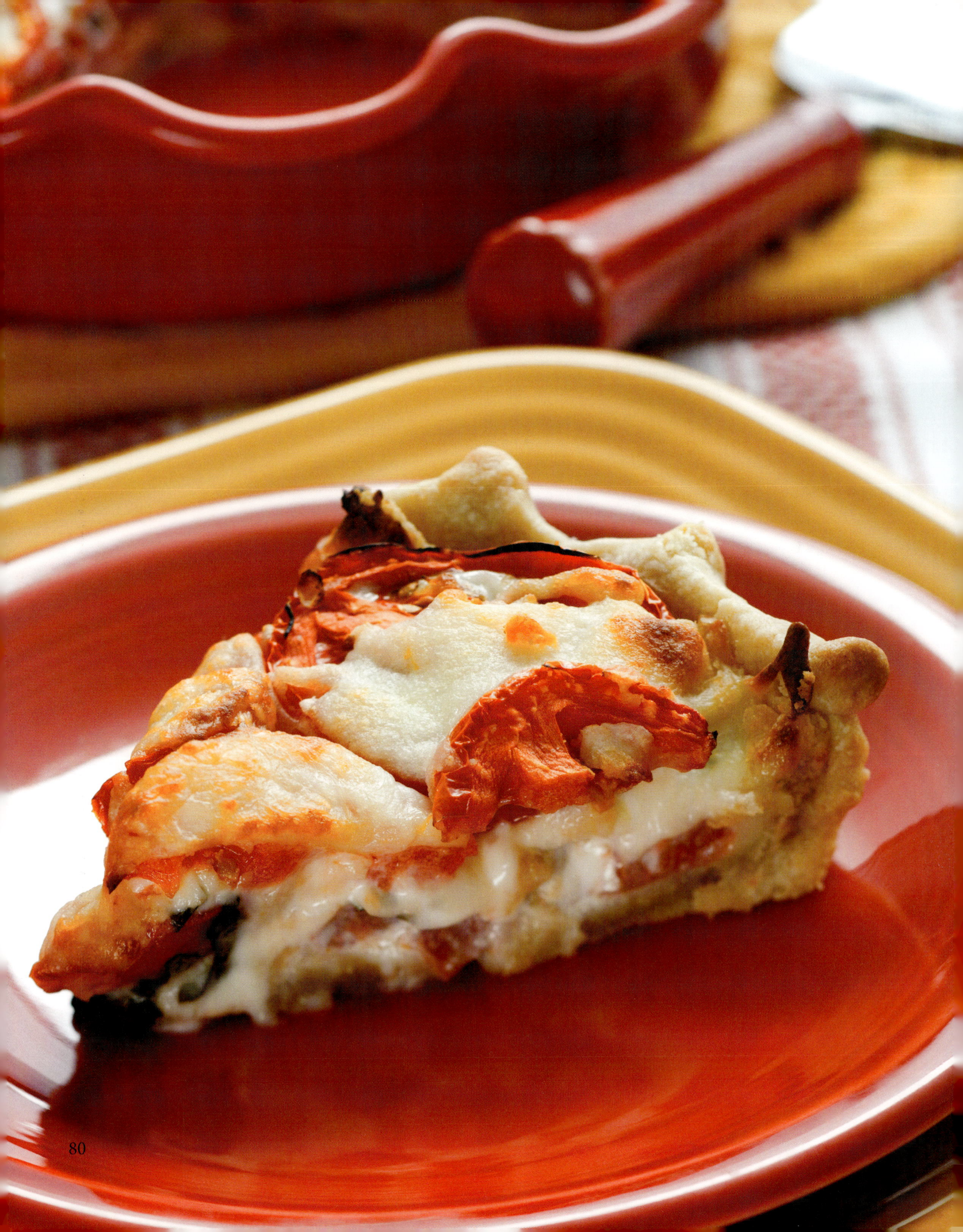

STEEPLECHASE PICNIC

Cathy's Tomato Pie

1 unbaked (9-inch) pie shell
½ cup (2 ounces) shredded mozzarella cheese
4 tomatoes
1 teaspoon salt
⅛ teaspoon white pepper
2 garlic cloves, minced
1 cup basil leaves, chopped
½ cup mayonnaise
1 cup (4 ounces) shredded mozzarella cheese
¼ cup (1 ounce) grated Parmesan cheese

Prick the pie shell with a fork and bake at 350 degrees for 10 minutes or just until beginning to brown. Sprinkle ½ cup mozzarella cheese over the hot crust and set aside to cool. Slice the tomatoes and drain well on paper towels. Arrange the tomatoes in the pie crust and sprinkle with the salt and white pepper. Sprinkle the garlic and basil over the tomatoes. Mix the mayonnaise, 1 cup mozzarella cheese and Parmesan cheese in a bowl. Spread evenly over the basil. Bake at 375 degrees for 45 to 60 minutes.

Serves 6

Liz's Ham and Swiss Quiche

1½ cups cubed cooked ham
1½ cups (6 ounces) shredded Swiss cheese or Havarti cheese
1 cup frozen chopped spinach, thawed and drained well
1 unbaked (9-inch) deep-dish pie shell
8 eggs, beaten
1 cup half-and-half
3 tablespoons honey mustard
2 tablespoons all-purpose flour
½ teaspoon salt
½ teaspoon dried thyme
⅛ teaspoon white pepper
2 tablespoons grated Parmesan cheese

Layer the ham, Swiss cheese and spinach in the pie shell. Whisk the eggs, half-and-half, mustard, flour, salt, thyme and white pepper in a bowl and pour into the pie shell. Sprinkle with the Parmesan cheese. Bake at 350 degrees for 40 to 50 minutes or until the crust is golden brown and the filling is set.

Serves 6 to 8

This lily-patterned quilt (ca. 1855) was handmade by Margaret Graham Scott in Alamance County. The art of quilting originally was born of necessity—to provide warm coverings for beds as well as hangings for doors and window. Quilts were made with homespun cloth, scraps, or wornout fabric.

81

SANDHILLS REGION

Sweet Potato Biscuits

Combine the sweet potatoes, sugar, margarine and milk in a large bowl and mix well. Add the shortening to the flour in a bowl and cut in with a pastry blender or fork until crumbly. Add to the sweet potato mixture and stir just until a dough forms. Roll out the dough on a floured surface and cut with a biscuit cutter. Arrange the biscuits on a nonstick baking sheet and let rise for 20 minutes. Bake at 425 degrees for 12 to 15 minutes.
Makes 5 dozen

2 cups mashed cooked sweet potatoes (6 to 8 sweet potatoes)
1 cup sugar
1/2 cup (1 stick) margarine, softened
1 cup milk
1 tablespoon shortening
4 cups self-rising flour, sifted

Country Ham with Bourbon Cream Sauce

Sauté the country ham in the butter in a sauté pan for 2 minutes on each side or until golden brown. Remove the ham and keep warm. Add the bourbon, cream and pepper to the sauté pan. Cook over medium heat until thickened, stirring constantly; do not boil. Remove from the heat and stir in the cream. Serve the ham on Sweet Potato Biscuits. Serve the bourbon cream sauce on the side.
Makes about 1/2 cup

12 ounces country ham
1/4 cup (1/2 stick) butter
2 tablespoons Gentleman Jack bourbon
1 1/4 cups heavy cream
Black pepper to taste

Mama Jo's Man Catcher Biscuits

Sprinkle the baking soda over the flour in a bowl. Cut in the shortening and butter with a pastry blender or fork until crumbly. Stir in the buttermilk until a thick dough forms. Pat or roll out the dough on a lightly floured surface to 1/2- to 3/4-inch thick. Cut the dough with a biscuit cutter and arrange the biscuits on a baking sheet lined with parchment paper. Bake at 450 degrees on the top rack in the oven for 5 to 7 minutes.
Makes 20 to 24
Note: You may use all butter instead of a butter and shortening combination.

1 scant teaspoon baking soda
2 cups self-rising flour
1/3 to 1/2 cup mixture of shortening and butter
3/4 to 1 cup good-quality full-fat buttermilk

STEEPLECHASE PICNIC

Grace's Blueberry Tea Cakes

2 cups sifted self-rising flour
¼ cup (½ stick) butter, softened
¾ cup sugar
1 egg
1 teaspoon vanilla exact
½ cup milk
1 cup (or more) blueberries

Topping
½ cup (1 stick) butter, softened
⅓ cup sugar
¼ cup all-purpose flour
½ teaspoon cinnamon

This is the recipe of a dear friend who was also the aunt of General Hugh Shelton. These cakes were her favorite blueberry dessert.

Combine the flour, butter and sugar in a bowl; whisk to blend. Add the egg, vanilla and milk; mix well. Fold in the blueberries. Spoon into a greased tea cake or muffin pan. Sprinkle with the topping. Bake at 350 degrees for 40 to 45 minutes or until the tea cakes test done.

For the topping: Combine the butter, sugar, flour and cinnamon in a small bowl. Mix together until crumbly. *Makes 1 dozen*
Note: This is really good served with a scoop of vanilla ice cream.

This blue transfer-printed pearlware platter (ca. 1825–1834) depicts the 1824 arrival of General Lafayette in New York, where he kicked off a "grand tour of the United States" to commemorate its 50th anniversary. The Marquis de Lafayette, who had played a significant role in the state during the Revolutionary War, was so beloved by North Carolinians that the residents of Cross Creek and Campbellton renamed their town Fayetteville, the first U.S. city to be named in his honor.

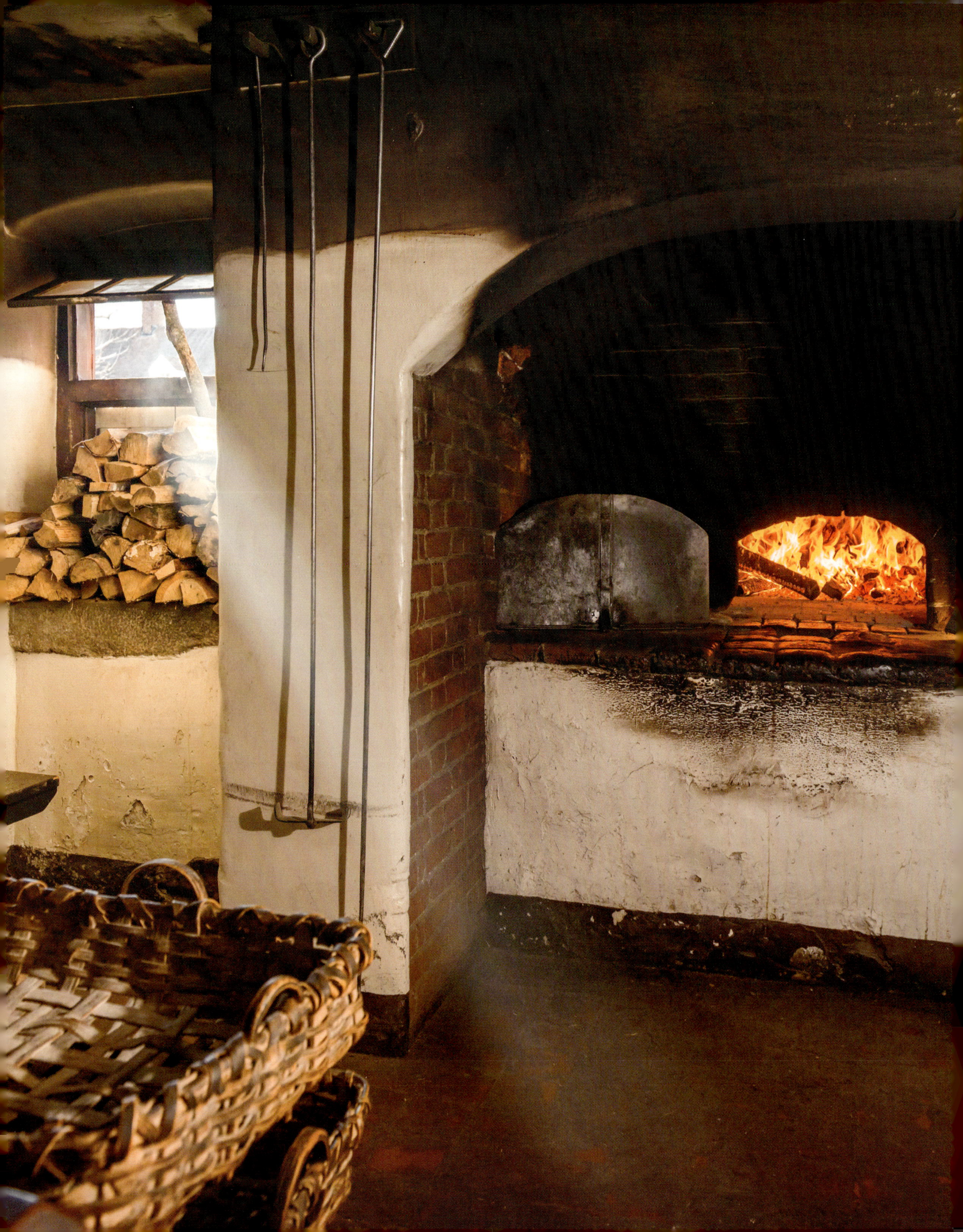

PIEDMONT REGION

The Piedmont Region is a happy combination of small cities and rural places. Generally, it is bordered by the Yadkin River to the south and the Dan River and the Commonwealth of Virginia to the north. The heart of the Piedmont Triad, anchored by Greensboro and Winston-Salem, is located here, along with pastoral Davie County and historic Caswell County. President George Washington, who visited five of the region's seven counties on his Southern Tour of 1791, declared that one of his best breakfasts of the trip was at Dobson's Tavern near present-day Kernersville.

In the mid-1700s Moravian settlers arrived in present-day Forsyth County and established Bethabara, Bethania, and Salem. Small, productive, and orderly, Salem thrived to become a long-running, successful settlement. Moravians came to be known for their devotion to hard work, worship, music, and food.

Moravian baking traditions persist to this day, both at home and commercially. Many travelers passing through Winston-Salem stop to stock up on Moravian cookies and sugar cakes. Tourists are welcome to visit Salem, now Old Salem, which is essentially a living history museum. Old Salem is also home to Salem College, an all-women's school established in 1772, making it the oldest college in North Carolina.

Davidson County is one of the state's barbecue meccas. Regardless of where you are in North Carolina, barbecue means pork; and Lexington is arguably ground zero for North Carolina's "western-style Q," which features pork shoulders with a sauce made of some combination of vinegar and ketchup. Every October since 1984 Lexington has held its popular barbecue festival.

Trucking and transportation are key businesses in the Triad, while High Point remains prominent in furniture and home furnishings. Cigarettes are still manufactured in Winston-Salem. However, healthcare is now one of the largest Piedmont employers, led by North Carolina Baptist Hospital and Wake Forest University Medical School, both located in Winston-Salem.

A great place for recreation, relaxation, and history education, Guilford Courthouse National Military Park is in the northern section of Greensboro. There, in March 1781, Lord Charles Cornwallis's British troops staged a sizable battle against forces led by American General Nathanael Greene. The British won the battle but suffered terrible casualties, causing some historians to award the Americans a moral and tactical victory. Those Revolutionary soldiers subsisted on various types of bread, corn, bits of pork or beef, and warm beer. Much better fare is available for today's Piedmont diners. Salute!

PIEDMONT REGION

CONTINENTAL BREAKFAST MENU

Iced Cinnamon Coffee

Fruit Salad Dressing

*Blueberry Pancakes or
Blueberry Muffins with Lemon Glaze*

Apple Sausage Bake

Cranberry Orange Scones

Coffee Cake

CONTINENTAL BREAKFAST

Iced Cinnamon Coffee

¼ cup sugar
½ cup water
10 cups strong coffee
Whipped cream
Cinnamon for sprinkling
Cinnamon sticks

Boil the sugar and water in a saucepan for 5 minutes. Chill in the refrigerator. Mix the sugar syrup with the coffee. Pour over ice in glasses. Top with whipped cream and sprinkle with cinnamon. Serve with a stick of cinnamon in each.

Serves 10 to 12

Fruit Salad Dressing

1 cup sugar
2 tablespoons all-purpose flour
½ teaspoon salt
4 eggs, lightly beaten
2 cups pineapple juice
¼ cup lemon juice
1 tablespoon butter
1 to 2 cups heavy whipping cream

Mix the sugar, flour and salt in a saucepan. Stir in the eggs. Whisk in the pineapple juice and lemon juice gradually. Cook over medium heat for 10 minutes or until thickened, stirring constantly. Remove from the heat and stir in the butter. Let cool to room temperature. Chill, covered, until cold. Beat the whipping cream in a bowl until firm peaks form. Fold in the chilled pineapple juice mixture. Use as a dressing for fruit salad, a pie topping or a dip for fresh fruit.

Makes 5 to 6 cups

Note: Feel free to alter the amount of whipped cream added to the pineapple juice mixture.

Bettie Archer Wrenn commissioned Traugott Leinbach, a silversmith and watchmaker from the Moravian community of Salem, to create this cup from silver coins she had saved. The cup was engraved "To Johney from Bettie" and was given to her brother, John Lawson Wrenn, who had entered the Confederate army. He carried the cup through four years of war.

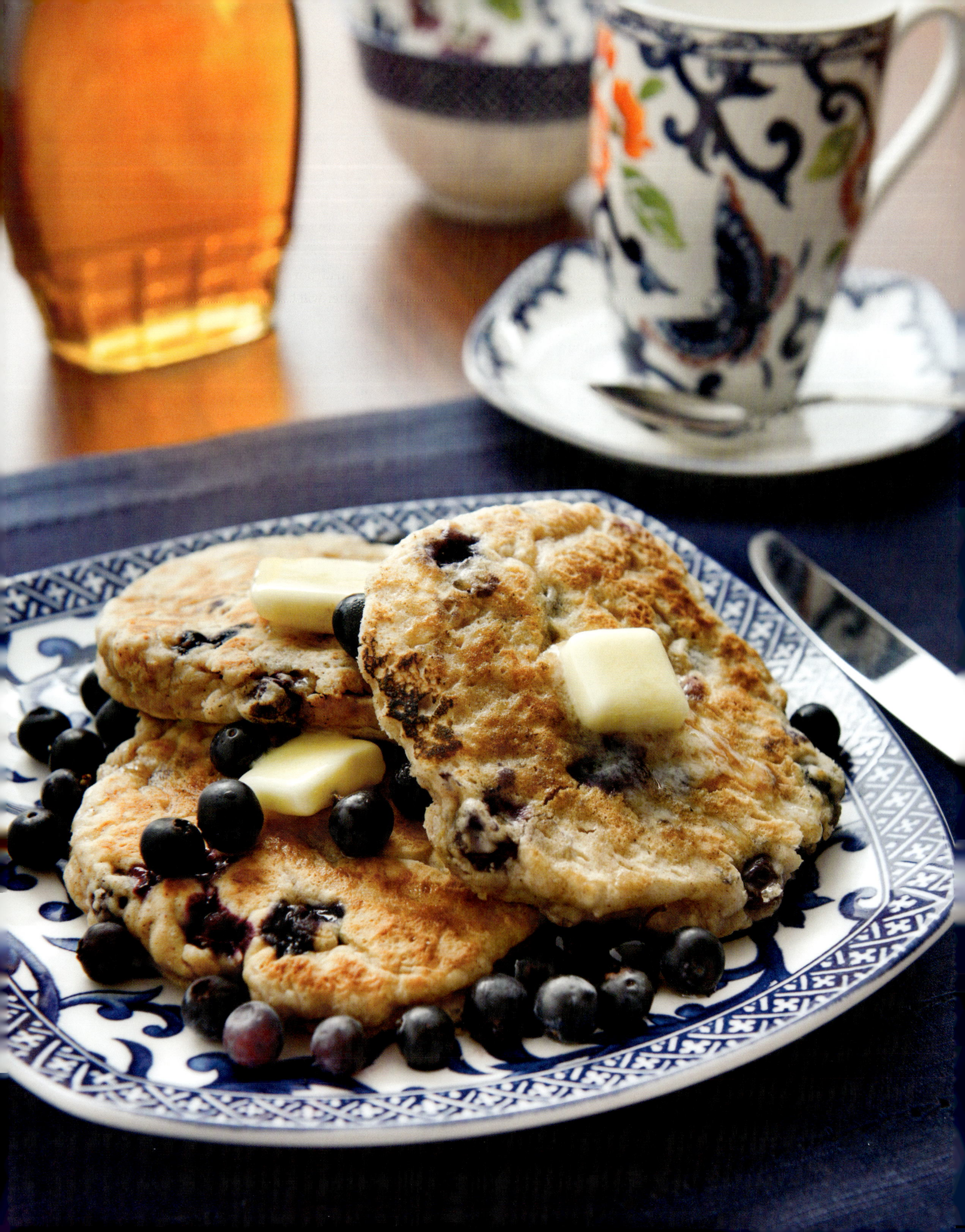

CONTINENTAL BREAKFAST

Blueberry Pancakes

1 1/4 cups flour
2 1/2 teaspoons baking powder
3 tablespoons sugar
3/4 teaspoon salt
3/4 teaspoon freshly grated lemon zest
1/2 teaspoon cinnamon
1 egg
3/4 cup whole milk
3 tablespoons melted butter
1/2 cup blueberries (fresh if available)
1 tablespoon butter for griddle
Confectioners' sugar

Whisk the flour, baking powder, sugar, salt, lemon zest and cinnamon together in a medium bowl. Mix egg, milk, and melted butter together in a small bowl. Add to the flour mixture and mix lightly. The batter will be very thick and not smooth. Fold in the blueberries.

Grease the griddle with 1 teaspoon of the butter (more if necessary) and drop batter on a medium hot griddle. You may need to spread the batter to make about a 3 inch pancake. Flip the pancake when you see the underside has turned nice and brown. Typically wait for bubbles to form on top of the pancake before flipping, but with this recipe you need to watch them carefully. I test one by cutting a piece out of one pancake to be certain batter has cooked. Sprinkle with powdered sugar and serve with fresh butter and warm syrup.

Note: Pancakes can be frozen after cooking or refrigerated the day before. Reheated on a baking sheet at 300 degrees until hot.

Janie's Bluberry Muffins with Lemon Glaze

1 egg
1 cup sugar
1/4 cup (1/2 stick) butter, melted and cooled
1 1/4 cups sour cream
2 cups unbleached flour
1 tablespoon baking powder
1/2 teaspoon salt
1 1/2 cups frozen blueberries
1/4 cup lemon juice
1/4 cup sugar
Grated lemon zest

Whisk the egg in a bowl for 20 seconds. Add 1 cup sugar and whisk well. Whisk in the melted butter gradually. Whisk in the sour cream gradually and set aside. Whisk the flour, baking powder and salt in a large bowl. Add the blueberries and toss gently to coat. Add the egg mixture and fold just until moistened. Fill well-greased muffin cups two-thirds full. Bake at 350 degrees for 25 to 30 minutes or until the muffins test done. Remove the muffins from the pan to a wire rack to cool. Simmer the lemon juice and 1/4 cup sugar in a saucepan until thickened, stirring frequently. Remove from the heat and let cool. Brush the lemon glaze over the tops of the cooled muffins and sprinkle with lemon zest.

Serves 12

PIEDMONT REGION

Apple Sausage Bake

Combine the apples, butter, lwmon juice, brown sugar and seasonings in a large skillet. Cook, covered, over medium heat until the apples are tender. Cook the sausage patties in a skillet until cooked through and crisp; drain. Cut into bite-sized pieces. Combine with the apple mixture in a baking dish. Bake at 350 degrees until heated through.

Serves 12

12 cooking apples, such as Golden Delicious, cored and sliced
6 tablespoons butter or margarine
Juice of 1/2 lemon
1/2 cup packed brown sugar
1 tablespoon cinnamon
1/2 teaspoon nutmeg
1/8 teaspoon salt
1 pound Neese's Sausage patties

Neese's Sausage is a family tradition that's never strayed from its original recipe for success: Fresh has always been better. When J.T. Neese developed the special recipe for Neese's Sausage in the early 1900s, he blended just the right amount of salt and seasonings, but never any added chemicals and preservatives. And that's just the way they do it today. This homegrown North Carolina business is run by the fourth generation of Neeses who are keeping the family tradition alive by making the best tasting, highest quality sausage and liver pudding products on the market.

While making sausage had been a popular way to preserve meats for hundreds of years, few tools were ever perfected to assist in the process. This metal meat grinder (ca. 1890–1930) is an example of early meat-processing equipment that helped revolutionize farm-based meat production and lead to the expansion of a commercial meat processing and packaging industry.

CONTINENTAL BREAKFAST

Cranberry Orange Scones

3 cups all-purpose flour
¹/₂ cup sugar
2¹/₂ teaspoons baking powder
¹/₂ teaspoon baking soda
1 teaspoon salt
2 tablespoons grated orange zest
³/₄ cup (1¹/₂ sticks) very cold butter, grated and frozen
1 cup chilled buttermilk
1¹/₂ cups orange-flavored dried cranberries
2 tablespoons Redi-Whip or whipped cream
1 teaspoon orange juice
Sparkling (sanding) sugar

Sift the first 5 ingredients together into a mixing bowl. Stir in the orange rind. Cut in the cold butter with a pastry cutter until mixture resembles coarse meal. Add the buttermilk gradually, stirring and tossing with a fork until moist clumps form and the dough comes together. Turn onto a lightly floured surface. Work in the cranberries, kneading about 4 turns. Shape into a 1- to 1¹/₂-inch-thick round; cut into 8 wedges. Place 2 inches apart on a baking parchment paper-lined baking sheet. Freeze for several hours to overnight. Spread a mixture of the whipped cream and orange juice on top of each scone with a pastry brush. Sprinkle with the sparkling sugar. Bake at 400 degrees for about 14 minutes or until the tops are golden brown.

Makes 8 scones

Coffee Cake

1 cup (2 sticks) butter or margarine, softened
2 cups sugar
2 eggs, beaten
2 cups cake flour, sifted
1¹/₄ teaspoons baking powder
¹/₄ teaspoon salt
1 cup sour cream
¹/₂ teaspoon vanilla exact
¹/₄ cup packed brown sugar
2 teaspoons cinnamon
1 cup chopped pecans

Cream the butter and sugar in a mixer bowl until light and fluffy. Add the eggs; mix well. Sift the flour, baking powder and salt together. Add to the creamed mixture alternately with the sour cream, mixing well after each addition. Blend in the vanilla. Combine the brown sugar, cinnamon and pecans in a bowl. Stir until crumbly. Spread half the crumb mixture over the bottom of a small greased bundt pan. Top with half the batter. Repeat the layers. Bake at 350 degrees for 1 hour or until the coffee cake tests done.

Serves 6 to 8

PIEDMONT REGION

FROM THE HEARTH SIMPLE MENU

Salem College Iced Tea

Salad for All Seasons

Simple Pasta with Basil or Chicken Pot Pie

Roasted Red Snapper with Garlic Butter

Orange Braised Carrots and Parsnips

Cornmeal Pecan Sandies

Moravian Sugar Cake Bread Pudding

FROM THE HEARTH SIMPLE

Salem College Iced Tea

4 (or more) mild mint sprigs, such as julep mint
6 to 8 whole cloves
12 cups water
1 family-size tea bag
1 1/2 cups packed light brown sugar
1 cup lemon juice
1 (12-ounce) can frozen orange juice concentrate
5 cups pineapple juice
Fresh mint

This sweet, fruit-flavored tea is the recipe of Jane Van Hoven of Home Moravian Church in Winston-Salem. It is a staple at Salem College, a women's college founded by the Moravian Church in 1772. It is North Carolina's oldest college and the oldest women's college by founding date in the United States.

Combine the mint sprigs, cloves and water in a large saucepan. Bring to a boil and reduce the heat. Simmer for 15 minutes and remove from the heat. Add the tea bag and let steep for 15 minutes. Strain through a wire mesh strainer into a very large heatproof pitcher or puch bowl; discard the solids. Add the brown sugar and stir until the sugar is dissolved. Stir in the lemon juice, orange juice and pineapple juice. Chill, covered, for 24 hours. Serve over ice and garnish with fresh mint.
Serves 10 to 15

Salad for All Seasons

1 head Bibb lettuce, torn into bite-size pieces
1/2 small head radicchio, torn into bite-size pieces
1/2 red onion, sliced
1/2 cup crumbled bleu cheese, feta cheese or goat cheese
1/2 cup blueberries or strawberries
1/2 cup dried cherries
1 (11-ounce) can mandarin oranges, drained, or fresh mandarin orange
1/2 cup toasted pine nuts or candied pecans
White Balsamic Vinaigrette (page 145) or bottled raspberry vinaigrette salad dressing

Layer the Bibb lettuce, radicchio, onion, cheese, blueberries, cherries, oranges and pine nuts in a large salad bowl. Drizzle with the vinaigrette and toss to coat. Serve immediately.
Serves 4 to 6

Note: Feel free to use your favorite fruits and nuts in this recipe. You can also use spring mixed greens instead of Bibb lettuce and radicchio.

This clay cup was made by Rudolf Christ (an apprentice to master potter Gottfried Aust), who worked in Salem from the 1780s to 1821. The green color on the exterior was achieved by adding copper oxide to the clear glaze.

PIEDMONT REGION

Alexa's Simple Pasta with Basil

Cut the basil into thin strips and line a large bowl with the basil strips. Sprinkle with the lemon zest and lemon juice. Add the hot pasta and sprinkle with the cheese and pepper. Drizzle with olive oil. Add the shrimp or chicken and toss to mix. Serve immediately.

Serves 4 to 6

Note: You may reserve some of the pasta cooking water to moisten the dish instead of using all olive oil.

1 cup basil leaves
Grated zest and juice of 1 lemon
Juice of 2 lemons
16 ounces linguini or favorite pasta, cooked and drained
1 cup (4 ounces) freshly grated Parmesan cheese
1 teaspoon freshly ground pepper
Extra-virgin olive oil
Cooked shrimp or poached chicken strips (optional)

Chicken Pot Pie

Spread the chicken in a 9×13-inch baking dish coated with nonstick cooking spray. Whisk the chicken soup and broth in a saucepan and cook over low heat until heated through. Pour evenly over the chicken. Add the celery and arrange the egg slices over the top. Beat the butter, flour and milk in a bowl. Spread evenly over the eggs. Place the baking dish on a baking sheet. Bake at 350 degrees for 1 hour and 20 minutes.

Serves 10 to 12

Note: You may use 4 chicken breasts and 4 chicken thighs instead of 1 whole chicken.

1 chicken, cooked, boned and chopped
1 (10 1/2-ounce) can cream of chicken soup
2 cups chicken broth
Steamed chopped celery (optional)
4 hard-cooked eggs, sliced
1/2 cup (1 stick) unsalted butter, softened
1 cup self-rising flour
1 cup milk

FROM THE HEARTH SIMPLE

Roasted Red Snapper with Garlic Butter

¼ cup (½ stick) unsalted butter, softened
1½ tablespoons chopped flat-leaf parsley
1 large garlic clove, peeled and minced
2 teaspoons chopped shallots
½ teaspoon Dijon mustard
1 tablespoon almond, rice or all-purpose flour
2 tablespoons freshly squeezed lemon juice
Salt and freshly ground pepper to taste
2 tablespoons canola oil
4 (7-ounce) skinless red snapper fillets
Lemon wedges

Combine the first 9 ingredients in a bowl; mix well and set aside. Heat the oil in a deep wide ovenproof skillet over medium-high heat. Season the fillets with salt and pepper. Cook for 4 minutes; turn the fillets over. Cook for 1 minute longer. Spoon 1 tablespoon of the butter mixture over each fillet. Bake in the skillet at 450 degrees for 2 minutes or just until the fish is cooked through and opaque in the center. Add any remaining butter mixture to the skillet, stirring to melt and combine with the pan juices. Spoon over the fish; garnish with lemon wedges. Serve immendiately.

Serves 4

Orange Braised Carrots and Parsnips

1 pound carrots with the greens attached
1 pound thin parsnips
⅓ cup small-diced shallots (1 large)
2 teaspoons grated orange zest
1¼ cups freshly squeezed orange juice, divided (about 3 oranges)
⅓ cup olive oil
6 sprigs fresh thyme, tied with kitchen string
Pinch of crushed red pepper flakes
Salt and freshly ground black pepper
2 tablespoons minced fresh flat-leaf parsley

Preheat the oven to 275 degrees. Trim and scrub or peel the carrots and parsnips. If the parsnips are thick, slice them into halves or quarters lengthwise so they are about the same width as the carrots. Place the carrots and parsnips in a saucepan or Dutch oven large enough for the vegetables to lie flat. Add the shallots, orange zest, ¾ cup of the orange juice, olive oil, thyme, red pepper flakes, 2 teaspoons salt and ½ teaspoon black pepper. Place the saucepan on the stove and bring to a boil over medium-high heat. Cover tightly with a lid or heavy-duty foil. Remove to the oven and cook for 1½ hours or until the carrots and parsnips are very tender. Discard the thyme bundle. Sprinkle with the remaining ½ cup orange juice and the parsley and season to taste. Serve hot, warm or at room temperature.

Serves 6

In the late 19th century, butter was often formed into shapes and stamped with an emblem or the maker's initials. These individualized stamps—such as this one (early 1900s), which features a stylized fern etching—helped make the product easily recognizable to customers.

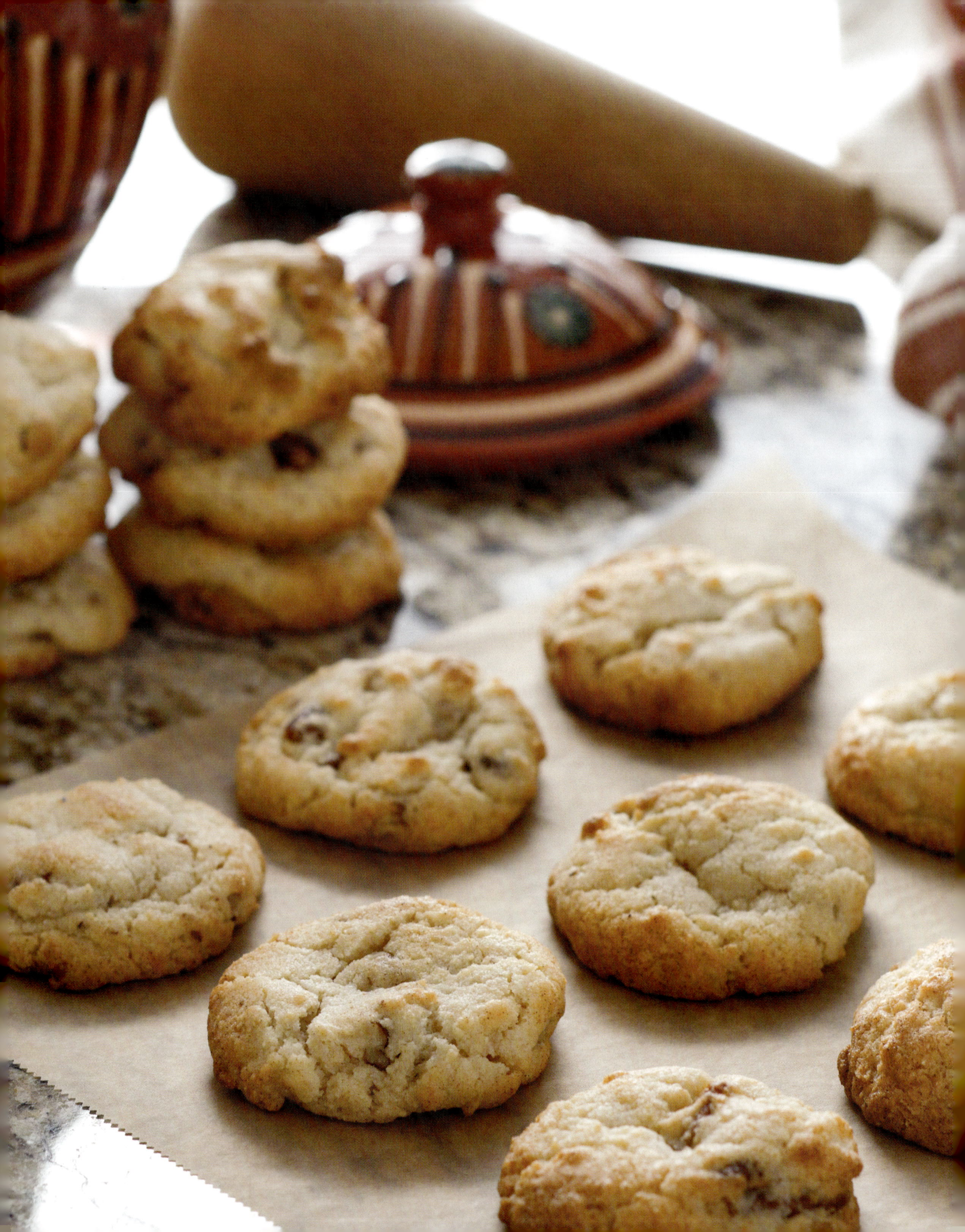

FROM THE HEARTH SIMPLE

Jeanne's Cornmeal Pecan Sandies

1 cup all-purpose flour
1/2 cup white cornmeal
1 teaspoon baking powder
1/2 teaspoon salt
1/2 cup (1 stick) butter, softened
1 cup sugar
1 egg
1 teaspoon vanilla extract
1/2 cup pecans, chopped

Jeanne's husband is the miller at Yates Mill, a historic Wake County site built in the 1750s. This recipe was a ribbon winner in the Yates Mill Cornmeal Cook-off.

Sift the flour, cornmeal, baking powder and salt together. Beat the butter and sugar in a mixing bowl until light and fluffy. Beat in the egg and vanilla. Stir in the dry ingredients. Stir in the pecans. Shape the dough into 1-inch balls. Arrange the balls on an ungreased cookie sheet and flatten slightly. Bake at 350 degrees for 11 to 13 minutes or until the edges begin to brown. Cool on the cookie sheet for 2 minutes. Remove to a wire rack to cool completely.

Makes 2 to 3 dozen sandies

Old Salem Moravian Sugar Cake Bread Pudding

2 (12-ounce) Moravian sugar cakes, cut into cubes
1 cup (2 sticks) butter, melted
1 1/4 cups sugar
5 eggs
2 1/2 cups heavy cream
Caramel sauce, warmed (optional)
Vanilla ice cream (optional)

Combine the cubed sugar cakes with the melted butter in a large mixing bowl; mix well. Whisk the sugar, eggs and cream together in a separate bowl. Add to the sugar cake mixture; mix well. Chill in the refrigerator for 1 hour to overnight. Spoon into individual oven-safe ramekins. Bake at 375 degrees for 12 to 15 minutes. Serve hot, each topped with a drizzle of warm caramel sauce and a scoop of vanilla ice cream, if desired.

Makes 6 servings

Use wide, shallow ramekins 5 to 6 inches in diameter to get a contrast of soft custard-soaked and crunchy cake.

Attributed to Solomon Loy, this earthenware plate (ca. 1820-1840) exemplifies the highly decorative and aesthetic quality of redware from Alamance County. Early Americans fired native clay at low temperatures to make this delicate pottery, which was commonly used due to its inexpensive nature.

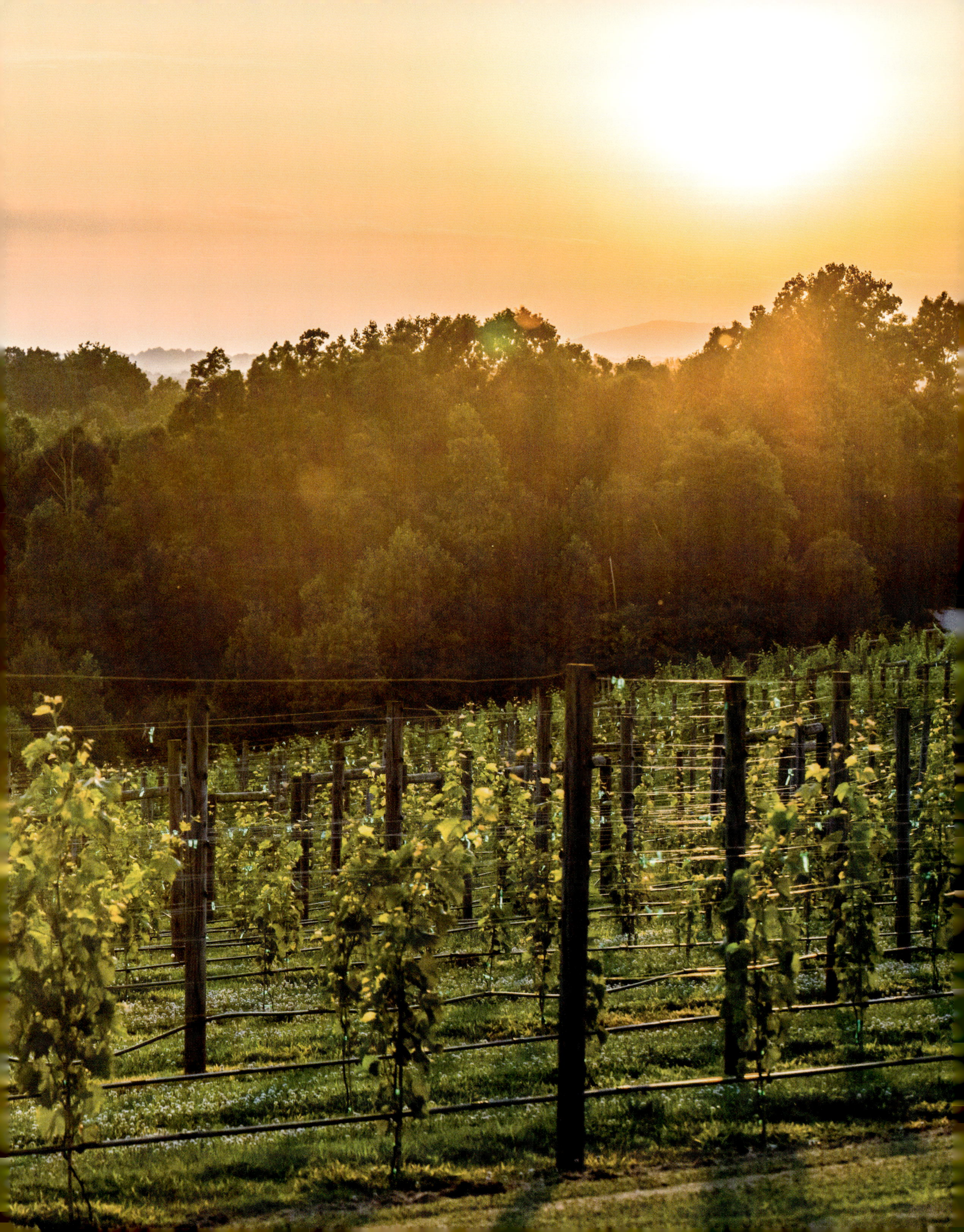

FOOTHILLS REGION

In the verdant and rolling Foothills Region that stretches from South Carolina to Virginia, one can look westward and glimpse distant Appalachian mountain ranges. The Foothills even feature a few small mountain ranges of their own, such as the Sauratown in Stokes County and Crowders and Kings Mountains in Gaston and Cleveland Counties.

This is a mineral-rich region. The rare gem, hiddenite, was discovered in Alexander County in the 1870s, and iron smelters were already at work in the southern counties by the late 1700s. During that period gold was discovered on John Reed's farm in Cabarrus County; and North Carolina subsequently led the nation in gold output until the California Gold Rush began in 1848. Today Reed Gold Mine State Historic Site preserves and interprets the history of gold mining in North Carolina.

Despite their natural beauty, the Foothills have a heritage of industry, including textiles, furniture, trucking, gravel, and mineral production. Gaston County, which has long been a leader in textiles, is named for William Gaston, a noted jurist and politician from New Bern. A Catholic, Gaston was the first student to enroll at Georgetown University when it opened in 1792. William Gaston probably never visited the area of his namesake since it wasn't until two years after his death that the county was organized and took his name.

The Catawba and Yadkin Rivers help drain the Foothills. These two rivers have their headwaters in the Mountain Region before winding their way through the Foothills en route to South Carolina. Along both rivers there are fish to be caught in Lake Norman, Lake Wylie, and High Rock Lake.

Salisbury, one of the oldest towns in the area, is the proud home of the popular soft drink Cheerwine, which many drink to chase their western-style barbecue. Widely recognized for its vineyards and wineries, the Yadkin Valley was approved in 2003 as a federal viticulture area. Apples and peaches are grown in Cleveland County; and small farms scattered throughout the region raise corn, tomatoes, melons, poultry, and livestock.

Charlotte, which has long been the largest city in North Carolina, is the biggest metro area between Atlanta and Washington, D.C., and is a major financial center. NASCAR, the Carolina Panthers, and the Charlotte Hornets all make the Queen City a great place for sports spectators and tailgaters.

Open land is rare near Charlotte; even Governor Cameron Morrison's old farm is now known as Southpark, a place of upscale shopping and offices. The upside to Charlotte's urban feel is its wonderful restaurants, handsome clubs, and charming homes, all great venues for a cocktail party.

FOOTHILLS REGION

UPTOWN POWER LUNCH MENU

Vichyssoise

Cold Cucumber Soup

Lime Basil Grilled Trout Fillets with Cantaloupe Garnish

Brussels Sprouts with Bacon

Fresh Fig & Warm Goat Cheese Salad with Fig Vinaigrette

Apple Chess Pie

Apple Walnut Cake

UPTOWN POWER LUNCH

Vichyssoise

5 tablespoons butter
6 onions, sliced
2 cups thinly sliced peeled potatoes
4 cups chicken stock
1 cup heavy cream
Dry sherry to taste (optional)
Salt and white pepper to taste
Minced parsley
Minced chives

Melt the butter in a saucepan over low heat. Add the onions and sauté for 5 minutes. Add the potatoes and stock and bring to a simmer. Cook until the potatoes are tender. Remove from the heat and purée the soup in a blender or food processor. Return the soup to the saucepan. Stir in the cream and sherry and season with salt and white pepper. Chill until cold. Serve the soup garnished with parsley and chives.

Serves 6

Note: This soup is also delicious served hot.

Cold Cucumber Soup

2 cucumbers, peeled and sliced
3 cups chicken broth
1/3 cup chopped onion
1 tablespoon all-purpose flour
1 bay leaf
1/2 teaspoon salt
1 cucumber, peeled and sliced
1 cup half-and-half
1/3 cup sour cream
2 tablespoons fresh lemon juice
Cucumber slices and fresh parsley

Combine 2 cucumbers, broth, onion, flour, bay leaf and salt in a saucepan. Simmer for 20 minutes, stirring occasionally. Remove and discard the bay leaf. Purée the mixture in a blender. Chill for 1 hour. Add 1 cucumber to the blender and purée. Remove to a bowl and stir in the half-and-half, sour cream and lemon juice. Chill until cold. Serve garnished with cucumber slices and parsley.

Serves 6

This metal box (ca. 1860–1900) belonged to Olivia Blount Grimes. Handwritten initials "J.G.B. Grimes" and the date of 1861 on the bottom of this portable metal container suggest that it likely first belonged to her father, John Gray Blount Grimes, who was the son of Civil War General Bryan Grimes. The decorative box was likely used to carry private papers and other personal items, though it was made about the time lunch boxes were replacing lunch baskets and also could have served that purpose.

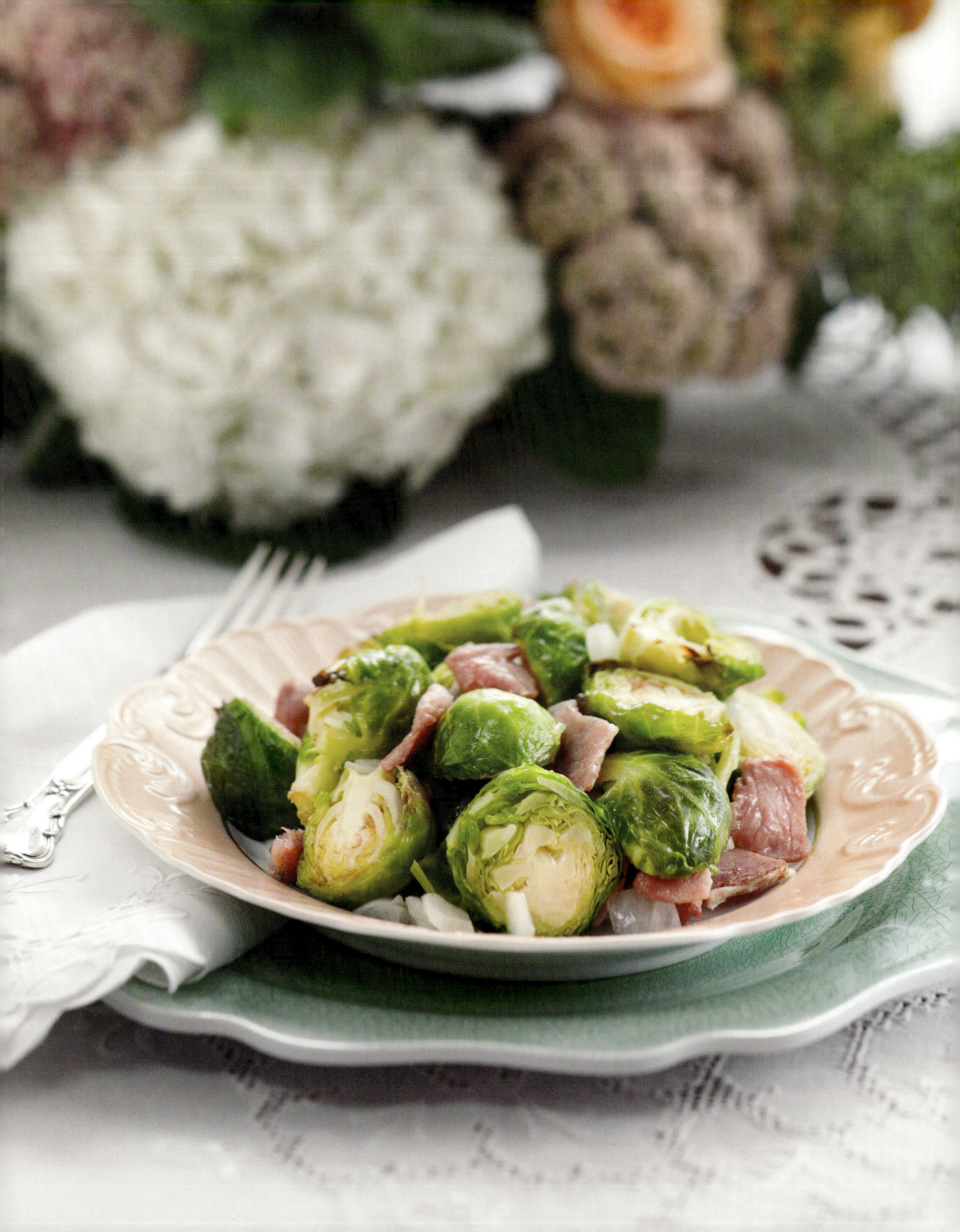

UPTOWN POWER LUNCH

Lime Basil Grilled Trout Fillets with Alicia's Cantaloupe Garnish

4 Sunburst trout fillets
Juice of 1 lime
1 handful fresh basil leaves
2 garlic cloves, chopped
¼ cup olive oil
⅛ teaspoon Lawry's seasoned salt
Freshly ground pepper to taste

Cantaloupe Garnish
1 large cantaloupe, peeled and seeds removed
½ red onion, chopped
½ cup cilantro, chopped
1 tablespoon (or more) freshly squeezed lime juice
Salt and pepper to taste

Marinate the trout fillets in a mixture of lime juice, basil, garlic, olive oil, seasoned salt and pepper in a glass dish or zip-lock bag for 1 hour or longer before grilling. Drain the fillets. Grill flesh side down on a well-oiled grill preheated to medium or medium-high for 3 to 4 minutes; flip the fillets to skin side down. Grill for 3 to 4 minutes longer. Trout may be sautéed in olive oil in a medium to large skillet over medium heat. Place flesh side down in hot olive oil in the skillet and cook for about 3 minutes. Flip the fish and cook for 2 to 3 minutes longer. Drain and keep warm. Serve with the Cantaloupe Garnish.

Cantaloupe Garnish
Cut the cantaloupe into bite-sized pieces. Combine all ingredients in a small bowl. Serve with the trout fillets.
Serves 4

Brussels Sprouts with Bacon

2 pounds brussels sprouts, washed, dried and cut into halves
⅓ cup extra-virgin olive oil
Salt and pepper to taste
¾ cup cooked chopped market-style bacon

Place the brussels sprouts in a stainless steel mixing bowl. Drizzle with the olive oil, tossing to coat. Season with salt and pepper. Spoon into a 9×13-inch baking dish. Roast at 450 degrees until evenly browned, tossing once after 5 minutes. Check for seasoning. Add the bacon, tossing to mix. Roast for 2 minutes longer.
Serves 8 to 10
Note: Leftovers can be served cold as a salad the next day.

This fork (ca.1760) was used by the Henry Weidner (Whitener) family, one of the first settlers in present-day Catawba County. Arriving around 1750, the family lived in a home inside a fort that was built for protection against natives.

FOOTHILLS REGION

Fresh Fig and Warm Goat Cheese Salad with Fig Vinaigrette

Shape the goat cheese into small rounds. Dip into the beaten egg; coat with panko bread crumbs. Place on a baking parchment paper-lined baking sheet. Chill until firm. Bake at 450 degrees until warm; do not melt. Divide the arugula, mixed greens, figs and walnuts among salad plates.

Combine the preserves, lemon juice, vinegars, basil and olive oil in a bowl; mix until blended. Serve with the salads.

Serves 8 to 10

1 large log goat cheese
1 egg, beaten
1 cup panko bread crumbs
5 cups arugula
5 cups mixed greens
14 to 16 fresh figs, cut into rounds
1 cup roasted walnuts

Fig Vinaigrette

3/4 cup good quality fig preserves, preferably homemade
1 tablespoon lemon juice
1 tablespoon balsamic vinegar
1 tablespoon white wine vinegar
2 teaspoons chopped fresh basil
4 to 6 tablespoons extra-virgin olive oil

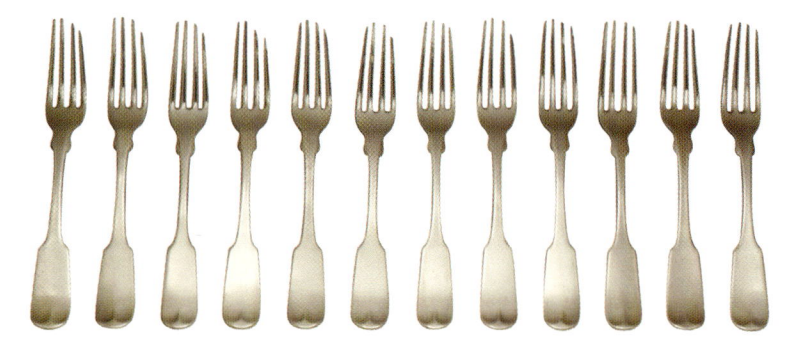

These silver forks (ca. 1850–1860) were crafted by Thomas Trotter in the later years of his life and career. Trotter apprenticed as a silversmith in Salisbury at the age of 18, opened a silver shop in Greensboro in the early 1820s, and settled in Charlotte in 1824. The store he built in 1850–1851 is the oldest remaining masonry structure in Charlotte.

UPTOWN POWER LUNCH

Mary's Apple Chess Pie

1 cup sugar
3 heaping tablespoons all-purpose flour
1/2 teaspoon cinnamon
1/8 teaspoon salt
3 eggs, beaten
1/2 cup (1 stick) butter, melted
1 teaspoon vanilla extract
2 to 3 cups chopped peeled Granny Smith apples
1 unbaked (9-inch) deep-dish pie shell
1/2 teaspoon cinnamon

Combine the sugar, flour, 1/2 teaspoon cinnamon and salt in a bowl and mix well. Add the eggs, melted butter and vanilla and mix well. Stir in the apples. Pour into the pie shell and sprinkle with 1/2 teaspoon cinnamon. Bake at 350 degrees for 45 to 50 minutes or until set. Remove to a wire rack to cool.

Serves 6

Note: In the summer when peaches and blueberries are plentiful, try using 3 chopped peaches plus 2 cups blueberries instead of apples for a delicious combination.

Apple Walnut Cake

2 cups all-purpose flour
2 teaspoons baking soda
2 teaspoons cinnamon
1 teaspoon salt
2 cups sugar
1/2 cup vegetable oil
2 eggs, beaten
2 teaspoons vanilla extract
4 cups (1/2-inch cubes) peeled Granny Smith apples
1 cup chopped walnuts

Sift the flour, baking soda, cinnamon and salt together. Mix the sugar and oil in a bowl. Stir in the eggs and vanilla. Add the dry ingredients and mix well. Stir in the apples and walnuts. The batter will be thick and very stiff. Pour into a greased and floured 12-cup bundt pan. Bake at 325 degrees for 1 hour or until a wooden pick inserted near the center comes out clean. Cool in the pan for 30 minutes. Invert onto a wire rack to cool completely. Serve with whipped cream.

Serves 16

Note: This cake can be made one day ahead. Store in an airtight container at room temperature.

FOOTHILLS REGION

COSMOPOLITAN COCKTAIL PARTY MENU

Cosmopolitan

Cold Pork Tenderloin

Shrimp with Rémoulade Sauce

Peach and Brie Quesadillas
with Lime Honey Dipping Sauce

Remember Me Olive Puffs

Cucumber Cheese Dip or Crab Tarts

Wild Mushroom & Onion Tartlets

Sour Lemon Bars

COSMOPOLITAN COCKTAIL PARTY

Mary Powell's Cosmo

1 ounce vodka
1 ounce Cointreau
1 ounce cranberry juice
Lime slice or orange twist

Combine all ingredients in a cocktail shaker. Shake vigorously with ice and strain into a chilled cocktail glass. Garnish with a lime slice or orange twist.

Makes 1

Hap's Cold Pork Tenderloin

1 (3-pound) pork tenderloin
2/3 cup soy sauce
2/3 cup packed brown sugar
1 tablespoon cornstarch
2 tablespoons vinegar
1 teaspoon ground ginger
3 garlic cloves
2/3 cup finely chopped candied or crystallized ginger

Marinate the pork tenderloin in a mixture of the next 6 ingredients in a 9×13-inch glass baking dish or large zip-lock bag for 6 to 8 hours or overnight. Bake at 350 degrees for 30 to 45 minutes per pound. Cool and drain, reserving the pan juices. Slice the tenderloin 1/4 inch thick and arrange on a small platter. Add the chopped ginger to the pan juices and drizzle over the tenderloin. Chill for 4 to 6 hours before serving.

Shrimp with Rémoulade Sauce

1/4 cup horseradish mustard
1/2 cup tarragon vinegar
2 tablespoons ketchup
1 tablespoon paprika
1/4 cup thinly sliced shallots
1 teaspoon salt
1/2 teaspoon cayenne pepper
1 garlic clove, thinly sliced
1/2 cup sliced green onions
1/2 cup chopped celery
1 cup vegetable oil
3 pounds cooked shrimp, peeled and de-veined

Process the mustard, vinegar, ketchup, paprika, shallots, salt, cayenne pepper, garlic, green onions, celery and oil in a blender to desired consistency. Pour over the shrimp in a bowl. Stir to coat the shrimp. Marinate, covered, in the refrigerator for 4 to 12 hours.

Serves 8

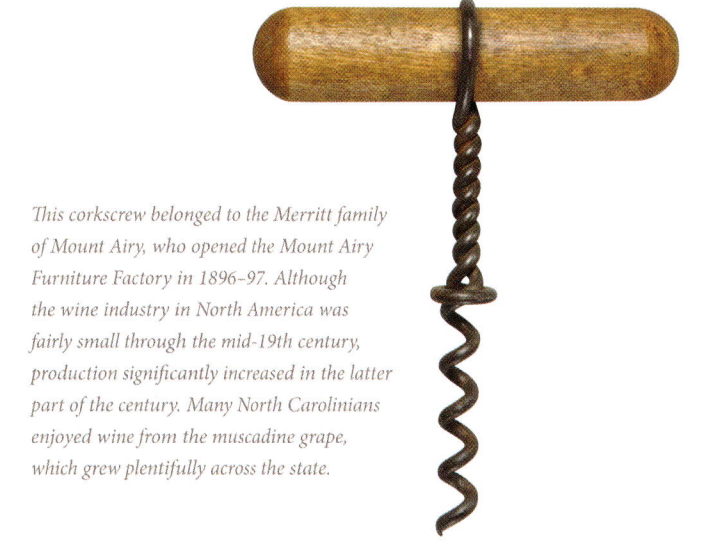

This corkscrew belonged to the Merritt family of Mount Airy, who opened the Mount Airy Furniture Factory in 1896–97. Although the wine industry in North America was fairly small through the mid-19th century, production significantly increased in the latter part of the century. Many North Carolinians enjoyed wine from the muscadine grape, which grew plentifully across the state.

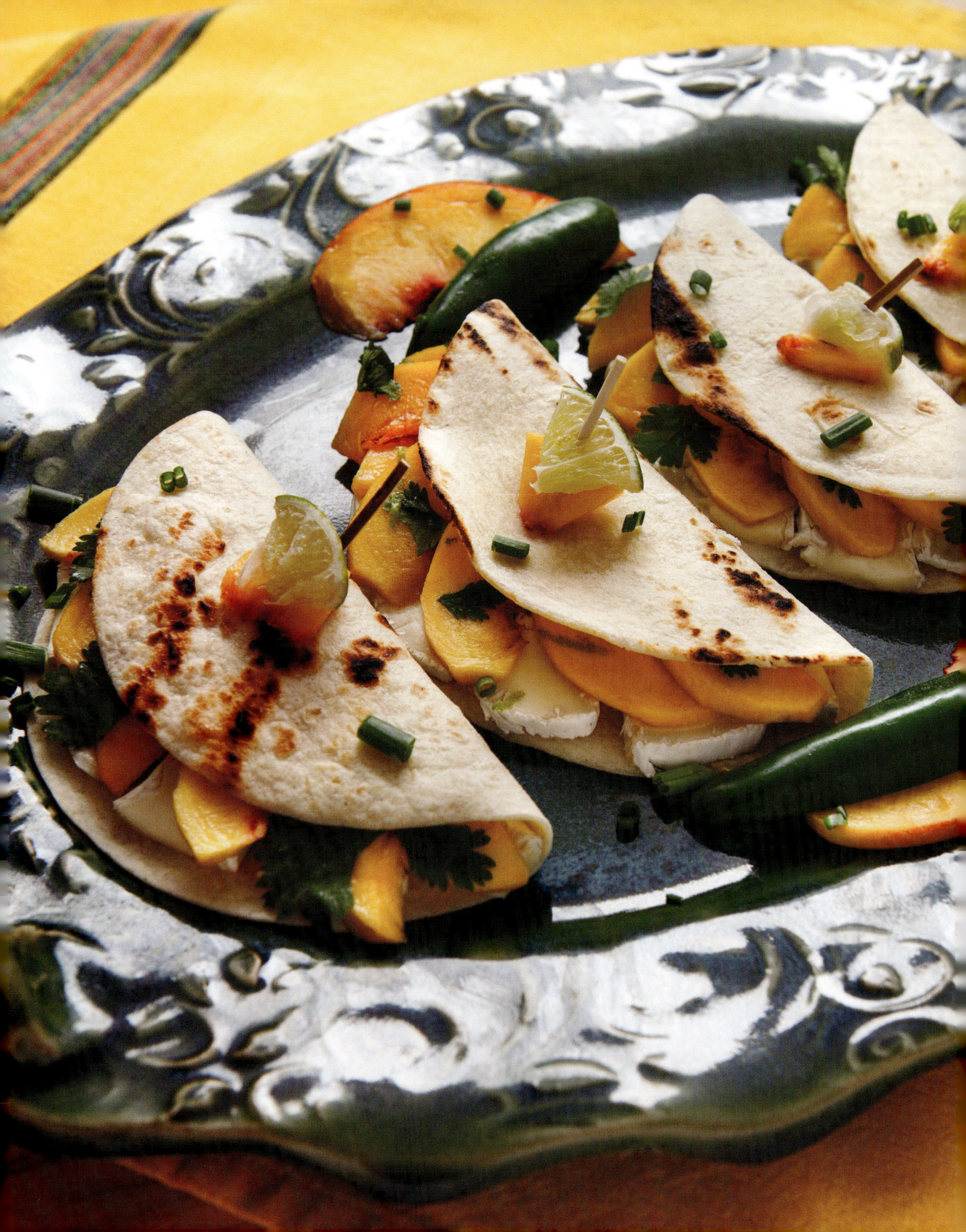

COSMOPOLITAN COCKTAIL PARTY

Carol's Peach and Brie Quesadillas with Lime Honey Dipping Sauce

2 tablespoons honey
1/2 teaspoon grated lime zest
2 teaspoons fresh lime juice
1 cup thinly sliced peeled firm ripe fresh peaches
1 tablespoon chopped fresh chives
1 teaspoon brown sugar
3 ounces Brie cheese, thinly sliced
4 (8-inch) fat-free flour tortillas

Whisk the honey, lime zest and lime juice in a small bowl and set aside. Combine the peaches, chives and brown sugar in a bowl and toss gently to mix. Spread one-half of the peach mixture and one-half of the cheese over each of two tortillas. Top with the remaining tortillas. Heat a nonstick skillet over medium-high heat and coat with nonstick cooking spray. Add one quesadilla to the skillet and cook for 2 minutes per side or until lightly browned and crisp. Remove to a cutting board and keep warm. Repeat with the remaining quesadilla. Cut each quesadilla into 6 wedges and serve with the lime-honey sauce for dipping.

Serves 6

Remember Me Olive Puffs

2 cups (8 ounces) finely shredded sharp Cheddar cheese
6 tablespoons margarine, softened
1 cup all-purpose flour, sifted
1/2 teaspoon salt
1 teaspoon paprika
Cayenne pepper to taste
48 pimento-stuffed green olives

Beat the cheese and margarine together in a bowl. Add the flour, salt, paprika and cayenne pepper and mix well. Dry the olives with a paper towel. Wrap a small amount of dough around each olive, enclosing completely. Arrange the olives on an ungreased baking sheet. Bake at 400 degrees for 10 to 15 minutes or until the bottoms are lightly browned.

Makes 4 dozen

Note: These may be frozen before baking and baked fresh whenever needed.

Cucumber Cheese Dip

1 large cucumber, seeded and diced
8 ounces cream cheese, softened
2 tablespoons lemon juice
Salt and pepper to taste

Combine the cucumber, cream cheese, lemon juice, salt and pepper in a bowl and mix well. Chill, covered, until ready to serve. Serve with thin wheat crackers.

Serves 8

Note: This is an easy and crowd-pleasing recipe for hot summer days.

FOOTHILLS REGION

Julie's Crab Tarts

To make the shells, mix the cheese, bread crumbs and chives in a bowl. Drizzle the melted butter over the bread crumb mixture and stir with a fork. Press about 2 teaspoons of the mixture onto the bottom of each of 24 miniature muffin cups. Set aside the remaining bread crumb mixture.

To make the filling, combine the cream cheese, Parmesan cheese, egg, sour cream, crab meat, lemon zest, chives and cayenne pepper in a bowl and mix well. Spoon equal portions into the prepared muffin cups and sprinkle each with equal portions of the remaining bread crumb mixture. Bake at 350 degrees for 25 to 30 minutes. Cool in the pan for 5 minutes. Run a small sharp knife around the edge of each muffin cup and gently remove the tarts. Serve immediately or let cool and chill for up to 3 hours. Reheat at 350 degrees for 8 to 10 minutes. You can also freeze these tarts. Reheat at 400 degrees for 10 to 15 minutes.

Serves 24

Note: This can also be made into small crab cakes.

Shells

1/2 cup (2 ounces) grated Parmesan cheese
1 cup panko bread crumbs
2 tablespoons minced chives
1/4 cup (1/2 stick) unsalted butter, melted

Filling

8 ounces cream cheese, softened
1/4 cup (1 ounce) grated Parmesan cheese
1 egg
1/4 cup sour cream
8 ounces crab meat
1/2 teaspoon grated lemon zest
1 tablespoon minced chives
1 pinch of cayenne pepper

Melissa's Wild Mushroom and Onion Tartlets

Heat the olive oil in a skillet. Add the onion and sauté until tender and golden brown. Sprinkle with the sugar, salt and pepper. Add the mushrooms and thyme and sauté over high heat for 5 minutes or until the mushrooms are tender. Remove from the heat and discard the thyme. Spread butter over one side of each slice of bread. Cut 24 circles from the bread with a 2-inch biscuit cutter. Fit each circle, buttered side down, into a miniature muffin cup. Spoon equal portions of the mushroom mixture into the bread cups. Sprinkle with equal portions of the cheese. Bake at 425 degrees for 10 to 15 minutes or until golden brown and bubbly. Serve immediately or let cool and chill. Reheat before serving.

Serves 24

Note: This is also delicious using button mushrooms.

2 tablespoons olive oil
1 large onion, chopped
1 tablespoon sugar
Salt and pepper to taste
1 1/2 cups finely chopped wild mushrooms (such as cremini, shiitake or portobello)
2 thyme sprigs
1/4 cup (1/2 stick) unsalted butter, softened
12 slices white bread
2 1/2 cups (10 ounces) shredded Gruyère cheese

COSMOPOLITAN COCKTAIL PARTY

Sour Lemon Bars

Crust
1 1/2 cups all-purpose flour
1/4 cup confectioners' sugar
Pinch of salt
1/2 cup (1 stick) chilled unsalted butter, cubed
1/2 teaspoon vanilla extract

Filling
5 eggs, at room temperature
2 cups granulated sugar
3 tablespoons all-purpose flour
2 1/2 tablespoons grated lemon zest
1 cup fresh lemon juice, strained
1/4 cup confectioners' sugar

To make the crust, line a 9×9-inch baking pan with baking parchment paper, allowing the parchment to extend over opposite sides of the pan. Butter the two exposed sides of the pan. Process the flour, confectioners' sugar and salt in a food processor. Add the butter and vanilla and pulse until the mixture is crumbly. Press evenly into the prepared pan. Bake at 350 degrees for 25 minutes or just until beginning to brown.

To make the filling, whisk the eggs in a bowl. Whisk in the granulated sugar. Whisk in the flour. Whisk in the lemon zest and lemon juice. Pour evenly over the hot crust. Bake at 325 degrees for 20 minutes or until the filling is set. Remove to a wire rack to cool completely. Chill for at least 6 hours. Lift out of the pan to a cutting board and peel back the parchment paper. Dust with the confectioners' sugar and cut into bars.

Serves 16

WHITE CHOCOLATE FRESH RASPBERRY MINIATURE TARTS

Place small baking cups in mini muffin tins. Melt 12 ounces of good white chocolate in the microwave. When melted, spoon enough to cover the bottom into each baking cup. Place 2 or 3 raspberries on top of the chocolate. Then cover with the remaining chocolate. Place in the refrigerator until set. Note: Will keep in a tin refrigerated for one week. Great for teas and cocktail parties.
Makes 16 to 18 tarts

This china plate was found in baggage belonging to Major Patrick Ferguson, a Scottish soldier in the British Army, by Major Joseph McDowell during the Battle at King's Mountain. McDowell was named an honorary militia general after the war and went on to serve the country in various political positions. When McDowell County was formed in 1842, it was named for Joseph McDowell.

111

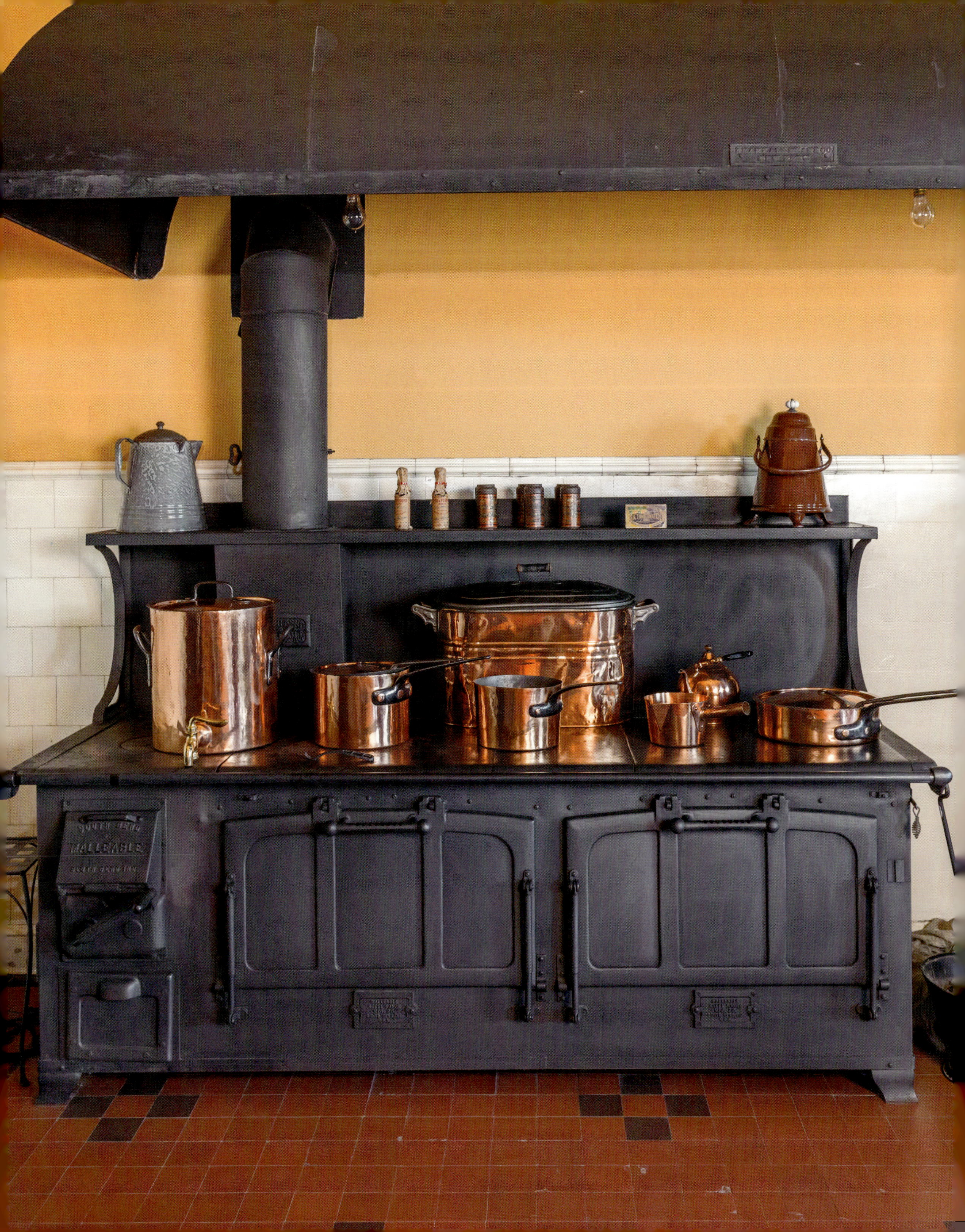
MALLEABLE

MOUNTAIN REGION

The Mountain Region spreads out from peaks and valleys to connect with four states—Georgia, South Carolina, Tennessee, and Virginia. Indeed, Murphy in the extreme southwest is closer to six state capitals than it is to Raleigh.

In this highest land of North Carolina, bakers should keep the elevation in mind before putting a cake in the oven, as air pressure is lower at higher elevations and thus affects baking. The Mountain Region is all part of the Appalachian chain, but the principal ranges are the Blue Ridge, the Great Smokies, and the Black Mountains.

Elevations in the region range from 1000 feet to nearly 6700 feet atop Mt. Mitchell, the highest point in the eastern United States. In 1857, UNC professor Elisha P. Mitchell died in a fall while measuring several peaks in the Black Mountains, including the one that ultimately became his namesake.

The Mountain Region has cooler weather than the rest of North Carolina, and hence a shorter growing season. The region is known for growing Christmas trees, evergreen shrubs, and apples. Years ago considerable moonshine was produced from corn not consumed by livestock, and a trout farm in Haywood County has been successful for over sixty years.

Since 1819 the Eastern Band of Cherokee has occupied the largest Indian reservation east of the Mississippi River, nearly 56,000 acres known as the Qualla Boundary. The Cherokees were once known for their dietary reliance on corn, beans, and squash; they referred to the food as the Three Sisters.

Asheville, which is the regional center for medicine, arts, and entertainment, enjoys significant tourist traffic. Nearby, the grand Biltmore Estate, built in the 1890s by George Washington Vanderbilt II, is a resplendent representative of the Gilded Age operated now by Vanderbilt descendants.

A much simpler home is the Gragg Cabin by the winding Yonahlossee Trail (US 221) between Linville and Blowing Rock. Built in the 1850s the house is of the saddlebag style—a large fireplace and chimney in the cabin center divides the house in two.

Parts of the Mountain Region felt the effects of the Civil War in the spring of 1865, when General George Stoneman's Union raiders crossed the Blue Ridge from Tennessee and stopped resistance in Watauga, Caldwell, and Wilkes Counties. The mountain folk were often forced to feed the invaders; today however, the tourist-centric region has a great reputation for happily hosting Yankees and visitors of all sorts.

MOUNTAIN REGION

DOWN HOME FAMILY-STYLE MENU

Hot Buttered Rum

Hot Apple Soup

Neese's Sausage Pinwheels

Apple Butter Pork Tenderloin

Southern Collards or Uptown Collards

Corn Light Bread

Applesauce Cake

DOWN HOME FAMILY-STYLE

Hot Buttered Rum Batter

1/2 cup (1 stick) butter, softened
1 pound dark brown sugar
1/4 teaspoon cinnamon
1/4 teaspoon nutmeg
1/4 teaspoon ground cloves
Dark rum

Cream the butter and brown sugar together in a bowl. Sprinkle in the spices and mix thoroughly. Store in the refrigerator in a covered container.

To make the drink: Place 1 heaping tablespoon of the batter in a mug. Add 1 1/2 ounces dark rum. Fill with boiling water. Stir and serve.

Hot Apple Soup

4 large apples, peeled and cored
1 large onion, chopped
1 tablespoon butter
4 cups chicken broth
3/4 teaspoon curry powder or to taste
Juice of 1/2 lemon
3 tablespoons butter
3 tablespoons all-purpose flour
1/4 cup half-and-half

Chop 2 of the apples and shred the remaining 2 apples. Sauté the onion in 1 tablespoon butter in a large saucepan until tender. Stir in the chopped apples, chicken broth, curry powder and lemon juice. Bring to a boil; reduce the heat. Simmer for 10 minutes. Melt 3 tablespoons butter in a separate large saucepan. Blend in the flour. Cook for 1 minute. Stir in the hot chicken broth mixture. Cook until thickened. Remove from the heat. Cool for several minutes. Process or purée in a food processor or blender. Return to the saucepan. Stir in the half-and-half and shredded apples. Heat to serving temperature and ladle into soup bowls.

Serves 6 to 8

Neese's Sausage Pinwheels

2 cups all-purpose flour
1 tablespoon baking powder
1 teaspoon salt
1/4 cup shortening
2/3 cup milk
1 pound hot Neese's sausage
Shredded cheese (optional)

Mix the flour, baking powder and salt together in a bowl. Cut in the shortening until crumbly. Add the milk and mix until a dough forms. Roll the dough into a 12" x 18" rectangle on a floured surface. Spread the sausage over the dough, leaving a border on all sides. Spread the cheese over the sausage. Roll as for a jelly roll, beginning with a long side. Chill, covered, for 1 hour. Cut the dough into 1/4-inch slices. Arrange the rolls on a baking sheet. Bake at 350 degrees for 20 minutes.

Makes 3 1/2 dozen

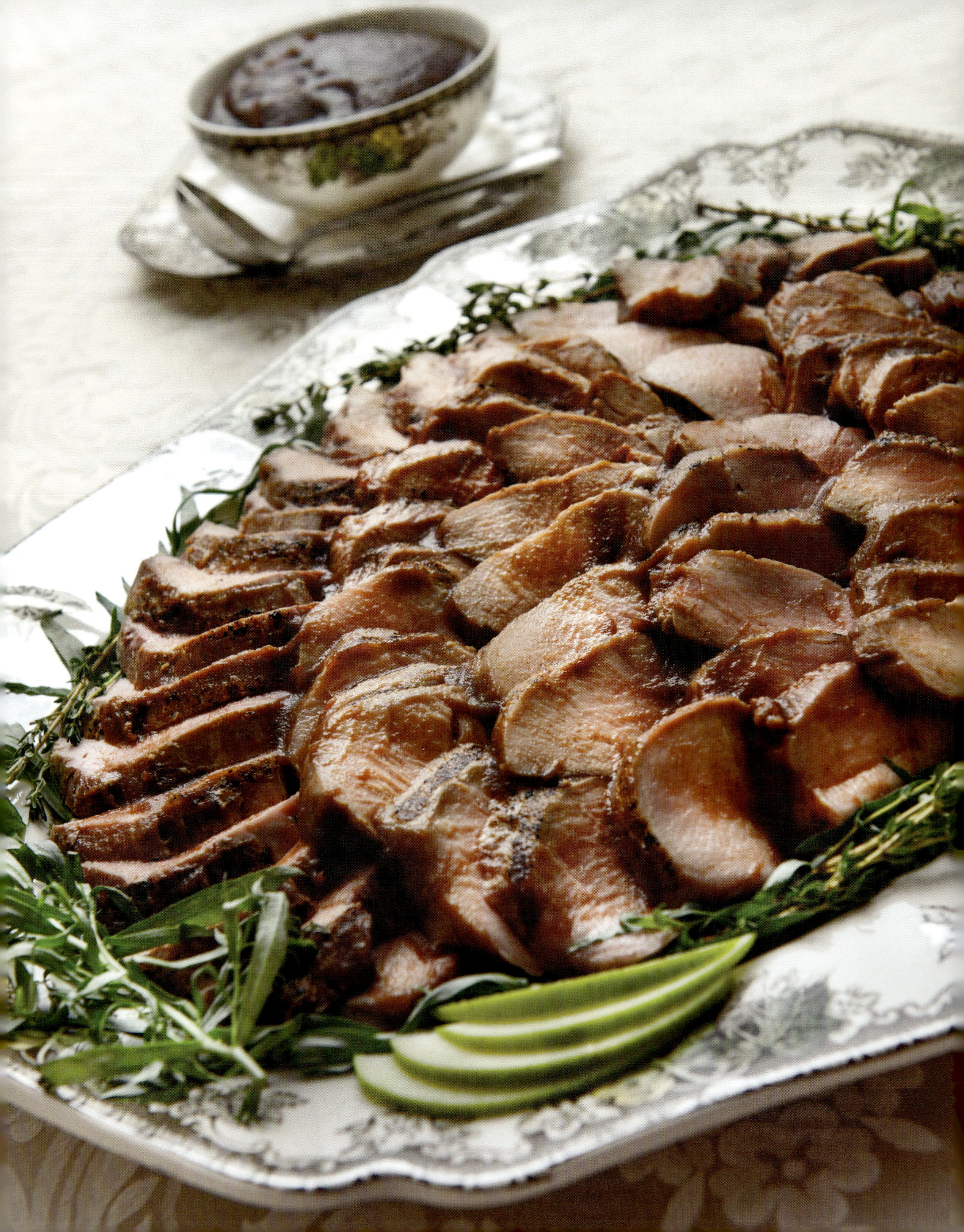

DOWN HOME FAMILY-STYLE

Apple Butter Pork Tenderloin

1 (1 1/2- pound) pork tenderloin
1/2 teaspoon salt
2 cups apple juice
1/2 cup apple butter
1/2 cup packed brown sugar
2 tablespoons water
1/2 teaspoon cinnamon
1/2 teaspoon ground cloves

Let the tenderloin stand until it returns to room temperature. Prick the tenderloin several times with a fork. Sprinkle with the salt and place in a 7×11-inch baking dish. Add the apple juice. Let stand, covered, at room temperature for 30 minutes or chill for 2 hours. Bake, uncovered, at 350 degrees for 15 minutes. Drain the liquid. Brush the tenderloin with a mixture of the apple butter, brown sugar, water, cinnamon and cloves. Bake for 15 minutes longer. Let stand for 15 minutes before slicing.

Cindy's Blue Ribbon Apple Butter

2 (106-ounce) cans applesauce, sweetened or unsweetened
12 cups (5 pounds) sugar
1 1/2 cups brown vinegar
2 tablespoons ground cinnamon
3/4 tablespoon ground allspice
3/4 tablespoon ground cloves

Combine the applesauce, sugar and vinegar in a large covered roasting pan. Bake, covered, for 7 hours, stirring occasionally. Be careful to avoid a steam burn when removing the top. When the sauce begins to thicken and the color is dark brown add the cinnamon, allspice and cloves. Mix well. Cover and bake for 30 minutes longer. Remove from the oven and ladle into hot canning jars. Invert the jars for 30 minutes to insure proper seal. There is no need to process the filled jars if they are sterile. Apple Butter makes a wonderful gift, especially accompanied with the recipe.

This plunge churn (ca.1850–1860) was a commonly used churn for home butter-making. Also known as an "up and down" churn, butter would have been made from cream by moving a staff, or dasher, in a vertical motion. This process would have agitated the cream, breaking down milk fats and subsequently forming clumps of butter grains.

APPLE BUTTER

Making apple butter has been an annual tradition in my family since the early 1800s. Great-grandparents, grandparents, aunts, uncles, spouses, and children all come together at the patriarchate's house in early autumn when the apples begin to fall. It is the children's job to collect the fruit and haul them to the coring tables to be washed, cut, cored, and cooked in large copper pots, one of which has been used now for 200 years and hangs on my side porch. The hot apples were then pressed through a sieve to be made into a sauce and stirred over a fire by a wooden paddle. At the end of the day-long process, secret spices were added and the apple butter was "jarred up," sealed, and cooled.

MOUNTAIN REGION

Southern Collards

Rinse the collards well and remove and discard the stems and center ribs. Cut the collards into 1 1/2-inch squares and set aside. Heat the bacon drippings in a large saucepan. Add the ham hocks and cook until lightly browned. Remove the ham hocks and set aside. Add the onion to the saucepan and sauté until tender. Add the garlic and sauté for 1 minute. Return the ham hocks to the saucepan and add the broth. Bring to a boil and reduce the heat. Simmer, covered, for 1 hour. Stir in the brown sugar, salt, cayenne pepper and black pepper. Add the collards gradually, pressing with a spoon to submerge in the liquid. Simmer, uncovered, for 50 to 60 minutes or until tender, stirring occasionally. Drain and serve.

Serves 8

Note: This may be made one day ahead. Chill until ready to serve and reheat just before serving.

3 pounds collards
3 tablespoons bacon drippings
2 ham hocks, scored
1 large onion, diced
2 garlic cloves, minced
10 cups low-sodium chicken broth
5 tablespoons brown sugar
1 1/2 teaspoons salt, or to taste
3/4 teaspoon cayenne pepper
Freshly ground black pepper to taste

Bo's Uptown Collards

Sauté the onions in the bacon drippings in a Dutch oven. Add the water, wine and sugar. Bring to a boil. Add the collards and bell pepper. Cook for about 45 minutes or until the collards are tender.

Serves 12

2 small onions, finely chopped
2 tablespoons bacon drippings
1 1/2 cups water
1 1/2 cups chablis or other white wine
1 tablespoon sugar
8 pounds collards, stems removed
1 red bell pepper, diced

DOWN HOME FAMILY-STYLE

Corn Light Bread

1 teaspoon baking soda
1 teaspoon salt
1/4 teaspoon baking powder
1/2 cup sugar
2 cups buttermilk
2 cups cornmeal
1/2 cup all-purpose flour
1/4 cup shortening
Additional cornmeal for dusting

Mix the baking soda, salt, baking powder and sugar in a bowl. Add the buttermilk and mix well. Beat in the cornmeal alternately with the flour. Melt the shortening in a 5×9-inch loaf pan in a 350-degree oven. Tilt the pan to coat with melted shortening. Dust the bottom of the hot pan with cornmeal and swirl the hot shortening into the batter. Pour the batter into the hot pan. Bake at 350 degrees for 1 to 1 1/4 hours or until the bread tests done.

Serves 12

Note: You may bake this in muffin cups and bake for 20 minutes or bake in an 8×8-inch baking pan or 9×9-inch baking pan and adjust the baking times.

Applesauce Cake

1 1/2 cups (3 sticks) butter, softened
1 1/2 cups sugar
2 eggs
1 teaspoon baking soda
1 1/2 cups applesauce
1 teaspoon cinnamon
1 teaspoon allspice
1/2 teaspoon nutmeg
Lemon flavoring to taste
1 1/2 cups chopped black walnuts
1 1/2 cups raisins
2 cups all-purpose flour
2 teaspoons baking powder

Brown Sugar Boiled Icing
3 cups packed brown sugar
1 cup cream
1/2 teaspoon vanilla extract

Beat the butter and sugar in a mixing bowl until light and fluffy. Add the eggs, one at a time, beating well after each addition. Dissolve the baking soda in the applesauce in a bowl and beat into the butter mixture. Stir in the cinnamon, allspice, nutmeg, lemon flavoring, walnuts and raisins. Sift the flour and baking powder together and stir into the batter. Pour into two greased 9-inch cake pans. Bake at 350 degrees for 35 to 45 minutes or until the cake tests done. Cool in the pan for 10 minutes. Remove to a wire rack to cool completely. Spread Brown Sugar Boiled Icing between the layers and over the top and side of the cake.

Brown Sugar Boiled Icing

Cook the brown sugar and cream in a saucepan to 235 degrees on a candy thermometer, soft-ball stage, stirring constantly. Remove from the heat and let cool. Beat until thick. Stir in the vanilla.

Serves 8 to 10

MOUNTAIN REGION

HORN OF PLENTY THANKSGIVING MENU

Cherry Pecan Brie

Thanksgiving Oysters

Butterball Turkey with Giblet Gravy

Multigrain Bread, Onion, Pecan & Golden Raisin Stuffing

Cranberry Salad

Sweet Potato Casserole

Roasted Broccoli with Parmesan Cheese

Bourbon Pecan Pie or Pumpkin Roll

HORN OF PLENTY THANKSGIVING

Kennedy's Cherry Pecan Brie

1/3 cup cherry preserves
1 tablespoon balsamic vinegar
1/8 teaspoon salt
1/8 teaspoon pepper
1 (16-ounce) Brie cheese, rind removed
Chopped pecans

Combine the preserves, vinegar, salt and pepper in a bowl and mix well. Place the cheese in a pie plate and spoon the cherry mixture over the Brie. Top with pecans. Bake at 350 degrees until the cheese is softened and beginning to melt. Serve with crackers or apple slices.

Serves 16

Thanksgiving Oysters

1 cup (2 sticks) butter
3/4 cup all-purpose flour
1 teaspoon paprika
1/2 teaspoon salt
1/4 teaspoon black pepper
Dash of cayenne pepper
1 garlic clove, minced
1 onion, chopped
1/2 green bell pepper, chopped
1 quart oysters
1 tablespoon lemon juice
2 teaspoons Worcestershire sauce
1/4 cup crushed crackers

Melt the butter in a large skillet over medium heat. Remove from the heat and whisk in the flour until smooth. Return to the heat and cook for 5 minutes or until light brown, stirring constantly. Stir in the paprika, salt, black pepper, cayenne pepper, garlic, onion and bell pepper. Cook for 5 minutes, stirring constantly. Drain one-half of the liquor from the oysters and add the oysters and remaining liquer to the skillet. Stir in the lemon juice and Worcestershire sauce. Pour into a greased shallow 2-quart baking dish and sprinkle with the crackers. Bake at 400 degrees for 20 minutes.

Serves 8 to 10

This silver tea service (ca.1930) is the work of silversmith William Waldo Dodge, Jr. Dodge was one of the leading figures in Asheville's architectural scene in the early 1920s and was a well-known silversmith. Arts and crafts influences could be seen in his pieces, which attracted patronage even during the Great Depression.

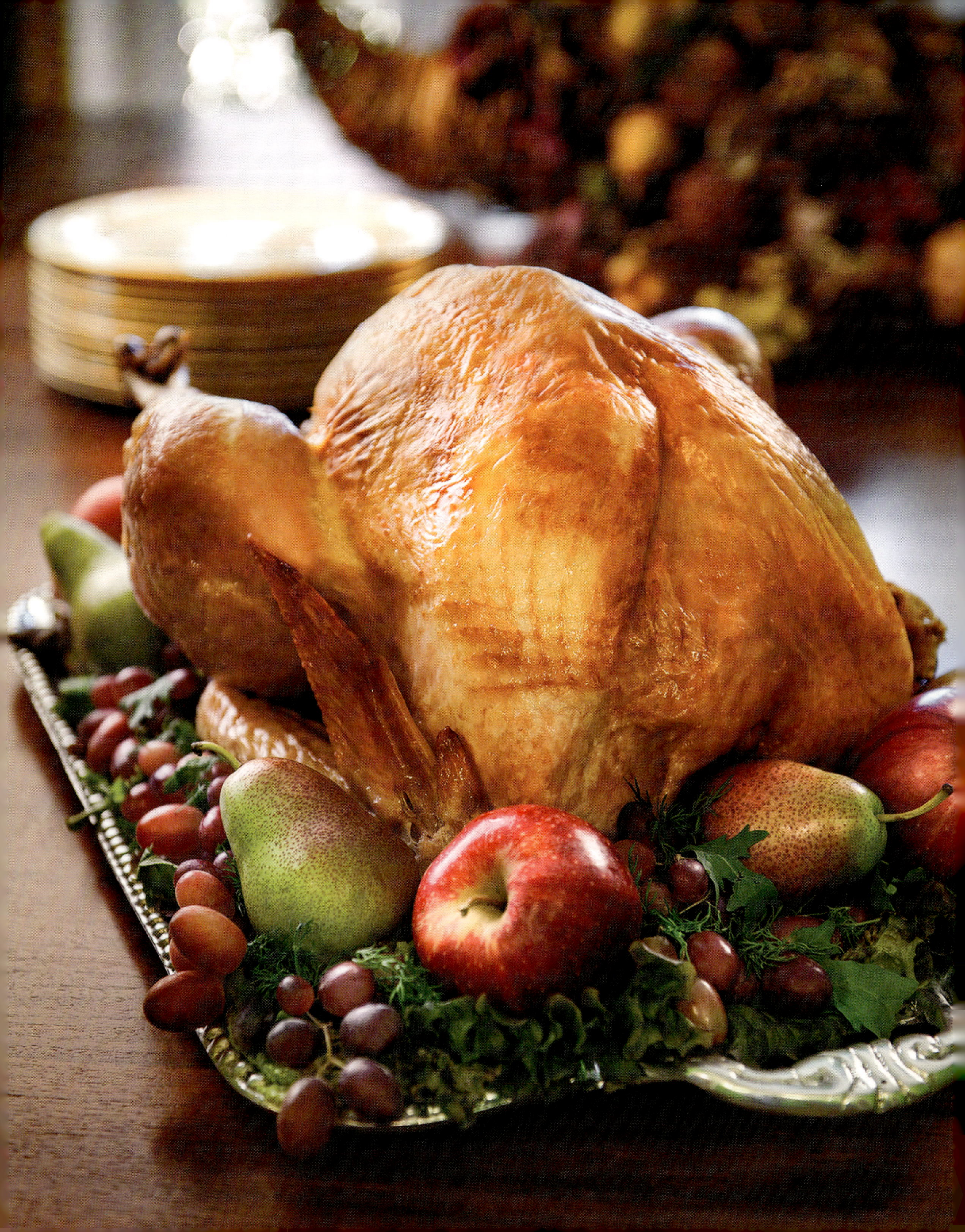

HORN OF PLENTY THANKSGIVING

Butterball Turkey with Giblet Gravy

1 (14-pound) turkey
2 onions, each cut into 8 wedges
3 ribs celery, each cut into thirds
1 cup fresh parsley leaves
4 garlic cloves, halved

Giblet Gravy
5 cups water
1/2 teaspoon salt
1/4 teaspoon black peppercorns
Nonstick cooking spray
3/4 cup all-purpose flour

Remove the heart, neck and gizzards from the turkey and place in a large saucepan. Add one-half of the onions, one-half of the celery, one-half of the parsley, one-half of the garlic, water, salt and peppercorns. Bring to a boil over medium-high heat, stirring occasionally. Reduce the heat to low. Simmer, covered, for 1 1/2 hours. Strain the broth through a wire mesh strainer into a bowl. Remove the meat from the bones and finely chop the neck meat, heart and gizzards. Chill the meat and broth separately, covered, until ready to use. Rinse the turkey and pat dry with paper towels. Place the remaining onion, celery, parsley and garlic in the turkey cavity. Place the turkey, breast side up, on a rack in a shallow roasting pan. Coat the turkey with nonstick cooking spray. Roast at 325 degrees for about 3½ hours or until 180 degrees on a meat thermometer inserted in the thickest part of the thigh. Cover the breast and drumsticks with foil after 2 hours of roasting to prevent overcooking. Remove the turkey to a serving platter and let rest for 15 minutes before carving.

For the gravy, strain the pan drippings into a 4-cup glass measuring cup. Skim 1/4 cup fat from the drippings and pour into a saucepan. Skim the remaining fat and discard. Add enough of the giblet broth to the measuring cup to make 4 cups. Whisk the flour into the fat. Whisk in the 4 cups liquid gradually. Bring to a boil over medium heat, stirring constantly. Cook until slightly thickened, stirring constantly. Stir in the reserved giblet meat and cook until heated through.

Serves 14

Turkey has a way of bringing people together. In fact, it's hard to think of Thanksgiving without it. The Butterball turkey was introduced in 1954, the product named for its broad breast and plump, round shape. Butterball, LLC was formed in 2006 and is a joint venture with Maxwell Farms Incorporated, an affiliate of the Goldsboro Milling Company (established in 1916), and Seaboard Corporation based in Kansas. Butterball, LLC, headquartered in Garner, is the largest producer of turkey products in the United States, and their plant in Mount Olive is the world's largest turkey plant.

MOUNTAIN REGION

Multigrain Bread, Onion, Pecan and Golden Raisin Stuffing

Arrange the bread in a single layer in a large roasting pan. Bake at 275 degrees for 25 minutes or until the bread is dry but not toasted, stirring frequently. Remove to a wire rack to cool. Bring the brandy and raisins to a boil in a small saucepan. Remove from the heat and let stand for 15 minutes. Heat the olive oil in a large skillet over medium-high heat. Add the onion, garlic and celery and sauté for 12 to 15 minutes or until the vegetables are tender. Combine the bread, raisins with liquid, onion mixture, pecans, parsley, sage, thyme and fennel seeds in a large bowl and toss to mix. Add the broth and egg and toss until equally moistened. Stuff into the turkey cavity just before roasting or spoon the stuffing into a buttered baking dish and bake at 325 degree for 45 minutes or until golden brown and crisp on top.

Serves 16

8 cups cubed multigrain bread
1/2 cup apple brandy or apple juice
3/4 cup golden raisins
1/3 cup olive oil
1 large onion, chopped
3 garlic cloves, minced
2 cups chopped celery
1 1/2 cups pecan halves, toasted and chopped
1 cup chopped fresh parsley
2 teaspoons dried sage, crushed
1 teaspoon dried thyme
1 teaspoon fennel seeds
2 cups chicken broth
1 egg, beaten

Robin's Cranberry Salad

Dissolve the gelatin in the boiling water in a bowl. Stir in the cranberry sauce. Chill for 15 minutes or until slightly thickened. Fold in the orange, apple and pecans. Pour into a gelatin mold lightly coated with nonstick cooking spray. Chill overnight or until firm. Dip the outside of the mold into warm water for a few seconds to loosen the gelatin. Unmold onto a serving plate covered with red or green leaf lettuce. Mix the mayonnaise, sour cream and sugar in a small bowl. Serve with the salad.

Serves 6 to 8

1 (3-ounce) package cherry gelatin
3/4 cup boiling water
1 (16-ounce) can whole cranberry sauce
1 orange, peeled, chopped and drained
1/2 cup diced peeled apple
1/2 cup chopped toasted pecans
Red or green leaf lettuce
1/2 cup mayonnaise
1/4 cup sour cream
1/3 cup sugar

HORN OF PLENTY THANKSGIVING

Sweet Potato Casserole

6 or 7 large sweet potatoes
Shortening
1/2 cup (1 stick) butter, cubed
1 1/4 cups granulated sugar
3/4 cup packed dark brown sugar
2 eggs
2 teaspoons vanilla extract
1/4 teaspoon salt
2 teaspoons dry sherry or brandy
2 tablespoons whole milk or evaporated milk
1 cup all-purpose flour
1/2 cup packed light brown sugar
1/2 cup packed dark brown sugar
1/2 cup (1 stick) butter, softened
1 cup broken pecans

Rub the potatoes with shortening and prick with a fork. Arrange on a foil-lined baking sheet. Bake at 400 degrees for 1 hour and 20 minutes or until tender. Remove to a wire rack to cool slightly. Peel the potatoes and place in a large mixing bowl. Add 1/2 cup cubed butter, granulated sugar, 3/4 cup dark brown sugar and eggs and beat until smooth. Beat in the vanilla, salt, sherry and milk. Pour into a 9×13-inch baking dish coated with nonstick cooking spray. Mix the flour, light brown sugar and 1/2 cup dark brown sugar in a bowl. Cut in 1/2 cup butter with a pastry blender or fork until crumbly. Stir in the pecans. Sprinkle over the sweet potatoes. Bake at 350 degrees for 45 minutes.

Serves 12

Note: This can be made ahead and frozen. Thaw before baking.

Roasted Broccoli with Parmesan Cheese

4 to 5 pounds broccoli
4 garlic cloves, peeled and thinly sliced
Good-quality olive oil
1 1/2 teaspoons kosher salt
1/2 teaspoon freshly ground black pepper
2 teaspoons grated lemon zest
2 tablespoons freshly squeezed lemon juice
3 tablespoons pine nuts, toasted
1/3 cup freshly grated Parmesan cheese
2 tablespoons julienned fresh basil leaves (about 12 leaves)

Preheat the oven to 425 degrees. Cut the broccoli florets from the thick stalks, leaving an inch or two of stalk attached to the florets, discarding the rest of the stalks. Cut the larger pieces through the base of the head with a small knife, pulling the florets apart. You should have about 8 cups of florets. Place the broccoli florets on a sheet pan large enough to hold them in a single layer. Toss the garlic on the broccoli and drizzle with 5 tablespoons olive oil. Sprinkle with the salt and pepper. Roast for 20 to 25 minutes or until tender-crisp and the tips of some of the florets are browned. Remove the broccoli from the oven and immediately toss with 1 1/2 tablespoons olive oil, lemon zest, lemon juice, pine nuts, cheese, and basil. Serve hot.

Salt cellars were an everyday fixture on dining tables in the 18th and 19th centuries until being replaced by the salt shaker, which was invented to address the problem of salt clumping. This blue cut glass salt cellar (ca.1880-1900) in a hobnail design would have been typical for the time and would have been accompanied with a salt spoon such as the one pictured (ca.1820-1840).

MOUNTAIN REGION

TURKEY LEFTOVERS

Butterball Turkey, Brie and Cranberry with Apple on Panini

Spread one side of each bread slice with butter. Spread the remaining side of one slice with dijonnaise. Spread the remaining side of the other slice with cranberry chutney. Layer the turkey, cheese, apple slices and spinach leaves over the chutney. Top with the remaining bread slice, buttered side up. Grill in a preheated panini pan for 4 to 6 minutes or until golden brown on both sides and the cheese is melted. Cut into halves and serve.

Serves 1

2 slices multigrain bread
1 tablespoon butter, softened
2 tablespoons cranberry chutney
1 tablespoon dijonnaise
3 ounces leftover sliced cooked turkey
2 ounces sliced Brie cheese
3 slices cored crisp unpeeled apple
Fresh spinach leaves

Butterball Turkey Ranch Pasta Salad

Cook the pasta using the package directions; drain and rinse with cold water. Combine with the broccoli, bacon, turkey, cheese, tomato and dressing in a large bowl. Add the green onions, salt and pepper; toss to mix. Chill, covered, for 2 hours or longer.

Serves 8

2 cups (8 ounces) uncooked penne
2 cups broccoli florets
6 slices fully cooked bacon, heated and chopped
2 cups chopped leftover cooked turkey
1 cup shredded Cheddar cheese
1 tomato, chopped
1 cup ranch dressing
$1/2$ cup sliced green onions
$1/2$ teaspoon salt
$1/4$ teaspoon pepper

HORN OF PLENTY THANKSGIVING

Jim's Bourbon Pecan Pie

½ cup (1 stick) butter
1 cup packed light brown sugar
1 cup light corn syrup
3 eggs, beaten
1 teaspoon vanilla extract, or to taste
2 tablespoons good-quality bourbon, or to taste
1 cup chopped pecans
1 unbaked (9-inch) deep-dish pie shell

This recipe combines ingredients noted by my grandmother and "Mama Dip." While I doubt the bourbon whiskey is a new addition (my Baptist and Presbyterian forebearers would never admit to this ingredient), it gives it a wonderful kick and the pie is the perfect complement to southern hospitality.

Melt the butter in a saucepan over medium heat. Stir in the brown sugar and corn syrup. Cook until the sugar is melted, stirring constantly; do not let boil. Remove from the heat and cool to room temperature. Stir in the eggs. Stir in the vanilla and bourbon. Stir in the pecans. Pour into the pie shell. Bake at 350 degrees for 55 minutes or until firm. Serve warm or at room temperature with a scoop of vanilla ice cream.

Serves 8

Pumpkin Roll

3 eggs
1 cup granulated sugar
⅔ cup canned pumpkin
1 teaspoon lemon juice
¾ cup all-purpose flour
1 teaspoon baking powder
½ teaspoon salt
1 teaspoon nutmeg
1 teaspoon ginger
2 teaspoons cinnamon
1 cup chopped pecans
Confectioners' sugar for dusting
6 ounces cream cheese, softened
¼ cup (½ stick) butter, softened
½ teaspoon vanilla extract
1 cup confectioners' sugar

Beat the eggs in a mixing bowl at high speed for 5 minutes. Gradually beat in the granulated sugar. Stir in the pumpkin and lemon juice. Mix the flour, baking powder, salt, nutmeg, ginger and cinnamon together and fold into the pumpkin mixture. Spread in a greased and floured 10×15-inch cake pan. Sprinkle with the pecans. Bake at 375 degrees for 15 minutes or until the cake tests done. Dust a clean kitchen towel with confectioners' sugar. Invert the cake onto the towel. Roll the warm cake in the towel as for a jelly roll from the short side and place on a wire rack to cool. Unroll the cooled cake carefully and remove the towel. Beat the cream cheese, butter and vanilla in a mixing bowl until light and fluffy. Beat in 1 cup confectioners' sugar. Spread over the cooled cake to the edge and reroll. Wrap in plastic wrap and chill. Cut into slices to serve.

Serves 8 to 10

Colonial settlers brought their pie recipes with them and adapted recipes to the ingredients and cooking techniques available to them in the New World. Early pies were made from berries and fruits that settlers learned about from Native Americans. Cooking pies in shallow pans allowed colonial cooks to stretch ingredients and to literally "cut corners." This pie crimper, or pastry cutter, (ca. 1875-1925) would have been used the late 19th and early 20th centuries.

BEVERAGES & APPETIZERS

Cherry Bounce

Cheerwine Punch

Bloody Marys

Minted Iced Tea

Toasted Bleu Cheese Rounds

Cheese Camellias

Mushroom Spread

Cheese Cookies

Cheese Straws

Buffalo Wing Dip

Corn Dip

Election Night Dip

King K Dip

Jalapeño Meat Dip

Eggplant Appetizer

Jalapeño Popper Dip

Oh, So Good

Shrimp Spread

Oysters

Scallop Skewers

Hot Crab Spread

Zesty Pickled Shrimp

Shrimp Dip

Stuffed Celery

Artichoke Squares

Manchego Stuffed Dates

BEVERAGES & APPETIZERS

Cherry Bounce

4 to 6 cups whole fresh sour cherries (preferably Morello), stems removed
2 cups sugar
Grated zest and juice of 1 lemon (optional)
4 allspice berries (optional)
Dash of ginger, bruised (optional)
2 cinnamon sticks, broken into pieces (optional)
2 to 4 whole cloves, bruised (optional)
1 (1/4-inch) piece fresh whole nutmeg, grated (optional)
4 cups favorite spirits (whiskey and brandy are traditional; vodka and bourbon and rye work, too)

In the late 1700s, North Carolina legislators traveled to rotating capital cities to meet and conduct the state's official business. In 1788 the Constitutional Convention met and decided the capital must be established within 10 miles of Isaac Hunter's tavern and plantation, a famous rest stop of the day. According to local legend, Joel Lane, who—like Isaac Hunter—operated a tavern and inn out of his house, relied upon a potent fruit and alcohol drink called Cherry Bounce to sway the legislators in favor of buying property from him, rather than Hunter. Cherry Bounce was such a favorite of General Washington's that it is documented he packed a "canteen" of it for a trip west across the Allegheny Mountains in September 1784.

Combine the cherries, sugar, lemon juice, allspice, ginger, cinnamon sticks, cloves and nutmeg in a large saucepan. Bring to a simmer for 20 minutes, stirring occasionally. Remove from the heat and let cool. Pour into a large glass jar with a tight-fitting lid and add the whiskey. Secure the lid and shake to mix well. Let stand in a cool dark place for 3 moths. Strain into a clean glass jar. Reserve the infused charries for garnishing, if desired. Will keep for up to 2 months.

Makes 4 cups

Cheerwine Punch

2 (2-liter) bottles Cheerwine
1 (2-liter) bottle Ginger ale
2 (46-ounce) cans unsweetened pineapple juice

Chill the soda, ginger ale and pineapple juice thoroughly. Pour into a large punch bowl and mix well. Serve immediately.

Makes 37 cups

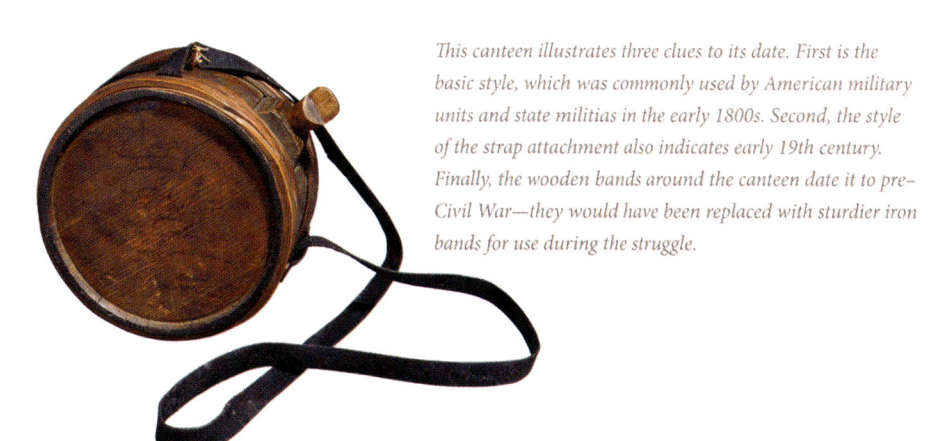

This canteen illustrates three clues to its date. First is the basic style, which was commonly used by American military units and state militias in the early 1800s. Second, the style of the strap attachment also indicates early 19th century. Finally, the wooden bands around the canteen date it to pre–Civil War—they would have been replaced with sturdier iron bands for use during the struggle.

BEVERAGES & APPETIZERS

Bloody Marys

Combine the tomato juice, lemon juice, Worcestershire sauce, pepper and celery salt in a large container with a tight-fitting lid. Seal the container and shake well. Add the vodka and shake well. Chill until ready to serve. Garnish with celery stalk, olive and lime. Additional garnishes; pickled asparagus, pickled okra, peppers or onions and shrimp or bacon.

Serves 8

1 (46-ounce) can Sacramento tomato juice
1/2 cup fresh lemon juice
1/3 cup Worcestershire sauce
3 tablespoons pepper
5 tablespoons celery salt
15 ounces vodka
Celery stalks, olives and lime slices

BEVERAGES & APPETIZERS

Minted Iced Tea

4 cups water
1/2 cup mint sprigs
5 English breakfast tea bags
1 cup freshly squeezed orange juice
1 tablespoon frozen orange juice concentrate
Fresh mint sprigs

Bring the water and 1/2 mint to a boil in a large stainless steel or enameled saucepan; remove from the heat. Add the tea bags. Let steep for 5 minutes to make a strong tea. Remove the tea bags; cool to room temperature. Stir in the orange juice and concentrate. Pour into a pitcher. Chill until serving time. Pour into ice-filled glasses. Garnish with fresh mint sprigs.

Makes 6 servings

Note: Bruise the mint sprigs to release the mint flavor.

Toasted Bleu Cheese Rounds

1/2 cup (1 stick) butter, softened
1 cup (4 ounces) crumbled bleu cheese
1/2 cup chopped toasted walnuts
1 small loaf sliced bread

Combine the butter, cheese and walnuts in a bowl and mix well. Cut rounds from the bread slices using a small biscuit cutter. Spread the cheese mixture over the bread rounds and arrange on a broiler pan. Broil until hot and bubbly.

Serves 15 to 20

Note: You may toast one side of the bread rounds before spreading the cheese mixture on the untoasted side.

Cheese Camellias

3/4 cup (1 1/2 sticks) butter, softened
1 1/2 cups (6 ounces) grated sharp Cheddar cheese
1/4 cup (1 ounce) grated Parmesan cheese
1 1/2 cups all-purpose flour
1 teaspoon salt
1/8 teaspoon (or more) cayenne pepper
Pecan halves

These are served at the Barker House tea parties in Edenton. The house was the home to Penelope Barker who organized a group of 51 women in October 1774 to sign a petition to King George III demanding the repeal of taxation on tea and other goods. It is considered to be the first female-driven political effort in the Western world. The house now serves as the Edenton Welcome Center and headquarters of the Edenton Historical Commission.

Beat the butter, Cheddar cheese and Parmesan cheese together in a bowl. Sift the flour, salt and cayenne pepper together and stir into the cheese mixture. Chill for 30 minutes. Roll out the dough on a floured surface and cut into rounds with a small biscuit cutter. Arrange the rounds on a nonstick baking sheet. Bake at 350 degrees for 12 minutes. Remove from the oven and gently press one pecan half on top of each round.

Serves 24

Note: If the dough seems too dry, stir in a small amount of water.

BEVERAGES & APPETIZERS

Mushroom Spread

Fry the bacon in a skillet until crisp. Remove the bacon with tongs to paper towels to drain. Remove and discard all but 3 tablespoons of bacon drippings from the skillet. Add the mushrooms, onion and garlic and sauté until the vegetables are tender and most of the liquid has evaporated. Whisk in the flour, salt and pepper and cook for 1 minute, stirring constantly. Add the cream cheese, Worcestershire sauce and soy sauce and cook over low heat until the cream cheese is melted, stirring frequently. Stir in the bacon and sour cream. Pour into a lightly greased baking dish. Bake at 350 degrees for 25 to 30 minutes. Garnish with chopped fresh parsley and serve.

Serves 12

- 4 slices bacon, chopped
- 12 ounces fresh mushrooms, finely chopped
- 1 onion, finely chopped
- 1 or 2 garlic cloves, pressed
- 2 tablespoons all-purpose flour
- $1/2$ teaspoon salt
- $1/4$ teaspoon pepper
- 8 ounces cream cheese, cubed
- 2 teaspoons Worcestershire sauce
- 1 teaspoon soy sauce
- $1/2$ cup sour cream

Cheese Cookies

Beat the butter and cheese together in a bowl. Add the flour, sugar, salt and cayenne pepper and mix well. Stir in the cereal. Chill for 20 minutes. Shape the dough into 1-inch balls. Arrange the balls on an ungreased cookie sheet and press to flatten. Press one pecan half on top of each cookie. Bake at 350 degrees for 10 to 15 minutes or until the edges are golden brown. Cool on the cookie sheet for 2 minutes. Remove to a wire rack to cool completely.

Makes 4 dozen

- 1 cup (2 sticks) butter, softened
- 10 ounces sharp Cheddar cheese, finely shredded (do not use pre-shredded)
- 2 cups self-rising flour
- 2 teaspoons sugar
- 1 teaspoon salt
- 1 to 2 teaspoons (or more) cayenne pepper
- 2 cups crisp rice cereal
- Pecan halves

Grandmother's Cheese Straws

Mix the cheese, flour, butter, salt and cayenne pepper in a food processor until a dough forms. Place the dough in a cookie press fitted with a star tip. Press desired length straws onto an ungreased baking sheet. Bake at 375 degrees for 7 to 9 minutes. Remove to a wire rack to cool.

Makes 2 dozen

- 1 cup (4 ounces) shredded sharp Cheddar cheese
- 1 cup all-purpose flour
- $1/2$ cup (1 stick) butter, softened
- $1/8$ teaspoon salt
- $1/8$ teaspoon cayenne pepper, or to taste

Economic situations improved for the middle and merchant classes during the early to mid-19th century, and one way these families could display their newfound affluence was to purchase silver serving pieces, such as these sterling silver tongs (ca. 1890). Driven in part by this increase in demand for silver, and also by silver exhibitions that promoted increasingly ornate pieces, the early 20th century ushered in a movement to further widen the gulf between utilitarian and artistic serving pieces.

BEVERAGES & APPETIZERS

Robin's Buffalo Wing Dip

3 large boneless skinless chicken breasts
Olive oil
Seasoned salt to taste
8 ounces light cream cheese, softened
$1/2$ to $3/4$ bottle Frank's hot sauce
1 (15-ounce) jar light chunky bleu cheese salad dressing
2 cups (8 ounces) shredded Monterey Jack cheese

Arrange the chicken in a 9×13-inch baking dish. Drizzle with a small amount of olive oil and sprinkle with seasoned salt. Bake at 350 degrees for 20 to 30 minutes or until the chicken is cooked through. Remove the chicken to a cutting board and let cool slightly. Shred the chicken and spread evenly in the baking dish. Combine the cream cheese, hot sauce and salad dressing in a bowl and mix well. Pour evenly over the chicken and cover with the Monterey Jack cheese. Bake at 350 degrees for 20 to 30 minutes or until bubbly. Stir to mix or serve layered. Serve hot with scoop-type chips or toasted bread rounds. This also freezes well.

Serves 20

Note: This is similar to the Buffalo Wing Dip sold at Ukrops grocery store in Richmond, VA. Ukrops sprinkles a small amount of shredded yellow Cheddar cheese over the top for color before baking.

Frances' Corn Dip

1 (11-ounce) can Mexicorn, drained
1 (4-ounce) can chopped green chiles
2 cups (8 ounces) shredded Colby-Jack cheese
$1/2$ cup (2 ounces) grated or shredded Parmesan cheese
1 cup mayonnaise

Combine the Mexicorn, green chiles, Colby-Jack cheese, Parmesan cheese and mayonnaise in a bowl and mix well. Spoon into a $1^{1}/_{2}$-quart baking dish. Bake at 350 degrees for 30 minutes or until heated through. Serve with tortilla chips.

Serves 10

Marcia's Election Night Dip

16 ounces cream cheese, softened
2 (16-ounce) cans black beans, rinsed and drained
1 large onion, chopped
1 jar raspberry salsa
4 cups (16 ounces) shredded Pepper Jack cheese

Spread the cream cheese in a baking dish. Layer the black beans, onion, salsa and Pepper Jack cheese over the cream cheese. Bake at 350 degrees for 30 minutes or until the cheese is melted and bubbly. Serve with lime-flavored tortilla chips.

Serves 20

Note: Raspberry salsa, such as Robert Rothschild Farm, can be found in upscale grocery stores and is a must for this recipe

BEVERAGES & APPETIZERS

King K Dip

Whisk the olive oil, vinegar and sugar in a large bowl. Add the beans, corn, green onions and cheese and toss to mix. Serve with scoop-type chips.

Serves 24

1/3 **cup olive oil**
1/3 **cup cider vinegar**
1/3 **cup sugar**
1 can black beans, rinsed and drained
1 can Shoe Peg corn, rinsed and drained
3 bunches green onions, chopped
1 block feta cheese, crumbled

Jalapeño Meat Dip

Brown the ground beef and sausage in a skillet, stirring until the meat is crumbly; drain. Add the onions and sauté until the onions are tender. Melt the cheese in the top of a double boiler over simmering water. Stir in the meat mixture, tomatoes and jalapeño chiles. Cook for 30 minutes, stirring occasionally. Serve hot with tortilla chips.

Serves 40

Note: This freezes well.

1 1/2 **pounds ground beef**
8 ounces bulk pork sausage
2 large onions, chopped
32 ounces Velveeta cheese, cubed
2 fresh tomatoes, chopped, or 1 (16-ounce) can tomatoes, drained and chopped
3 large or 4 small jalapeño chiles, chopped

Jennie's Eggplant Appetizer

Heat 1/4 cup olive oil in a large skillet. Add the onion and garlic and sauté until tender. Stir in the eggplant and salt. Cook, covered, for 15 minutes or until the eggplant is tender, adding additional olive oil, 1 tablespoon at a time, if needed. Stir in the tomato paste, vinegar and brown sugar. Bring to a boil and stir in the olives. Remove from the heat and stir in the artichokes, tarragon, basil and oregano. Let cool to room temperature. Serve with pita wedges.

Serves 18

1/4 **cup olive oil**
1 onion, chopped
2 to 3 garlic cloves, minced
1 large eggplant, peeled and cubed
1/2 **teaspoon salt**
Additional olive oil
2 tablespoons tomato paste
1/4 **cup red wine vinegar**
1 tablespoon brown sugar
1 cup pitted green olives, chopped
1 (6-ounce) jar marinated artichoke hearts, chopped
Pinch of tarragon
Pinch of basil
Pinch of oregano

BEVERAGES & APPETIZERS

Jalapeño Popper Dip

16 ounces cream cheese, softened
1 1/4 cups mayonnaise
1 cup (4 ounces) shredded Mexican blend cheese
1/2 cup (2 ounces) grated Parmesan cheese
1 (4 ounce) can chopped green chiles
1 (4 ounce) can sliced jalapeño chiles
1 cup panko bread crumbs
1/2 cup (2 ounces) grated Parmesan cheese
1/4 cup (1/2 stick) butter, melted

Process the cream cheese, mayonnaise, Mexican cheese, 1/2 cup Parmesan cheese, green chiles and jalapeño chiles in a food processor until blended. Spoon into a greased 2-quart baking dish. Mix the bread crumbs, 1/2 cup Parmesan cheese and melted butter in a bowl. Sprinkle evenly over the dip. Bake at 375 degrees for 20 minutes or until bubbly and golden brown; do not overbake. Serve with butter crackers or baguette slices.

Note: Feel free to double the amount of jalapeño chiles if you want a really spicy dip.

Serves 10

Oh, So Good

1 pound very lean bacon, cut into pieces
8 ounces sharp Cheddar cheese, cut into pieces
1 onion, cut into pieces
Triscuit crackers or party rye bread

Grind the bacon, cheese and onion in a food grinder or finely chop in a food processor. Spread over crackers or party rye bread and arrange on a baking sheet. Broil 6 or 7 inches from the heat source until golden brown and bubbly. Serve immediately.

Serves 40

Note: The uncooked spread freezes well.

Cathy's Shrimp Spread

1 1/2 pounds deveined peeled cooked shrimp, chopped
1/2 cup finely chopped red onion
1 1/2 cups finely chopped celery
8 ounces cream cheese, softened
1/4 cup sour cream
1 tablespoon mayonnaise
3 tablespoons fresh dill weed, minced
1/2 teaspoon freshly ground black pepper
Cayenne pepper to taste
Salt to taste
Additional fresh dill weed

Mix the shrimp, onion and celery in a large bowl. Beat the cream cheese, sour cream and mayonnaise in a bowl. Stir into the shrimp mixture. Add 3 tablespoons dill, black pepper, cayenne pepper and salt and mix well. Garnish with fresh dill weed. Serve in endive cups or with your favorite crackers.

Serves 16

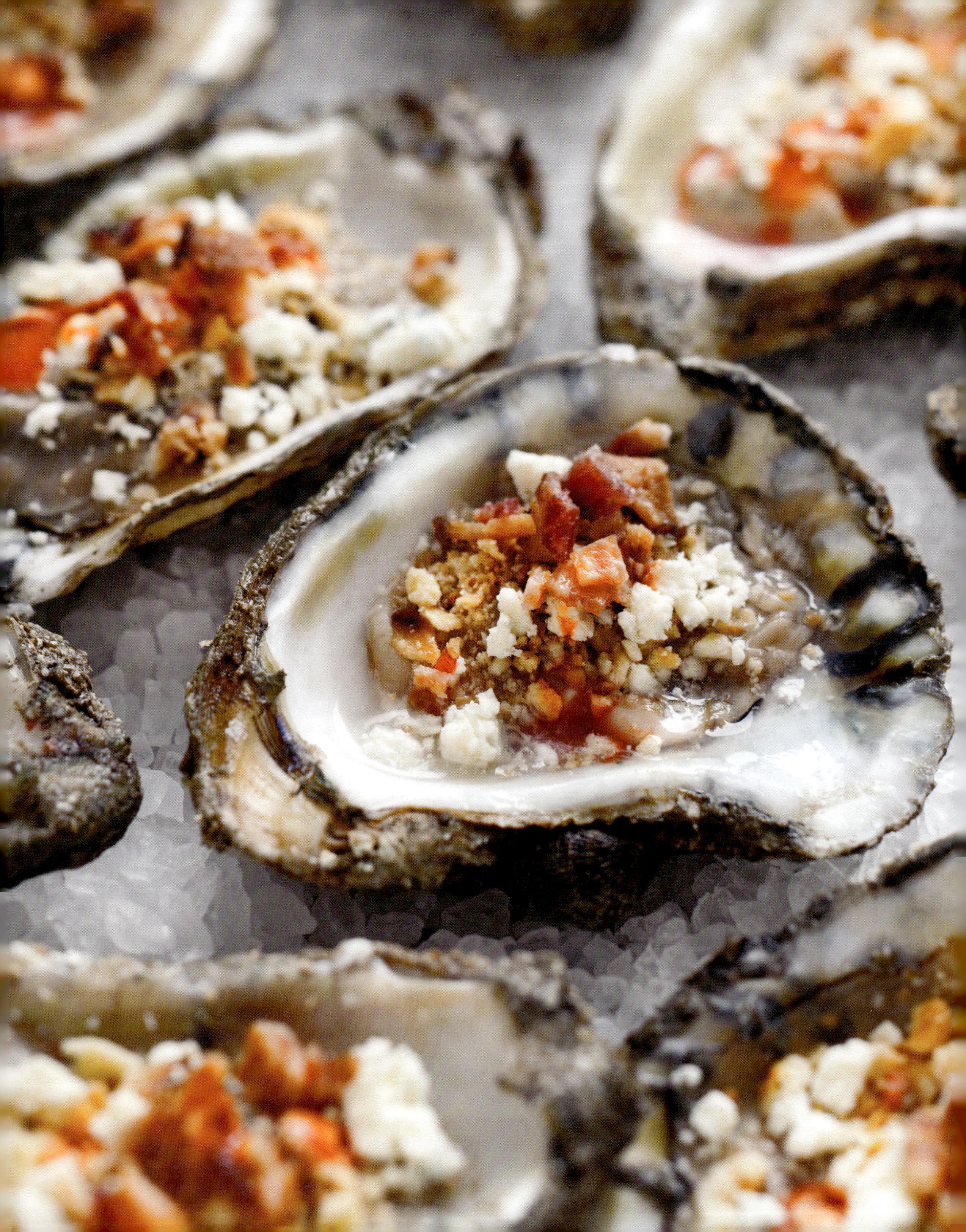

BEVERAGES & APPETIZERS

Those Oysters Dick Fixes

Rock salt
12 large oysters on the half shell
1/2 cup crushed butter crackers
1/3 cup (5 tablespoons) butter, melted
1/2 cup (2 ounces) crumbled bleu cheese
6 slices bacon, crisp-cooked and crumbled
Tabasco sauce

We call this "Oysters Dick-afellers" here in Washington…

Cover the bottom of a broiler pan with rock salt. Insert the oysters in their shells partway into the salt. Top the oysters evenly with the cracker crumbs and drizzle evenly with the melted butter. Add the cheese and bacon evenly on top. Add one or two drops of Tabasco sauce on each oyster. Broil until bubbly and the edges of the oysters curl. Serve immediately.

Serves 12

Edwina's Scallop Skewers

6 tablespoons olive oil or a combination of olive oil and vegetable oil
2 tablespoons red wine vinegar
1 tablespoon Dijon mustard
1 teaspoon salt
1 1/2 pounds small scallops
Bamboo skewers soaked in water
Bacon slices cut into 1/2-inch pieces
Bottled cocktail onions
Small button mushrooms

Whisk the olive oil, vinegar, Dijon mustard and salt in a bowl. Stir in the scallops. Marinate in the refrigerator for 3 hours to overnight. Remove the skewers from the water. Remove the scallops from the marinade and thread one scallop, one bacon piece, one onion and one mushroom onto each skewer. Arrange the skewers on a broiler pan. Broil 8 inches from the heat source until the scallops and bacon are cooked through, turning once during cooking. Remove to a chafing dish to keep warm.

Serves 12 to 14

Note: After removing the scallops from the marinade, you may bring the marinade to a boil in a saucepan and boil for 5 minutes. Add to the cooked scallop skewers in the chafing dish.

Melissa's Hot Crab Spread

24 ounces cream cheese, softened
1 to 1 1/2 pounds back-fin crab meat
1 garlic clove, minced
2 teaspoons dry mustard
1/2 cup mayonnaise
1/4 cup dry white wine
Juice of 1 large lemon
1/3 cup dry sherry
1 1/2 teaspoons salt, or to taste
1 to 2 dashes of Worcestershire sauce
1 to 2 dashes of Tabasco sauce
3 dashes of pepper

Combine the cream cheese, crab meat, garlic, mustard, mayonnaise, wine, lemon juice, sherry, salt, Worcestershire sauce, Tabasco sauce and pepper in a bowl and mix well. Spoon into a baking dish. Bake at 350 degrees for 20 to 30 minutes or until heated through. Serve with pita chips, crackers or toasted baguette slices.

Serves 24

BEVERAGES & APPETIZERS

Zesty Pickled Shrimp

Whisk the oil, vinegar, capers, hot sauce, lemon zest, lemon juice, sugar and celery salt in a large bowl. Stir in the onion, bay leaves, shrimp and lemon slices. Cover with plastic wrap and chill overnight. Remove and discard the bay leaves before serving.
Serves 8 to 10

1 cup safflower oil
1/3 cup white vinegar
3 tablespoons capers with juice
1 tablespoon hot red pepper sauce
1 1/2 teaspoons grated lemon zest
1 tablespoon fresh lemon juice
1/4 cup sugar (optional)
1 teaspoon celery salt (optional)
1 onion, thinly sliced
6 bay leaves
2 pounds cooked shrimp, peeled and deveined
Thinly sliced lemon (optional)

Linda's Shrimp Dip

Combine the cream cheese, mayonnaise, salt and white pepper in a bowl and mix well. Add the lemon juice, ketchup and onion and mix well. Stir in the shrimp. Chill until ready to serve. Serve with crackers.
Serves 12

8 ounces cream cheese, softened
3/4 cup mayonnaise
Salt to taste
White pepper or cayenne pepper to taste
Juice of 2 lemons
2 tablespoons ketchup
1 small onion, grated
1 pound cooked shrimp, peeled, deveined and chopped

Stuffed Celery

Combine the cream cheese, salt, Worcestershire sauce and milk in a bowl and mix well. Fill the celery ribs with the cream cheese mixture. Arrange in an airtight container and cover with a damp paper towel before sealing. Chill until ready to serve. *Serves 12 to 15*

12 ounces cream cheese, softened
1 teaspoon salt
2 1/2 to 3 tablespoons Worcestershire sauce
1 tablespoon milk
6 large ribs celery, cut into 4 or 5 pieces

BEVERAGES & APPETIZERS

Artichoke Squares

3 (6-ounce) jars marinated artichoke hearts
1 garlic clove, crushed
1/2 cup chopped onion
4 eggs
1/4 cup seasoned bread crumbs
8 ounces extra-sharp Cheddar cheese, finely shredded
2 tablespoons minced fresh parsley
1/4 teaspoon salt
1/8 teaspoon dried oregano
1/8 teaspoon pepper
1/8 teaspoon Tabasco sauce

Carefully drain the oil from the top of one jar of marinated artichokes into a skillet and heat over medium heat. Add the garlic and onion and sauté for 5 minutes. Set aside. Drain the liquid from the remaining jars of artichokes and finely chop all the artichokes. Beat the eggs in a bowl until foamy. Stir in the bread crumbs, cheese, parsley, salt, oregano, pepper and Tabasco sauce. Fold in the chopped artichokes. Fold in the onion mixture. Spoon into a greased 9×9-inch baking pan. Bake at 325 degrees for 30 minutes. Remove to a wire rack to cool completely. Cut into small squares and arrange on a nonstick baking sheet. Heat at 325 degrees for 10 to 12 minutes and serve.

Serves 12

Note: This also freezes well. Thaw and reheat following the above directions.

Manchego Stuffed Dates

24 Medjool dates
16 ounces Manchego cheese, cut into twenty-four 1 1/2×1/4-inch pieces
8 slices thick cut bacon, cut into thirds
Smoked paprika

Cut a lengthwise slit in the side of each date and remove the pit. Insert one piece of cheese into each date. Sprinkle one side of the bacon slices generously with paprika. Wrap one piece of bacon around each date with the paprika side against the date. Secure the bacon with a wooden pick. Arrange the dates in a shallow baking pan lined with baking parchment paper. Bake at 425 degrees for 8 minutes. Turn the dates over and bake for 8 minutes longer or until the bacon is cooked through. Remove the dates to a serving platter and remove the wooden picks. Serve warm.

Serves 18 to 24

HESTER'S SAUSAGE DIP

Brown 1 pound of sausage in a saucepan, stirring until crumbly; drain. Add 16 ounces of cubed cream cheese and cook until the cheese is melted, stirring constantly. Stir in 2 cans of tomatoes with green chiles. Pour into a heatproof dish to serve or pour into a chafing dish to keep hot for serving.

Serves 16

SOUPS & SALADS

SOUPS & SALADS

Asparagus Soup

Down East Clam Chowder

Clam Chowder

Cream of Crab Soup

Day Ahead Green Salad

Cold Lemon Chicken Salad

Wedge Salad

Arugula & Watermelon Salad

Ginger Salad Dressing

Kale Salad

Til's Corn Bread Salad

SOUPS & SALADS

Asparagus Soup

1 pound asparagus
1/4 cup (1/2 stick) unsalted butter
1/2 cup chopped onion
2 tablespoons all-purpose flour
4 cups chicken broth, heated
2 egg yolks
1/2 cup heavy cream
Lemon juice to taste
Salt and white pepper to taste
1 to 2 tablespoons dry sherry
Minced chives

Break off and discard the tough ends of the asparagus. Peel the bottom third of the stems. Cut the stems into 1-inch pieces and set aside the tips. Melt the butter in a saucepan. Add the onion and sauté until tender. Add the asparagus stem pieces and sprinkle with the flour. Cook for 3 minutes, stirring constantly. Whisk in the broth. Bring to a boil, whisking constantly. Reduce the heat and simmer for 15 minutes or until the asparagus is tender. Remove from the heat and purée the soup in a food processor. Return the soup to the saucepan. Stir in the asparagus tips and simmer for 5 minutes. Beat the egg yolks and cream in a bowl. Whisk 1 cup of the hot soup gradually into the egg yolks. Whisk the mixture slowly into the soup. Simmer for 3 minutes; do not let boil. Stir in the lemon juice, salt, white pepper and sherry. Serve garnished with chives.

Serves 6

Sarah's Down East Clam Chowder

2 large white potatoes, diced
2 sweet onions, diced
4 slices bacon
1 (51-ounce) can Cape May chopped clams
2 pounds fresh clams in shells or 2 (6-ounce) cans minced clams
1 tablespoon Worcestershire sauce
Several dashes of Texas Pete hot sauce
Salt and pepper to taste
2 tablespoons all-purpose flour or cornmeal

The chef at the Atlantic Beach Dunes Club shared this recipe when I was a little girl, and it quickly became a family favorite. While I have added and changed some things over the years, it remains a special dish that is served every Christmas for our family oyster roasts. It is wonderful to be able to continue this tradition and share it with the younger members of our family.

Combine the potatoes and onions in a large saucepan and add just enough water to cover the vegetables. Cook until the vegetables are tender. Fry the bacon in a skillet until crisp. Remove the bacon with tongs to paper towels to drain. Crumble the bacon and add to the potatoes. Stir several tablespoons of bacon drippings into the potato mixture and simmer for 1 minute. Stir in the chopped clams with juice, fresh clams, Worcestershire sauce, hot sauce, salt and pepper. Whisk in the flour. Cook until thickened, stirring constantly. Serve with coleslaw, corn bread, oysters and steamed or fried shrimp. This soup is wonderful to eat while waiting for those oysters to steam and be shucked.

Serves 8

SOUPS & SALADS

Jesse Boy Clam Chowder

Add enough water just to cover the clams in a large saucepan. Bring to a simmer and cook for 10 minutes or until the clams have opened. Remove the clams with a slotted spoon to a work surface and let cool. Strain the cooking liquid through a wire mesh strainer into a bowl. Measure 4 cups of cooking liquid and set aside. Remove the clams from the shells and chop. Discard any clams that did not open. Sauté the bacon in a heavy saucepan over medium-high heat until the bacon is beginning to brown and much of the fat is rendered. Add the onions and sauté until the onions are tender. Add the potatoes and sauté for 1 minute. Stir in the flour. Cook for 1 minute, stirring constantly. Stir in the half-and-half and reserved cooking liquid gradually. Bring to a boil, stirring constantly. Stir in the chopped clams, salt and pepper. Reduce the heat and simmer until ready to serve.
Serves 6

Note: If you do not have 4 cups of cooking liquid, add bottled clam juice to make up the difference. If fresh clams aren't available, you may use two 8-ounce bottles of clam juice and two 8-ounce cans of minced clams.

4 dozen clams in shells, scrubbed
4 ounces bacon or salt pork, diced
2 onions, finely chopped
4 potatoes, diced and cooked
2 tablespoons all-purpose flour
2 to 3 cups half-and-half
Salt and pepper to taste

Cream of Crab Soup

Melt the butter in a large saucepan. Stir in the flour. Cook for 1 minute, stirring constantly. Stir in the broth gradually. Cook over medium heat until the sauce is thickened, stirring constantly. Stir in the crab meat, half-and-half, sherry, salt and white pepper. Cook over low heat for 10 to 15 minutes or until heated through; do not let boil.
Serves 8

1/4 cup (1/2 stick) butter
1/4 cup all-purpose flour
1 1/4 cups chicken broth
1 pound back-fin crab meat, drained and flaked
5 cups half-and-half
1/2 cup dry sherry
1 teaspoon salt
1/4 teaspoon white pepper

This coin-silver ladle (ca. 1807–1838) was made by Fayetteville silversmith John Selph. As silver was not mined in the United States until the middle of the 19th century, silversmiths used coin or bullion, often from England, as the raw material they needed to create their goods. By melting coins, those few people who had silver were able to retain the value of their carefully attained wealth while enjoying useable items for both everyday life and display.

SOUPS & SALADS

Day Ahead Green Salad

Iceberg lettuce, cut into bite-size pieces
Fresh spinach, cut into bite-size pieces
1 (10-ounce) package frozen peas, thawed
1 to 2 bunches green onions, chopped
8 slices bacon, crisp-cooked and crumbled
5 hard-cooked eggs, sliced
1 cup sour cream
1/2 cup mayonnaise
1 envelope Italian salad dressing mix
Croutons (optional)

Layer the lettuce, spinach, peas, green onions, bacon and eggs in a 9×13-inch baking dish. Combine the sour cream, mayonnaise and salad dressing mix in a bowl and mix well. Spread over the top of the salad. Chill, covered, for 24 hours. Sprinkle with croutons and serve.

Serves 8 to 10

Note: Feel free to double the amount of the sour cream mixture.

Cold Lemon Chicken Salad

1/4 cup (1/2 stick) butter
6 whole boneless skinless chicken breasts, split
1/2 cup white wine
1/3 cup lemon juice
Salt and pepper to taste
1 1/2 cups mayonnaise
1/4 cup lemon juice

Melt the butter in a skillet. Add the chicken breasts and brown on both sides. Remove the chicken to a baking dish. Add the wine to the skillet and cook until the liquid is reduced to 1/3 cup, stirring constantly. Stir in 1/3 cup lemon juice, salt and pepper. Pour over the chicken. Bake, covered, at 350 degrees for 30 minutes or until the chicken is cooked through, basting with pan juices several times. Remove the pan juices to a saucepan and cook until reduced by one-half. Pour over the chicken and chill overnight. Mix the mayonnaise and 1/4 cup lemon juice in a bowl. Spread over the chicken and serve.

Serves 6

SOUPS & SALADS

Wedge Salad

Cook the bacon in a medium skillet over medium-low heat for 5 to 7 minutes or until crisp, stirring frequently; remove to a paper towel-lined plate. Cut the lettuce into 4 wedges. Place the lettuce on plates and spoon bleu cheese dressing over the lettuce. Top with bacon, red onion, and crumbled blue cheese. Add any combination of the croutons, dried cranberries, diced avocado, fresh tarragon, chorizo, toasted almonds or fried shallots on top.

4 servings

4 ounces bacon, chopped
1 small head iceberg lettuce
Bleu cheese salad dressing
$1/4$ small red onion, thinly sliced
Crumbled bleu cheese
Croutons
Dried cranberries
Diced avocado
Fresh tarragon
Chorizo
Toasted almonds
Fried shallots

BLEU CHEESE SALAD DRESSING

Combine 1 cup mayonnaise, $1/2$ cup sour cream, 2 tablespoons minced onion, 1 tablespoon fresh lemon juice, 4 ounces crumbled bleu cheese, $1/2$ teaspoon Worcestershire sauce and 1 tablespoon white wine vinegar in a bowl; mix well. Chill for 1 hour.

Marge's German Slaw

Combine the cabbage, onion, bell pepper and carrot in a large bowl and sprinkle with salt. Sprinkle with the celery seeds. Heat the sugar and the vinegar in a saucepan until the sugar is dissolved, stirring frequently; do not let boil. Pour over the cabbage mixture and mix well. Chill until ready to serve.

Serves 12

1 head of cabbage, grated
1 onion, finely chopped
1 red bell pepper, finely chopped
1 carrot, grated (optional)
Salt
1 teaspoon celery seeds
1 cup sugar
1 cup vinegar

SOUPS & SALADS

Arugula and Watermelon Salad

1 pound baby arugula
1 (4-pound) seedless watermelon, cut into ¾-inch cubes
⅔ cup olive oil
5 tablespoons fresh lemon juice
1½ teaspoons kosher salt
2 cups (8 ounces) shaved Parmesan cheese
Salt and pepper to taste

Mix the arugula and watermelon in a large bowl. Whisk the olive oil, lemon juice and kosher salt in a small bowl. Pour over the arugula and watermelon and toss to coat. Divide among salad plates and top with equal portions of the cheese. Sprinkle with salt and pepper and serve.

Serves 12

Alice's Ginger Salad Dressing

1 cup vegetable oil
¼ cup vinegar
¼ cup soy sauce
2 to 3 tablespoons ketchup
2 tablespoons sugar
½ teaspoon salt
¼ teaspoon pepper
1 onion, chopped
1 rib celery, chopped
2 (2- to 3-inch) pieces fresh ginger, chopped

This simple yet delicious recipe was shared by a co-worker at North Carolina State University and a special friend for 50 years. Alice is a talented cook who enjoys identifying food categories and their different ingredients. You could say she is a "Food Detective!"

Process the oil, vinegar, soy sauce, ketchup, sugar, salt, pepper, onion, celery and ginger in a blender for 10 to 15 seconds. Use over salad greens or as a dip.

Makes 3½ cups

WHITE BALSAMIC VINAIGRETTE

Combine 1 rounded tablespoon Dijon mustard, 1 teaspoon salt and ½ teaspoon pepper in a bowl. Whisk in ⅓ cup white balsamic vinegar. Add ¾ cup extra-virgin olive oil very gradually, whisking constantly until emulsified. Store in a glass jar in a dark location away from the heat for up to 3 weeks. Shake vigorously before using. May use canola oil if you are not an olive oil fan.

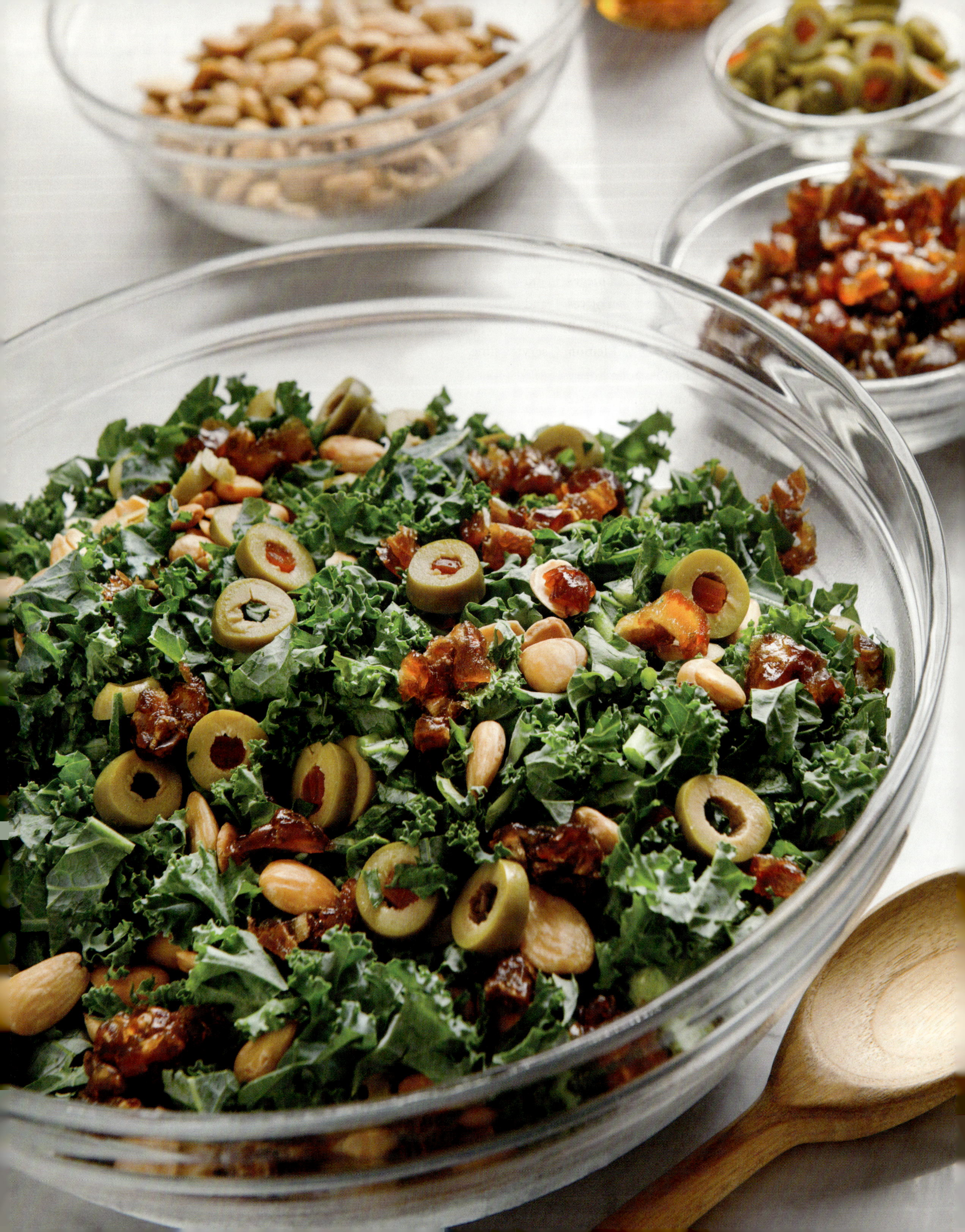

SOUPS & SALADS

Kathy's Kale Salad

8 cups fresh curly kale, torn into pieces
½ cup chopped dates
½ cup roasted almond pieces
½ cup sliced green olives
¼ cup olive oil
Grated zest and juice of 1 lemon
1 tablespoon honey
salt and pepper to taste

Combine the kale, dates, almond pieces and olives in a large salad bowl. Mix the olive oil, lemon zest, lemon juice and honey in a small bowl until blended. Add to the salad and toss to coat. Serve immediately or may make ahead one day earlier and store, covered, in the refrigerator until serving time.

Makes 8 servings

Til's Corn Bread Salad

1 package corn bread mix
1 tablespoon butter
2 to 3 green onions, chopped
6 to 8 ounces bacon, crisp-cooked and crumbled, or 1 jar bacon bits
1 tomato, chopped
1 green bell pepper, chopped
1 rib celery, chopped
Mayonnaise

Prepare and bake the corn bread according to the package directions. Let cool and crumble into a large bowl. Melt the butter in a skillet. Add the green onions and sauté until tender. Add to the corn bread. Add the bacon, tomato, bell pepper and celery and toss to mix. Add just enough mayonnaise to moisten the bread and toss to coat.

Serves 8

This Wedgwood serving bowl is number 1 of 100 commissioned by Ivey's Carolinas department stores in 1985. The fine earthenware bowls commemorate the 400th anniversary of the Roanoke Voyages and feature coastal American Indian motifs. The voyages were funded by Sir Walter Raleigh and resulted in the first explorers and colonists to what became the North Carolina coast.

MAIN DISHES & ENTRÉES

- Steak Diane
- Beef Stew
- Chemistry Roast
- Lamb and Butternut Squash Stew
- Pork Tenderloin with Glazed Onions
- Neese's Sausage Chili
- Macadamia-Encrusted Grouper
- Crab Cakes
- Hot Panned Oysters
- Seafood Quiche
- Shrimp and Grits
- Fish Stew
- Vodka Pasta with Shrimp
- Hatteras Rockfish Stew
- Brunswick Stew
- Brunswick Stew Customized
- Chicken Chili
- Three Bean Chili
- Oriental Chicken Salad
- Sesame Chicken and Asparagus Salad
- New Old Fashioned Chicken Pastry
- Hot Chicken Salad
- Barbecued Chicken
- Chicken Salad Soufflé
- Quail
- Egg and Mushroom Casserole
- Cheese Pastry Casserole

MAIN DISHES & ENTRÉES

Steak Diane

3 tablespoons butter
1 tablespoon minced shallots
1 pound beef tenderloin, thinly sliced
1 tablespoon chopped chives
1 tablespoon chopped parsley
1 tablespoon Worcestershire sauce
1 tablespoon A.1. steak sauce
Salt and pepper to taste

Melt the butter in a large skillet. Add the shallots and sauté until tender. Add the beef and brown on both sides. Stir in the chives, parsley, Worcestershire sauce, steak sauce, salt and pepper and cook to the desired doneness.

Serves 2

Beef Stew

1 1/2 teaspoons olive oil
1 1/2 pounds (1-inch) beef cubes
3 1/2 cups (8 ounces) halved mushrooms
2 cups diagonally cut carrots
1 1/2 cups coarsely chopped onions
1 1/2 cups sliced celery
2 garlic cloves, minced
1 1/2 cups water
1 1/2 cups cabernet sauvignon
1/2 teaspoon dried thyme
1 1/4 teaspoons kosher salt
1/4 teaspoon coarsely ground pepper
2 (14-ounce) cans no-salt-added stewed tomatoes
2 bay leaves
1 (2-ounce) can sliced black olives
1 tablespoon light brown sugar
2 tablespoons red wine vinegar
1/4 cup chopped flat-leaf parsley

Heat the olive oil in a large heavy saucepan over medium-high heat. Add the beef and sauté for 5 minutes or until browned on all sides. Remove the beef to a bowl. Add the mushrooms, carrots, onions, celery and garlic to the saucepan and cook for 5 minutes, stirring occasionally. Add the beef to the pan. Stir in the water, wine, thyme, salt, pepper, tomatoes and bay leaves and bring to a boil. Reduce the heat and cover. Simmer for 1 hour. Drain the olives. Stir the olives and brown sugar into the stew and simmer for 30 minutes or until the beef is tender. Remove and discard the bay leaves. Stir in the vinegar and sprinkle with the parsley.

Serves 6

MAIN DISHES & ENTRÉES

Chemistry Roast

Sprinkle the roast with meat tenderizer and prick the roast all over with a fork. Place the roast in a large bowl or baking dish. Melt the butter in a skillet. Add the sesame seeds and sauté until toasted. Remove from the heat and stir in the coffee, soy sauce, Worcestershire sauce, vermouth and onion. Pour over the roast. Cover and marinate in the refrigerator overnight, turning once. Remove the roast and discard the marinade. Grill the roast over a charcoal fire for 45 minutes or to desired doneness, turning several times during grilling. Slice and serve.

Serves 12

1 (6-pound) beef chuck roast
Unseasoned meat tenderizer
2 tablespoons butter
1 tablespoon sesame seeds
1/2 cup strong brewed coffee, chilled
1/2 cup soy sauce
1 1/2 tablespoons Worcestershire sauce
1 tablespoon dry vermouth
1 large onion, chopped

Jill's Lamb and Butternut Squash Stew

Heat the olive oil in a large Dutch oven over medium-high heat. Add the lamb and sauté for 10 minutes. Add the onions and sauté for 5 minutes. Add the garlic, squash, jalapeño chiles, salt, pepper, coriander and cumin and stir well. Stir in the wine, stock and tomatoes with juice and bring to a boil. Remove from the heat and cover. Bake at 275 degrees for 4 hours, checking occasionally to see if more liquid is needed. Add a combination of stock and wine, 1 cup at a time, if needed. Garnish with chopped fresh parsley or cilantro and serve over rice or mashed potatoes.

Serves 12

Note: You may need to brown the lamb in batches, adding more olive oil as needed.

1/3 cup olive oil
4 to 5 pounds lamb shoulder or leg, cut into 1 1/2-inch cubes
3 onions, coarsely chopped
1 tablespoon minced garlic
1 butternut squash, peeled and cut into 1 1/2-inch cubes
2 jalapeño chiles, seeded and minced
1 tablespoon coarse salt
1 teaspoon freshly ground pepper
1 tablespoon ground coriander
1 tablespoon ground cumin
1 1/2 cups burgundy or other dry red wine
2 cups beef stock
1 (28-ounce) can plum tomatoes, coarsely chopped
Chopped fresh parsley or cilantro
Hot cooked rice or mashed cooked potatoes

MAIN DISHES & ENTRÉES

Pork Tenderloin with Glazed Onions

2 (1½-pound) pork tenderloins, trimmed
2 tablespoons unsalted butter
2 large Vidalia onions or other sweet onions, sliced
2 tablespoons dark brown sugar
2 tablespoons balsamic vinegar
½ cup golden raisins
Salt and freshly ground pepper to taste

Arrange the tenderloins in an oiled roasting pan just large enough to fit them. Melt the butter in a skillet over medium heat. Add the onions and sauté for 2 to 3 minutes or until tender. Stir in the brown sugar, vinegar, raisins, salt and pepper. Sauté for 3 to 5 minutes or until the onions are glazed. Spoon the onions over the pork. Roast at 375 degrees to 150 degrees on a meat thermometer, about 35 minutes. Remove the pork to a cutting board and cover loosely with foil. Let rest for 5 minutes before slicing. Serve topped with the onions.

Serves 6

Dale's Sausage Chili

1 pound Hot Neese's Sausage
1 pound Mild Neese's Sausage
1 medium onion
2 (15-ounce) cans kidney beans or pinto beans, drained and rinsed
1 (28-ounce) can of crushed tomatoes
1 (15-ounce) can tomato sauce
1 (6-ounce) can tomato paste
3 teaspoons chili powder
1 cup water
1 (11-ounce) can Mexicorn

Brown sausage and drain. Add other ingredients. Simmer for 30 minutes. Serve with oysterettes or cornbread.

Chartered in 1962, the North Carolina Pork Council is dedicated to ensuring a socially responsible and profitable state pork industry. Every day, the efforts of our pork producers demonstrates their dedication to producing safe and nutritious pork products for a hungry world. They work diligently to provide a healthy and wholesome product you can safely serve your family.

MAIN DISHES & ENTRÉES

Gert's Crab Cakes

My mother was born and raised in Point Lookout, Maryland. I grew up eating crabs at an early age. When I moved to Duck on the seafood-rich Outer Banks 34 years ago, I brought my mother's recipe with me.

Mix the crab meat, egg, mayonnaise, Worcestershire sauce, mustard and seasonings in a bowl gently. Try not to break up the crab lumps. Add the crushed crackers. The crackers act as a binder to hold the cakes firmly together, so the amount may vary by a cracker or two according to the temperature of the kitchen. You want the mixture to be firm enough to stay together when you hand press them. Shape into 6 crab cakes; place on a plate. Chill for 1 to 6 hours. Fry the crab cakes in a cast-iron pan with about ¼ inch of olive oil until the cakes are golden on each side. Drain on a paper towel and serve.

Makes 6 crab cakes

1 pound lump crab meat, flaked
1 egg
3 tablespoons Hellmann's mayonnaise
2 dashes of Worcestershire sauce
¾ tablespoon yellow mustard
Pinch of dried tarragon
½ teaspoon pepper
½ teaspoon Old Bay seasoning
⅓ teaspoon garlic powder
⅓ teaspoon dry mustard
8 to 10 saltine crackers, crushed
Olive oil

MAIN DISHES & ENTRÉES

Alicia's Macadamia Encrusted Grouper

2 slices whole wheat bread
³/₄ cup macadamia nuts
2 tablespoons minced shallots
2 tablespoons minced fresh parsley
2 tablespoons lime juice
¹/₄ cup grainy Dijon mustard
¹/₄ teaspoon Tabasco sauce
1 large grouper fillet

Pulse the bread in a food processor to make crumbs. Remove to a bowl. Pulse the nuts in a food processor to chop. Add to the bread crumbs. Add the shallots and parsley and mix well. Whisk the lime juice, Dijon mustard and Tabasco sauce in a small bowl. Coat the fish with the mustard mixture and place in a greased shallow baking dish. Top evenly with the nut mixture. Bake at 425 degrees for 10 minutes per inch of thickness or until the fish begins to flake.

Serves 4 to 6

Hot Panned Oysters

1 quart North Carolina Select oysters
¹/₂ cup (1 stick) butter
¹/₄ large rib celery, finely chopped
Salt and pepper to taste
6 tablespoons Worcestershire sauce
20 drops of Tabasco sauce
1 sleeve saltine crackers, crushed

Remove the oysters from the shells and remove any bits of shell. Drain the oysters well in a colander; do not rinse. Melt the butter in a shallow baking dish in the oven. Remove from the oven when the pan is hot and the butter is melted and tilt to coat the bottom of the baking dish with melted butter. Layer the oysters, celery, salt, pepper, Worcestershire sauce, Tabasco sauce and crushed crackers one-half at a time into the baking dish. Bake at 275 degrees for 1 hour.

Serves 6

Betty Anne's Seafood Quiche

3 tablespoons butter
2 tablespoons minced shallots
1 cup lightly cooked peeled shrimp, cut into large pieces
¹/₄ teaspoon salt, or to taste
1 pinch of pepper, or to taste
2 tablespoons dry vermouth or white wine
1 tablespoon tomato paste
3 eggs
1 cup heavy whipping cream
1 partially baked (9-inch) pie shell
¹/₄ cup shredded Gruyère cheese

Melt the butter in a skillet. Add the shallots and sauté for 2 minutes. Add the shrimp and sauté gently for 2 minutes. Sprinkle with the salt and pepper. Stir in the vermouth and boil for 30 seconds. Stir in the tomato paste. Remove from the heat and let cool slightly. Beat the eggs and cream in a bowl. Stir in the shrimp mixture. Pour into the pie shell and sprinkle with the cheese. Bake at 375 degrees for 25 to 30 minutes or until puffed and golden brown.

Serves 6

MAIN DISHES & ENTRÉES

Shrimp and Grits à la Edwina

Bring the water and salt to a boil in a saucepan. Whisk in the grits gradually. Cook over medium-low heat for 10 minutes, stirring frequently. Stir in the cheese and cayenne pepper. Stir in the garlic, mushrooms, fresh tomatoes and sun-dried tomatoes. Spoon evenly into a 9×13-inch baking dish. Press the shrimp into the grits. Top with the green onions and sprinkle with the lemon juice. Sprinkle the bacon over the top. Bake at 350 degrees for 20 to 25 minutes.

Serves 8

Note: This is a great buffet or dinner party dish.

6 cups water
1 teaspoon salt
1 1/2 cups quick-cooking grits
2 cups (8 ounces) shredded sharp Cheddar cheese
1/8 to 1/4 teaspoon cayenne pepper
1 tablespoon chopped garlic
3 cups sautéed mixed mushrooms, such as button and shiitake
2 cups diced fresh red tomatoes
3/4 cup sun-dried tomatoes, chopped
2 pounds cooked shrimp, peeled and deveined
1 1/2 cups chopped green onions
2 tablespoons fresh lemon juice
1 pound bacon, crisp-cooked and crumbled

Sarah Ellen's Fish Stew

This was a recipe of my father's, a native of Lenoir County. He served North Carolina in the House of Representatives and the State Senate. Fish stews in Eastern North Carolina, such as this one, have a time-honored reputation of being served at political and social gatherings.

Pour the bacon drippings into a large heavy stockpot. Alternate layers of the fish, onions and potatoes in the stockpot until all of the ingredients are used. Top with the tomato soup, barbecue sauce, chile pods, salt and black pepper. Add just enough water to the stockpot to reach the top layer of the ingredients. Bring to a boil and reduce the heat; do not stir. Simmer for 1 1/2 hours; do not stir. Break the eggs, one at time, into a small bowl and carefully slide into the stew. Simmer for 20 minutes or until the eggs are cooked through. Serve with pickles and crackers or corn bread and have Tabasco sauce on hand for guests to add to taste.

Serves 20

3/4 to 1 cup bacon drippings
5 pounds firm fish fillets, cut into 1 1/2-inch pieces
5 pounds onions, diced
5 pounds potatoes, cut into small chunks
1 (10-ounce) can tomato soup
1 small bottle barbecue sauce
Dried red chile pods or red pepper flakes to taste
Salt and black pepper to taste
20 medium eggs

MAIN DISHES & ENTRÉES

Vodka Pasta with Shrimp

1/2 cup vodka
1/2 teaspoon red pepper flakes
1/2 cup (1 stick) butter
1 cup heavy cream
1 (8-ounce) can tomato sauce
2 cans diced tomatoes, drained
1 pound deveined peeled fresh shrimp
16 ounces bowtie pasta, cooked and drained
1/2 teaspoon salt
1/2 teaspoon black pepper
Shredded Parmesan cheese

Mix the vodka and red pepper in a small bowl. Let stand for 2 hours to overnight. Heat the vodka and red pepper in a large nonstick skillet until hot. Remove from the heat and carefully ignite with a long match. Add the butter after the flames have died down. Cook over medium-low heat until the butter is melted. Stir in the cream, tomato sauce and tomatoes and cook until heated through. Add the shrimp and cook for 2 minutes or until the shrimp turn pink. Stir in the pasta, salt and black pepper and cook for 2 minutes or until heated through. Serve topped with cheese.

Serves 4 to 6

Hatteras Rockfish Stew

8 ounces bacon, chopped
1 cup chopped yellow onion
1/2 cup chopped celery
6 tablespoons butter, softened
10 tablespoons all-flour
2 tablespoons minced shallots
1 tablespoon minced garlic
4 cups chicken stock or fish stock
3 potatoes, peeled and diced
3 pounds rockfish fillets, cut into 2-inch pieces
6 to 8 green onions, chopped
1/2 cup minced parsley
1 1/2 teaspoons minced thyme
1 teaspoon salt
1/2 teaspoon pepper
1/2 cup brandy
1/2 cup sherry
1 1/2 cups heavy cream, at room temperature

The town of Weldon, NC is known as the "Rockfish Capital of the World," due to its proximity to the Roanoke River, where fishermen flock to catch the striped bass that are locally dubbed "rockfish."

Sauté the bacon, yellow onion and celery in a large heavy saucepan over medium heat until the bacon is cooked through and the onion is tender. Add the butter and cook until the butter is melted. Stir in the flour and reduce the heat. Cook for 5 minutes, stirring constantly. Add the shallots and garlic and cook for 3 minutes, stirring constantly. Add the stock gradually and cook until thickened, stirring constantly. Stir in the potatoes and simmer for 30 minutes. Stir in the fish, green onions, parsley, thyme, salt and pepper. Warm the brandy and sherry in a small saucepan over low heat. Remove from the heat and carefully ignite with a long match. Stir into the stew when the flames have died down. Simmer for 10 minutes. Stir in the cream and simmer until heated through.

Serves 6

MAIN DISHES & ENTRÉES

Bateman Brunswick Stew

Place the chickens and onions in a large stockpot and cover with water. Bring to a boil over medium heat. Reduce the heat and simmer until the chicken is cooked through and falling off the bone. Remove the chickens from the broth to a cutting board and let cool. Strain the broth and reserve. Remove the chicken from the bones and shred with 2 forks or clean hands. Return the shredded chicken to the stockpot. Dice the potatoes and add along with the string beans. Add the tomatoes, Shoe Peg corn, yellow corn, cream-style corn and lima beans. Add enough of the reserved stock to cover all the ingredients. Bring to a simmer over medium-low heat, stirring occasionally. Brown the ground beef and sausage in a skillet, stirring until the meat is crumbly; drain. Add the meat to the stockpot. Cook for $1\frac{1}{2}$ to 2 hours, stirring occasionally. Stir in the garlic, cayenne pepper, black pepper, salt, Worcestershire sauce and ketchup. Simmer for 30 minutes longer.

Serves 30 to 40

2 whole chickens
4 sweet onions, finely chopped
1 (39-ounce) can string beans and potatoes, drained
2 (28-ounce) cans crushed tomatoes
1 (12-ounce) package frozen Shoe Peg corn
1 (6-ounce) package frozen yellow corn kernels
2 (15-ounce) cans cream-style corn
2 (12-ounce) packages frozen baby lima beans
$1\frac{1}{2}$ pounds ground beef
8 ounces bulk pork sausage
2 tablespoons minced garlic
1 teaspoon cayenne pepper
1 tablespoon freshly ground black pepper
1 tablespoon salt
$\frac{1}{4}$ cup Worcestershire sauce
Ketchup to taste

Brunswick Stew Customized

Sauté the chicken breasts in a nonstick skillet until cooked through. Remove the chicken to a cutting board and let cool. Combine the stock, corn, beans, tomatoes, sweet onions and red onion in a 12-quart stockpot and bring to a boil. Reduce the heat and stir in the ketchup, Worcestershire sauce, vinegar, brown sugar, hot sauce, salt and pepper. Shred the cooled chicken and add to the pot. Stir in the bacon. Simmer for 1 to 2 hours, stirring occasionally. Serve with corn bread.

Note: Customize your Brunswick Stew by adding one or more of the following: 2 cups cut okra, 1 jar roasted red peppers, chopped, 8 ounces chopped mushrooms, $1\frac{1}{2}$ pounds boiled white potatoes, diced, chopped garlic or 1 pound Eastern North Carolina pork barbecue.

Serves 16 to 20

4 large boneless skinless chicken breasts
4 cans chicken stock
2 cups frozen corn kernels
2 cups frozen butter beans
3 cans diced tomatoes
3 sweet onions, chopped
1 red onion, chopped
1 cup ketchup
5 tablespoons Worcestershire sauce
$\frac{1}{2}$ cup cider vinegar
$\frac{1}{2}$ cup packed brown sugar
2 teaspoons hot red pepper sauce
2 teaspoons salt
Pepper to taste
1 pound thick cut bacon, crisp-cooked and crumbled

MAIN DISHES & ENTRÉES

Chicken Chili

2 tablespoons olive oil
2 poblano chiles
1 large red bell pepper, chopped
1 sweet onion, chopped
3 garlic cloves, minced
2 (14-ounce) cans diced zesty chili-style tomatoes
3 cups shredded cooked chicken (about 1 pound)
1 (16-ounce) can navy beans
1 (15-ounce) can black beans, rinsed and drained
1 (12-ounce) can beer
1 envelope white chicken chili seasoning mix

Heat the olive oil in a large saucepan over medium-high heat. Add the chiles, bell pepper, onion and garlic and sauté for 8 minutes or until the vegetables are tender. Stir in the tomatoes, chicken, navy beans, black beans, beer and chili seasoning mix. Bring to a boil and reduce the heat to low. Simmer for 1 hour, stirring occasionally. Serve in bowls topped with shredded Cheddar cheese, chopped cilantro, sour cream, sliced black olives, chopped red onion and/or crushed tortilla chips.

Serves 9

Annette's Three Bean Chili

1 (15-ounce) can no-salt-added red kidney beans, rinsed and drained
1 (15-ounce) can small white beans, rinsed and drained
1 (15-ounce) can very low sodium black beans, rinsed and drained
1 (14^1/$_2$-ounce) can diced tomatoes and green chiles
2 chicken breasts, cooked and chopped
^{1}/$_3$ link turkey kielbasa
1 cup beer or chicken broth
3 tablespoons chocolate syrup
1 tablespoon chili powder
1 teaspoon Cajun seasoning
Sour cream
Shredded cheddar cheese

Combine the kidney beans, white beans, black beans, undrained tomatoes, chicken, turkey kielbasa, beer, chocolate syrup, chili powder and Cajun seasoning in a slow cooker. Cook, covered, on Low for 6 to 8 hours or on High for 2 to 4 hourse. Serve topped with sour cream and cheese, if desired.

Serves 4-6

Note: The flavor is best if you mix and refrigerate overnight before cooking.

This cast-iron cooking pan (ca. 1860–1880) exemplifies what was once commonly called a "spider." Spiders were transitional pans that still had legs, to keep them out of hot coals and ash, but introduced long, stiff handles off one or two sides, instead of looped handles that could be hung from a hook or rack. Spiders bridged the gap between cookware that was designed for use in hearth cooking and campfires and implements that were more practical for cookstoves.

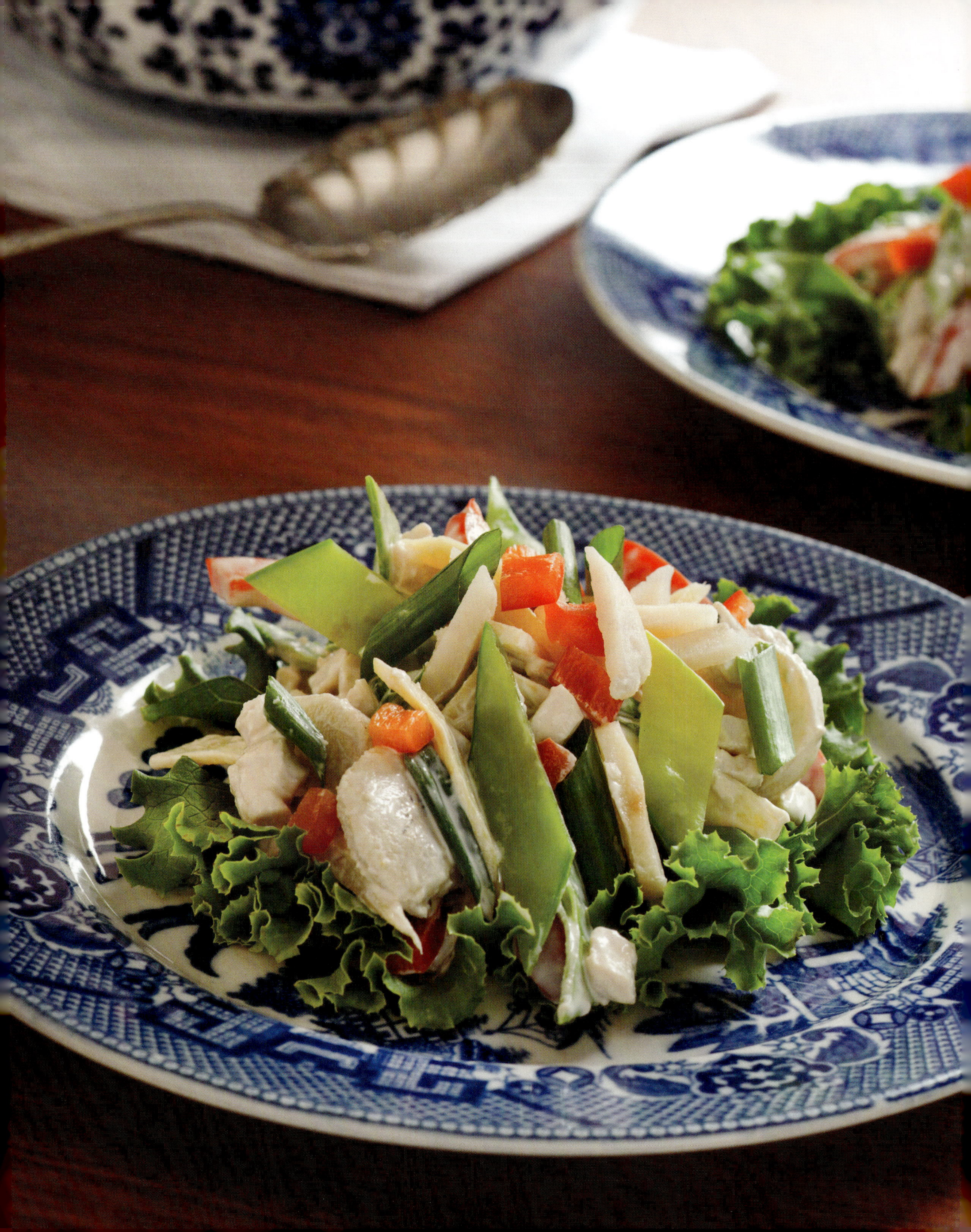

MAIN DISHES & ENTRÉES

Joanna's Oriental Chicken Salad

5 ounces shell pasta, cooked and drained
1 pound chicken, cooked and diced
1 can water chestnuts, drained and sliced
1 can bamboo shoots, drained
4 ounces snow peas, trimmed and sliced diagonally
$1/3$ cup finely chopped scallions
1 red bell pepper, cut into thin strips
1 cup mayonnaise
$1/4$ to $1/2$ cup soy sauce
1 to 3 teaspoons minced fresh ginger
$1/8$ teaspoon pepper

Combine the pasta, chicken, water chestnuts, bamboo shoots, snow peas, scallions and bell pepper in a large bowl and toss to mix. Combine the mayonnaise, soy sauce, ginger and pepper in a bowl and mix well. Add to the salad and toss to coat. Chill for at least 8 hours before serving.

Serves 8

Note: Leave out the pasta and this makes a delicious sandwich filling.

Sesame Chicken and Asparagus Salad

8 ounces linguini
2 boneless skinless chicken breasts, poached and cut into thin 2-inch strips
3 garlic cloves, minced
2 tablespoons red wine vinegar
2 tablespoons brown sugar
6 tablespoons chunky peanut butter
$1/2$ cup soy sauce
6 tablespoons sesame oil
1 tablespoon hot chile oil
5 tablespoons sesame seeds, toasted
1 pound thin asparagus, trimmed and cut diagonally into 1-inch pieces
3 scallions, white part and 3 inches green part, cut into thin 2-inch strips
1 small cucumber, halved, seeded and cut into $1/4$-inch pieces
1 tablespoon sesame seeds, toasted

Cook the linguini in a saucepan of boiling salted water until al dente; drain. Rinse under cold water and drain well. Remove to a large bowl. Add the chicken and toss to mix. Process the garlic, vinegar, brown sugar, peanut butter and soy sauce in a food processor. Add the sesame oil and chile oil gradually, processing constantly until smooth. Add to the linguini mixture. Add 5 tablespoons sesame seeds and toss to coat. Blanch the asparagus in a saucepan of boiling water for 1 minute; drain. Rinse under cold water and pat dry. Mound the linguini mixture on a large platter and arrange the asparagus over the top. Sprinkle with the scallions, cucumber and 1 tablespoon sesame seeds. Serve at room temperature.

Serves 6

MAIN DISHES & ENTRÉES

Lou's New Old Fashioned Chicken Pastry

Cover the chicken with water in a 6-quart saucepan and add 1 teaspoon salt. Bring to a boil and reduce the heat. Simmer until the chicken is cooked through and the leg bone separates when moved. Remove from the heat. Remove the chicken from the broth to a cutting board and let cool. Remove the chicken from the bones and chop. Skim the fat from the surface of the broth and discard. Bring the chicken broth to a rolling boil. Add the dumpling strips to the broth one at a time, stirring after every 4 or 5 strips are added. Reduce the heat and simmer for 20 minutes. Stir in the chicken, soup and chicken stock. Bring back to a boil over medium heat, stirring frequently. Season with salt and pepper and serve.

Serves 8

- 1 (4- to 5-pound) chicken
- 1 teaspoon salt
- 1 (24-ounce) package Annie's frozen flat dumpling strips
- 2 (10-ounce) cans low-fat cream of chicken soup
- 1 1/2 cups chicken stock
- Salt and pepper to taste

Hot Chicken Salad

Mix the chicken and celery in a bowl. Stir in the onion, lemon juice, salt and cayenne pepper. Add the mayonnaise, almonds and stock and mix well. Spoon into a 3-quart shallow baking dish. Mix the cheese and potato chips in a bowl and sprinkle evenly over the top. Bake at 375 degrees for 20 minutes; do not overcook.

Serves 10 to 12

- 6 cups diced cooked chicken (about 8 chicken breasts)
- 3 cups diced celery
- 2 to 3 teaspoons grated onion
- 3 to 4 tablespoons lemon juice
- 1 to 1 1/2 teaspoons salt
- Dash of cayenne pepper
- 2 cups mayonnaise
- 1/2 to 1 cup slivered almonds
- 2 tablespoons chicken stock
- 1 cup (4 ounces) shredded mild Cheddar cheese
- 1 1/3 cups crushed potato chips

MAIN DISHES & ENTRÉES

Cindy's Barbecued Chicken

²/₃ cup vegetable oil
1¼ cups cider vinegar
1 teaspoon black pepper
²/₃ teaspoon chile pepper
1 teaspoon Texas Pete hot sauce
½ cup lemon juice
1 teaspoon salt
²/₃ teaspoon cayenne pepper
2 tablespoons Worcestershire sauce
Dash of garlic salt
4 bone-in chicken breasts

My great-grandfather, Papa Minton, owned a store in Ferguson. It was a popular stopping place for enthusiastic pioneer participants in the "Daniel Boone Wagon Train." Each June, from 1963-1973, hundreds of folks brought their wooden wheeled wagons and travelled in caravan for four days in commemoration of the 300th Anniversary of the Carolina Charter. This dish was a great favorite of the wagon train participants. This is the recipe of my paternal grandparents' from Wilkes County.

Mix the oil, vinegar, black pepper, chile pepper, hot sauce, lemon juice, salt, cayenne pepper, Worcestershire sauce and garlic salt in a saucepan. Cook over medium heat until hot, stirring frequently; do not let boil. Place the chicken in a sealable container and pour the sauce over the chicken. Seal the container and marinate in the refrigerator overnight. Remove the chicken to a hot grill and cook until the chicken is cooked through. Discard the marinade.

Serves 4

This plate (ca. 1661) reportedly belonged to George and Ann Durant, who moved into what was then known as the Virginia frontier of "Roanoke," adjacent to the Albemarle Sound (in present-day Perquimans County), in 1661. Their new home was used for council meetings, assemblies, and even court—so frequently that George often served as an attorney or jurist and that a set of stocks was erected on his property. Ann is also recognized as an attorney—the first woman to act as an attorney in the province of Carolina (1673).

MAIN DISHES & ENTRÉES

Sara's Chicken Salad Soufflé

Combine the chicken, celery, onion, bell pepper, mayonnaise, salt and pepper in a bowl and mix well. Spread one-third of the bread cubes over the bottom of a greased 9×13-inch baking dish. Spread the chicken salad over the bread in the baking dish. Top evenly with the remaining bread cubes. Mix the milk and eggs in a bowl and pour evenly over the bread. Chill, covered, for 2 hours to overnight. Spread the mushroom soup evenly over the bread. Bake at 350 degrees for 40 minutes. Sprinkle with the cheese and bake for 10 minutes longer.

Serves 10 to 12

3 cups chopped cooked chicken
1/2 cup chopped celery
1/2 cup chopped onion
1/2 cup chopped green bell pepper
1/2 cup mayonnaise
3/4 teaspoon salt
Dash of pepper
6 slices white bread, crusts removed, cubed
1 1/2 cups milk
2 eggs, beaten
1 (10-ounce) can cream of mushroom soup
1/2 cup (2 ounces) shredded sharp Cheddar cheese

Quail

Season the quail with salt and pepper and dredge in flour. Melt the butter in a large skillet. Add the quail and cook for 10 minutes or until browned on all sides. Remove the quail to a platter and add the onion and mushrooms to the skillet. Sauté until the vegetables are tender but not browned. Add the quail, consommé and wine to the skillet and cover. Simmer for 30 to 45 minutes or until the quail is cooked through. Stir in the orange juice and bring to a boil. Remove from the heat and serve with wild rice.

Serves 6

6 quail, split down the back
Salt and pepper to taste
All-purpose flour
6 tablespoons butter
1/2 cup chopped onion
1 1/2 cups chopped mushrooms
1 cup beef consommé or bouillon
3/4 cup wine
1/3 cup orange juice
Hot cooked wild rice

MAIN DISHES & ENTRÉES

Helen's Egg and Mushroom Casserole

4 hard-cooked eggs, sliced
2 tablespoons butter
1 pound mushrooms, chopped
1/4 cup (1/2 stick) butter
1/4 cup all-purpose flour
2 cups milk
4 ounces sharp Cheddar cheese, shredded
Salt to taste

This recipe was introduced into our family friend that had lived in upstate New York and Vermont. Her northern cuisine was quite different from the southern cooking we were used to making a meal at her home a divine culinary experience.

Arrange the egg slices in a 9×13-inch baking dish. Melt 2 tablespoons butter in a skillet. Add the mushrooms and sauté until tender. Spoon the mushrooms evenly over the eggs. Melt 1/4 cup butter in a saucepan. Stir in the flour. Cook for 1 minute, stirring constantly. Stir in the milk. Cook until thickened, stirring constantly. Add the cheese and cook until the cheese is melted, stirring frequently. Pour evenly over the mushrooms and season with salt. Bake at 350 degrees for 30 minutes.
Serves 4 to 6

Cheese Pastry Casserole

1 (8-count) can refrigerator crescent rolls
8 ounces cream cheese, softened
4 ounces Monterey Jack cheese, shredded
4 ounces Swiss cheese, shredded
4 ounces Muenster cheese, shredded
4 ounces sharp Cheddar cheese, shredded
1 egg, lightly beaten
1/4 to 1/2 bunch parsley, chopped
Melted butter
1/2 cup chopped sesame seeds

Unroll the crescent dough and divide in half. Press one-half of the dough onto the bottom of a nonstick 8×8-inch baking pan, pressing the perforations to seal. Combine the cream cheese, Monterey Jack cheese, Swiss cheese, Muenster cheese and Cheddar cheese in a bowl and mix well. Mix the egg and parsley in a bowl. Add to the cheese and mix well. Spread over the dough in the baking pan. Press the remaining dough to a square to fit the pan and fit over the cheese mixture in the pan. Brush with melted butter and sprinkle with the sesame seeds. Bake at 350 degrees for 30 minutes or until golden brown. Cut into squares and serve warm with strawberry preserves on the side.
Serves 6

VEGETABLES & SIDE DISHES

Creamed Asparagus Parmesan

Green Bean Sauté

Baked Beans

Sweet Fig Pickles

Mulberry Hill Inn Chutney

Baked Pineapple

Bleu Cheese Soufflé

Vidalia Onion Soufflé

Corn & Basil Tart

Stuffed Potatoes

Mashed Sweet Potatoes with Apple Streusel

Sweet Potato Pudding

Spinach Supreme

Zucchini Rounds with Tomato Sauce

Sweet Potato Balls

German Slaw

Spoon Bread

VEGETABLES & SIDE DISHES

Creamed Asparagus Parmesan

1/4 cup (1/2 stick) butter
2 to 3 tablespoons chopped green onions
1/4 teaspoon curry powder
1/2 teaspoon salt
1/3 cup all-purpose flour
2 cups whole milk, or 1 2/3 cups milk plus 1/3 cup white wine
2 (8-ounce) cans asparagus tips, drained
1/3 cup shredded Parmesan cheese

Melt the butter in a saucepan. Add the green onions, curry powder and salt and cook for several minutes, stirring frequently. Stir in the flour. Cook for 1 minute, stirring constantly. Stir in the milk gradually. Cook until thickened, stirring constantly. Stir in the asparagus. Pour into a baking dish and sprinkle with the cheese. Bake at 400 degrees for 15 to 20 minutes.

Serves 6

Green Bean Sauté

2 tablespoons sesame oil
1 garlic clove, minced
1 tablespoon sesame seeds, toasted
1/2 teaspoon red pepper flakes
2 tablespoons soy sauce
8 ounces French green beans, trimmed
Sesame seeds

Heat the sesame oil in a skillet over medium heat. Add the garlic and sauté until tender. Stir in 1 tablespoon sesame seeds, red pepper and soy sauce and reduce the heat to low. Add the green beans and sauté for 25 minutes or until tender-crisp. Garnish with additional sesame seeds and serve immediately.

Serves 4

Winnie's Baked Beans

1 to 2 teaspoons olive oil, vegetable oil or canola oil
2 cups chopped onions
1 pound ground beef
2 (16-ounce) cans pork and beans
1 can red kidney beans
1 cup packed brown sugar
1 cup ketchup
2 teaspoons prepared mustard
1 teaspoon salt
1 teaspoon vinegar

Heat the olive oil in a skillet. Add the onions and sauté until tender. Add the ground beef and cook, stirring until the meat is crumbly; drain. Combine the pork and beans, kidney beans, brown sugar, ketchup, mustard, salt and vinegar in a bowl and mix well. Stir in the ground beef and onion mixture. Pour into a greased baking dish. Bake at 400 degrees for 30 minutes or until thick and bubbly.

Serves 10 to 15

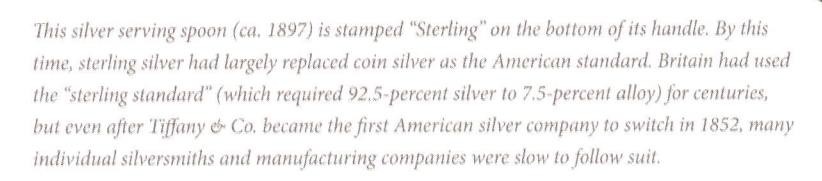

This silver serving spoon (ca. 1897) is stamped "Sterling" on the bottom of its handle. By this time, sterling silver had largely replaced coin silver as the American standard. Britain had used the "sterling standard" (which required 92.5-percent silver to 7.5-percent alloy) for centuries, but even after Tiffany & Co. became the first American silver company to switch in 1852, many individual silversmiths and manufacturing companies were slow to follow suit.

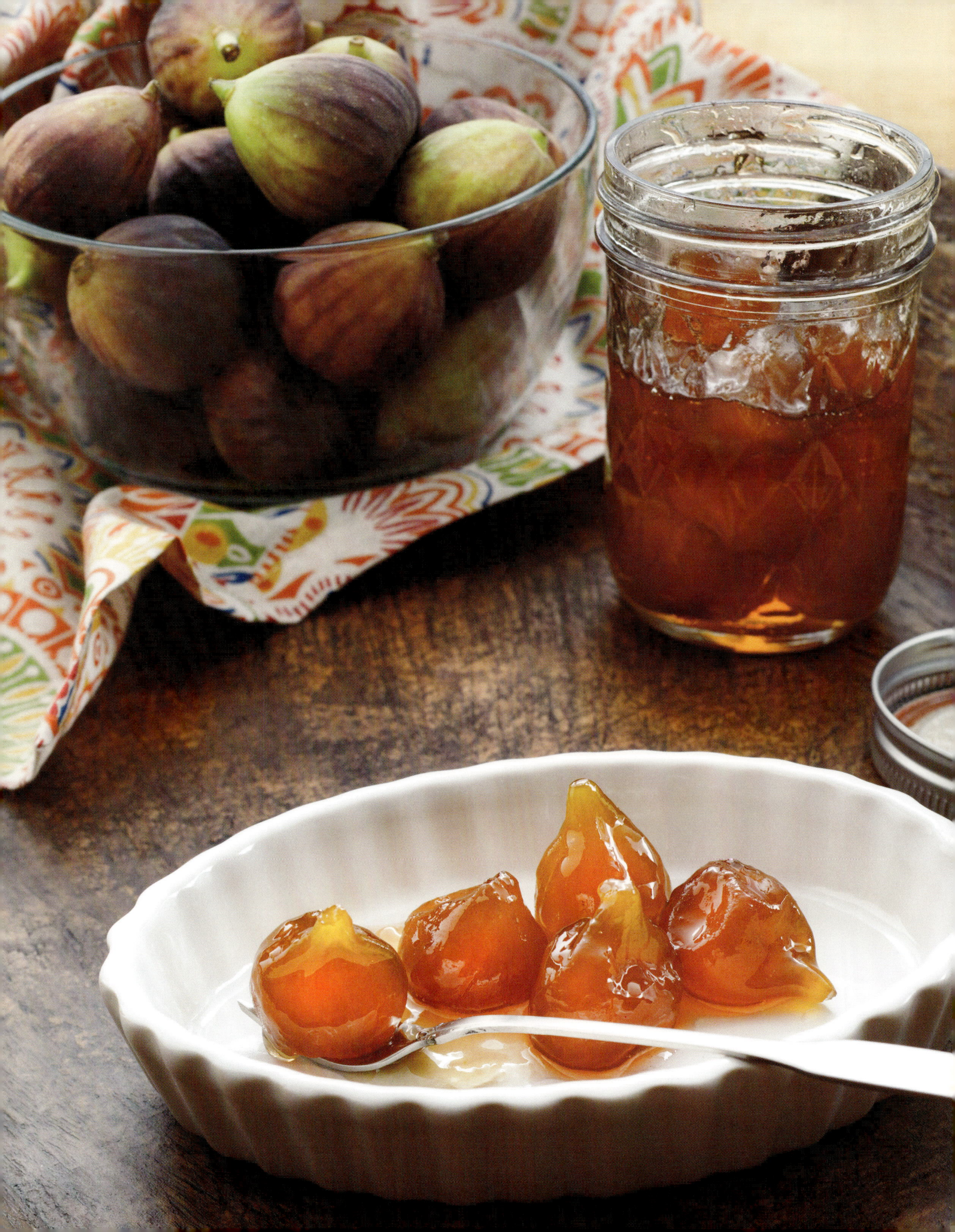

VEGETABLES & SIDE DISHES

Kay's Sweet Fig Pickles

4 pounds figs, stems attached
1 tablespoon baking soda
4 pounds sugar
2 cups vinegar
3 tablespoons pickling spice, tied in a cheesecloth bag

Cover the figs and baking soda with boiling water in a large nonreactive saucepan. Let stand for 5 minutes. Drain in a colander and rinse with water. Return the figs to the saucepan and add the sugar, vinegar and pickling spice. Bring to a boil, stirring frequently. Boil for 15 minutes, stirring frequently. Remove from the heat. Let soak, covered, for 24 hours. Drain, reserving the syrup. Bring the reserved syrup to a boil and pour over the figs. Repeat the soaking, draining and heating process two times. Bring the figs and liquid to a boil and boil for 15 minutes. Remove and discard the cheesecloth bag. Pack the figs and syrup into hot sterilized canning jars, leaving 1/2 inch headspace. Seal with two-piece lids. Process in a boiling water bath for 10 minutes.

Makes 4 pints

Mulberry Hill Inn Chutney

1 pound apples, chopped
1 pound red plums, chopped
1 pound pears, chopped
1 pound apricots, chopped
1 onion, chopped
1 (12-ounce) box white raisins
1 1/2 cups cider vinegar
Grated zest and juice of 1 orange
2 cups packed brown sugar
1 teaspoon allspice

Combine the apples, plums, pears, apricots, onion, raisins, vinegar, orange zest and orange juice in a large saucepan. Bring to a boil, stirring frequently. Reduce the heat to medium and simmer for 45 minutes, stirring occasionally. Stir in the brown sugar and allspice. Simmer over low heat for 1 hour or until thickened, stirring occasionally. Pack the chutney into hot sterilized canning jars, leaving 1/2 inch headspace. Seal with two-piece lids. Process in a boiling water bath for 10 minutes or store in the refrigerator.

Serves 12

Best if stored in a cool dark place for 6 months to allow time for flavors to develop.

Ruth's Baked Pineapple

3 eggs
1 (15-ounce) can crushed pineapple
1/2 cup sugar
2 tablespoons all-purpose flour
4 slices bread, cubed
1/2 cup (1 stick) butter, melted

Beat the eggs in a mixing bowl for 2 minutes. Stir in the undrained pineapple and sugar. Sprinkle the flour over the pineapple and mix well. Pour into a baking dish. Top with the bread cubes and drizzle with the melted butter. Bake at 400 degrees for 30 to 40 minutes.

Serves 6

VEGETABLES & SIDE DISHES

Jessica's Bleu Cheese Soufflé

Sprinkle the gelatin over the water in a small saucepan and let stand for a few minutes. Cook over low heat until the gelatin is dissolved, stirring constantly. Remove from the heat. Beat the butter, cream cheese and bleu cheese in a mixing bowl until smooth. Beat in the egg yolk, Dijon mustard and gelatin. Beat the egg white in a mixing bowl until stiff peaks form. Fold into the cheese mixture. Fold in the whipped cream. Attach a collar of oiled waxed paper or foil to a soufflé dish, using a string or rubber band to hold it in place. Spoon the cheese mixture into the soufflé dish to the top of the collar. Chill for several hours to overnight. Remove the collar and serve with crackers or fresh vegetables.

Serves 12

Note: If you are concerned about using raw eggs, use eggs pasteurized in their shells, which are sold at some specialty food stores.

- 1 envelope unflavored gelatin
- 2 tablespoons cold water
- 1/4 cup (1/2 stick) unsalted butter
- 4 ounces cream cheese, softened
- 4 ounces bleu cheese
- 1 egg yolk
- 1 teaspoon Dijon mustard
- 1 egg white
- 1/2 cup heavy whipping cream, whipped

Martha's Vidalia Onion Soufflé

This is a dish that has been passed down through four generations. It began with my grandmother, who passed it down to my father, then to me, and then to my own daughters. They now serve it at Thanksgiving and Christmas. Delicious!

Melt the butter in a large skillet over low heat. Add the onions and a pinch of salt. Cook for 40 minutes or until golden brown, stirring occasionally. Remove from the heat and let cool. Whisk the flour, baking powder and 1 teaspoon salt in a small bowl. Beat the eggs and cream in a large bowl. Stir in the cheese. Whisk in the dry ingredients. Fold in the onions. Spoon into eight buttered ramekins or a buttered 9×13-inch baking dish. Bake at 350 degrees for 20 minutes for ramekins or 45 minutes for a baking dish or until set and golden brown on top.

Serves 8

- 1/2 cup (1 stick) unsalted butter
- 4 pounds Vidalia onions or other sweet onions, thinly sliced
- Pinch of salt
- 3 tablespoons all-purpose flour
- 2 teaspoons baking powder
- 1 teaspoon salt
- 6 eggs
- 2 cups heavy cream
- 3/4 cup (3 ounces) freshly grated Parmigiano-Reggiano cheese

VEGETABLES & SIDE DISHES

Corn and Basil Tart

5 tablespoons butter, softened
2 tablespoons sugar
1/2 teaspoon salt
1 egg
1 cup yellow cornmeal
2/3 cup all-purpose flour
2 eggs
1 cup half-and-half or cream
1 1/2 cups fresh corn kernels
1/2 cup coarsely chopped basil
1/2 teaspoon salt
1/4 teaspoon pepper
Chopped tomatoes for garnish

Beat the butter in a mixing bowl at medium speed for 30 seconds. Beat in the sugar and 1/2 teaspoon salt. Beat in 1 egg. Beat in the cornmeal. Beat in most of the flour, stirring in the final amount. Shape the dough into a disk and wrap in plastic wrap. Chill for 30 to 60 minutes. Pat the dough evenly onto the bottom and up the side of a 9-inch tart pan with a removable side. Line the pastry shell with foil or baking parchment paper and place pie weights in the pastry shell. Bake at 350 degrees for 10 minutes. Remove the foil and weights and bake for 4 to 6 minutes longer. Remove to a wire rack. Whisk 2 eggs and half-and-half in a bowl. Stir in the corn, basil, 1/2 teaspoon salt and pepper. Pour into the pastry shell. Bake at 350 degrees for 35 to 40 minutes or until set. Let cool for 10 minutes. Remove the side of the pan and cut the tart into wedges. Garnish with chopped tomatoes and serve.

Serves 6 to 8

Flo's Stuffed Potatoes

8 large russet potatoes
Vegetable oil
3/4 cup (1 1/2 sticks) butter
5 tablespoons grated Parmesan cheese
1/4 cup crumbled cooked bacon
2 tablespoons sour cream
2 tablespoons chopped chives
2 teaspoons salt
1 teaspoon pepper
Paprika

This recipe was perfected for the Angus Barn Menu.

Coat the potatoes with oil and bake at 400 degrees for 45 minutes to 1 hour or until tender. Cut each potato in half lengthwise and scoop the pulp into a mixing bowl. Add the butter, cheese, bacon, sour cream, chives, salt and pepper and beat for 3 minutes. Mound equal portions of the mixture into the potato shells and sprinkle with paprika. Arrange the stuffed potatoes on a baking sheet. Bake at 400 degrees until lightly browned and heated through.

Serves 16

Note: These freeze well and can be reheated from frozen.

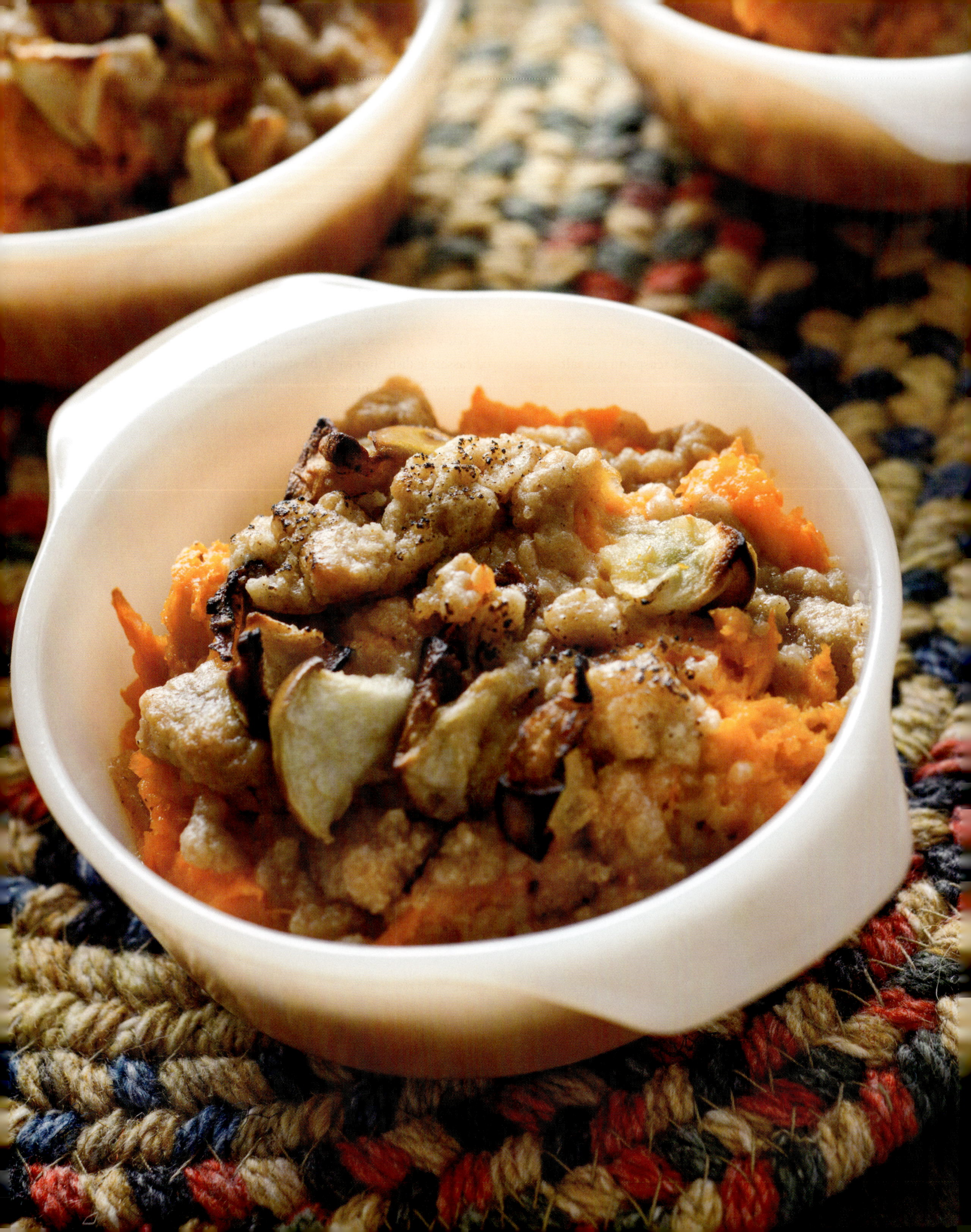

VEGETABLES & SIDE DISHES

Jill's Mashed Sweet Potatoes with Apple Streusel

Mashed Sweet Potatoes
2 1/2 **pounds sweet potatoes**
1/4 **cup (1/2 stick) butter**
1 **teaspoon vanilla extract**
1 **teaspoon sea salt**

Streusel Topping
1/2 **cup packed brown sugar**
1/2 **cup granulated sugar**
1/4 **cup (1/2 stick) butter**
1/4 **teaspoon cinnamon**
1/4 **teaspoon salt**
1/2 **teaspoon vanilla extract**
1 **cup all-purpose flour**
4 **Granny Smith apples, diced**

Slit each potato in the center to create a pocket. Roast at 350 degrees for 1 hour or until tender. Let cool to the touch. Remove the skins. Mash the sweet potatoes with the butter, vanilla and salt with a masher or mixer. Spoon into a buttered or sprayed casserole dish. Top with the streusel topping. Bake at 350 degrees for about 20 minutes.

For the topping, mix the brown sugar, granulated sugar, butter, cinnamon, salt and vanilla in a bowl. Cut in the flour; fold in the diced apples.

Note: If you make this ahead and then bake it at the time of service, you will need to bake it for about 50 to 60 minutes to fully heat the sweet potato dish.

Stag's Sweet Potato Pudding

1/4 **teaspoon cinnamon**
1/8 **teaspoon nutmeg**
1/8 **teaspoon allspice**
1/8 **teaspoon ginger**
1/8 **teaspoon ground cloves**
Pinch of salt
1 1/2 **cups sugar**
1/2 **teaspoon vanilla extract**
1 **cup whole milk**
2 **eggs, lightly beaten**
2 **cups grated sweet potatoes**
1/2 **cup (1 stick) butter, melted**

Combine the cinnamon, nutmeg, allspice, ginger, cloves, salt and sugar in a bowl and mix well. Stir in the vanilla, milk and eggs. Add the sweet potatoes and melted butter and mix well. Pour into a baking dish. Bake at 350 degrees for 1 hour or until set.

Serves 6

VEGETABLES & SIDE DISHES

Spinach Supreme

Cook the spinach in a saucepan of boiling water. Drain the spinach through a wire mesh strainer into a bowl. Measure 1 1/2 cups of cooking liquid, adding water if needed to make 1 1/2 cups. Set aside the cooked spinach. Melt the butter in a saucepan. Stir in the flour. Cook for 1 minute, stirring constantly. Stir in the reserved cooking liquid, salt and pepper. Cook until thickened, stirring constantly. Remove from the heat and stir in the lemon juice. Let cool to warm. Stir in the eggs. Cook for 1 to 2 minutes, stirring constantly. Remove from the heat and stir in the spinach, cheese and nutmeg. Pour into a greased ring mold. Bake at 350 degrees for 30 minutes or until set. Unmold and serve.

Serves 8

Note: You may use a baking dish instead of a ring mold and increase the baking time.

2 (10-ounce) packages frozen chopped spinach
3 tablespoons butter
3 tablespoons all-purpose flour
1 teaspoon salt
1/2 teaspoon pepper
Juice of 1 lemon
2 eggs, beaten
1 cup (4 ounces) grated Parmesan cheese
Dash of nutmeg

Zucchini Rounds with Tomato Sauce

To make the sauce, heat the butter and oil in a saucepan. Add the onion and sauté until tender. Process the tomatoes for a few seconds in a blender and add to the onion. Stir in the basil, oregano, salt and pepper. Simmer for 20 to 30 minutes, stirring occasionally. Stir in the zucchini and cook just until the zucchini is tender. Keep warm.

To make the rounds, mix the baking mix, cheese and pepper in a bowl. Add the eggs and stir just until moistened. Fold in the zucchini. Dollop 2-tablespoon portions into a hot nonstick skillet and fry for 2 to 3 minutes per side. Serve warm with the tomato sauce.

Serves 4

Sauce
2 tablespoons butter
1 tablespoon vegetable oil
1 onion, chopped
1 (20-ounce) can tomatoes
1/4 teaspoon basil
1/4 teaspoon oregano
Salt and pepper to taste
1 zucchini, chopped

Rounds
1/3 cup Bisquick baking mix
1/4 cup (1 ounce) grated Parmesan cheese
1/8 teaspoon pepper
2 eggs, lightly beaten
2 cups shredded unpeeled zucchini

VEGETABLES & SIDE DISHES

Sweet Potato Balls

4 or 5 large sweet potatoes
24 large marshmallows
1 (16-ounce) package flaked coconut

Boil or bake the sweet potatoes until tender. Peel the potatoes and mash well in a bowl. Enclose each marshmallow in equal portions of sweet potato to form a ball. Roll the balls in coconut and arrange in a shallow baking pan coated with nonstick cooking spray. Bake at 450 degrees for 10 minutes or until lightly browned.

Makes 2 dozen

Note: These may be made ahead and reheated just before serving.

Evelyn's Spoon Bread

2 medium eggs
1 cup whole milk
2 cups buttermilk
1 cup coarsely ground cornmeal
1 teaspoon baking powder
1 teaspoon baking soda
1 teaspoon salt
Pinch of sugar
1/4 cup (1/2 stick) butter

This is the recipe of a dear family friend who lived in Duplin County most of her life. She was an avid public servant, a member of the Woman's Club, and a volunteer with the Red Cross. The many gatherings she hosted in her home were legendary for good food and good conversation. This particular dish has been cherished by my family for as long as I can remember.

Beat the eggs in a bowl. Stir in the whole milk, buttermilk and cornmeal. Add the baking powder, baking soda, salt and sugar and mix well. Melt the butter in a 9×13-inch baking pan in the oven. Remove the pan from the oven and tilt to coat the bottom of the pan with melted butter. Pour the batter into the hot pan. Bake at 350 degrees for 30 minutes.

Serves 10 to 12

Manufactured by G. T. Glascock and Sons in Greensboro, this cast-iron Dutch oven is just one example of the breadth of style and products made by this foundry, which actually specialized in making coal- and wood-fueled stoves. Today, their products are highly sought after by collectors.

SWEETS & DESSERTS

SWEETS & DESSERTS

Holiday Fruit Bars

Old Fashioned Peanut Brittle

Russian Rocks

Grand Marnier Soufflé

Cold Strawberry Soufflé

Angel Food Cake Dessert

Lemon Curd

Southern Banana Pudding Parfait

Blueberry Pudding

Lemon Chess Tarts

Lemon Pie

Chocolate Seduction Pie

Peanut Butter Pie

Caramel Cake

Crumb Cake

Orange Date Nut Cake

Pear & Dried Cherry Frangipane Cake

Cheesecake

Chocolate Mousse

SWEETS & DESSERTS

Big Kay's Holiday Fruit Bars

½ cup (1 stick) butter, softened
1½ cups packed dark brown sugar
2 eggs, well beaten
1 teaspoon vanilla extract
1 cup all-purpose flour
2 cups chopped nuts
8 ounces candied cherries, finely chopped
8 ounces candied pineapple, finely chopped

My beloved aunt brought these to every Thanksgiving and Christmas for my entire life, and it has remained a favorite dish for three generations!

Beat the butter and brown sugar in a mixing bowl until light and fluffy. Beat in the eggs and vanilla. Beat in the flour. Spread the nuts over the bottom of a greased and floured 10×10-inch baking pan. Spoon the dough evenly over the nuts and press down gently with clean damp hands. Top evenly with the cherries and pineapple. Bake at 350 degrees for 20 to 25 minutes. Remove to a wire rack. Cool completely before cutting into squares.

Makes 2 to 3 dozen

This coin-silver tea service (ca. 1840–1850) features fleur-de-lis–inspired feet and scallop-decorated rims. By the 1840s, as evening meals were served later and later, afternoon tea—complete with light sandwiches or cakes—became a common occurrence for wealthier families and provided an opportunity to display one's wealth to invited guests.

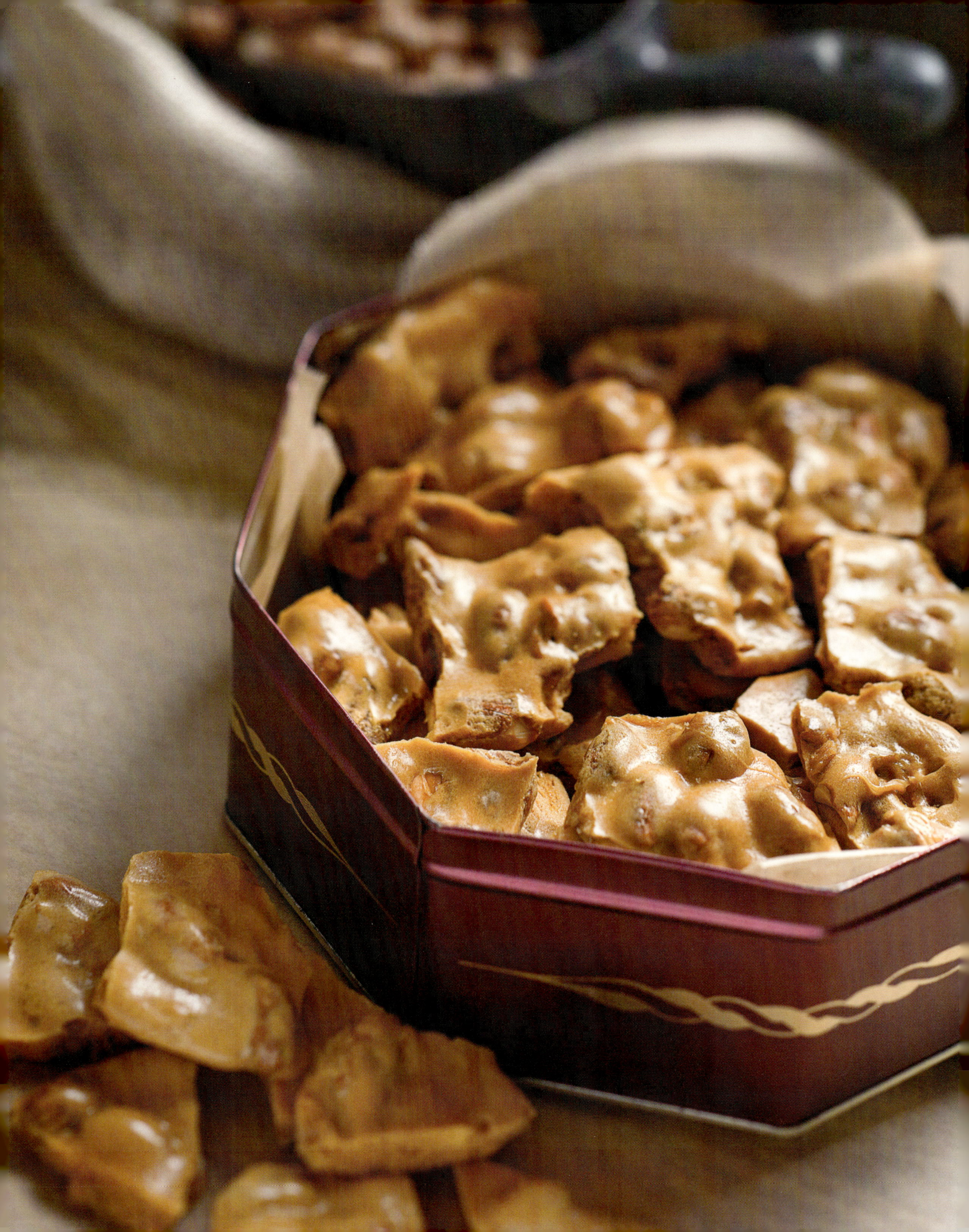

SWEETS & DESSERTS

Old Fashioned Peanut Brittle

1 cup light corn syrup
1/3 cup water
2/3 cup sugar
1/4 teaspoon salt
1 1/4 cups raw peanuts
2 tablespoons butter, softened
1/2 teaspoon vanilla extract
1 heaping tablespoon baking soda

Combine the corn syrup, water, sugar, salt and peanuts in a 4-quart saucepan and stir until the sugar is dissolved. Bring to a boil over medium heat, stirring occasionally. Cook until the mixture is an amber color, being careful that it doesn't scorch and stirring only occasionally. Remove from the heat and stir in the butter and vanilla. Add the baking soda and mix well. Pour the mixture into a lightly buttered 10×15-inch baking pan, spreading with a wooden spoon to fill the pan. Let cool. Invert the brittle onto a work surface and wipe the butter from the surface with a paper towel. Break into pieces and store in an airtight container.

Makes 1 1/4 pounds

Mrs. Broughton's Russian Rocks

2 3/4 cups all-purpose flour
1 teaspoon baking soda
2 teaspoons cinnamon
3/4 teaspoon ground cloves
1 cup (2 sticks) butter, softened
1 1/4 cups packed brown sugar
3 eggs
1 pound pecans, chopped
1 pound raisins

Mrs. J. Melville Broughton was North Carolina's First Lady from 1941–1945.

Mix the flour, baking soda, cinnamon and cloves together. Beat the butter and brown sugar in a mixing bowl until light and fluffy. Add the eggs, one at a time, beating well after each addition. Beat in the dry ingredients. Fold in the pecans and raisins. Drop by spoonfuls onto a greased cookie sheet. Bake at 300 to 325 degrees for 20 minutes. Cool on the cookie sheet for 5 minutes. Remove to a wire rack to cool completely.

Makes 3 dozen

SWEETS & DESSERTS

Grand Marnier Soufflé

Grease a 2-quart soufflé dish with 1 tablespoon butter. Dust with 3 tablespoons granulated sugar and set aside. Bring the milk and 3/4 cup granulated sugar to a boil in a saucepan, stirring frequently. Reduce the heat to low. Melt 1/4 cup butter in a saucepan. Stir in the flour. Cook for 1 to 2 minutes, stirring constantly. Stir in the hot milk mixture gradually. Cook over medium heat until thickened, stirring constantly. Beat the egg yolks in a large bowl until thick and pale yellow. Stir in the Grand Marnier. Beat some of the hot white sauce into the egg yolks to warm the yolks. Beat in the remaining white sauce. Beat the egg whites in a bowl until stiff peaks form. Fold carefully into the egg yolk mixture. Pour into the soufflé dish. Bake at 400 degrees for 20 to 25 minutes. Dust with confectioners' sugar and serve immediately.

Serves 4 to 6

1 tablespoon butter, softened
3 tablespoons granulated sugar
2 cups milk
3/4 cup granulated sugar
1/4 cup (1/2 stick) butter
1/3 cup all-purpose flour
5 egg yolks
1/4 cup Grand Marnier
7 egg whites
Confectioners' sugar

Cold Strawberry Soufflé

Sprinkle the gelatin over the water in a small saucepan and let stand for 5 minutes. Cook over low heat until the gelatin is dissolved, stirring constantly. Remove from the heat and let cool. Purée the strawberries and sugar in a blender. Beat the whipping cream with the egg whites in a mixing bowl until firm peaks form. Fold in the puréed strawberries and liqueur. Pour into a soufflé dish. Chill for several hours to overnight. Serve garnished with additional whipped cream and whole strawberries.

Serves 6 to 8

Note: If you are concerned about using raw egg whites, use whites from eggs pasteurized in their shells, which are sold at some specialty food stores, or use an equivalent amount of meringue powder and follow the package directions.

4 1/2 teaspoons unflavored gelatin
1/4 cup cold water
2 cups strawberries or raspberries
3/4 cup sugar, or to taste
1 1/2 cups heavy whipping cream
2 egg whites
2 tablespoons Grand Marnier (optional)
Whipped cream
Whole strawberries

SWEETS & DESSERTS

Angel Food Cake Dessert

1 envelope unflavored gelatin
1/2 cup cold water
4 egg yolks
2 tablespoons all-purpose flour
3/4 cup sugar
2 cups whole milk
Pinch of salt
1 teaspoon vanilla extract
4 egg whites
1/2 cup heavy whipping cream, whipped
1 baked angel food cake, torn into pieces
Additional whipped cream
Maraschino cherries or grated fresh ginger

My grandmother, the wife of E. C. Brooks, who was president of NC State College from 1923–1934, served this dessert many times.

Soften the gelatin in the water in a small bowl. Whisk the egg yolks, flour and sugar in a saucepan. Whisk in the milk, salt, vanilla and dissolved gelatin. Cook until the mixture is slightly thickened, stirring constantly. Pour into a large bowl and let cool to lukewarm. Beat the egg whites in a bowl until stiff. Fold into the milk mixture. Fold in the whipped cream. Fold in the cake pieces. Spoon into a 9×13-inch baking dish and chill until set. Cut into squares and serve each topped with whipped cream and a maraschino cherry or grated fresh ginger, if desired.

Serves 12

Note: If you are concerned about using raw egg whites, use eggs pasteurized in their shells, which are sold at some specialty food stores, or use an equivalent amount of meringue powder and follow the package directions.

Lemon Curd

3 lemons
1 cup sugar
2 eggs
3 egg yolks
1/2 cup (1 stick) unsalted butter, softened

Grate the zest from the lemons and set aside. Juice the lemons to get 1/3 cup lemon juice. Mix the sugar, eggs and egg yolks in a saucepan. Stir in 1/3 cup lemon juice gradually. Cook over low heat to 168 degrees on a candy thermometer, stirring constantly; do not let boil. Remove from the heat and whisk the mixture until slightly cooled. Stir in the lemon zest. Stir in the butter, 1 tablespoon at a time. Let cool completely. Store in a covered container in the refrigerator for up to 2 weeks. Stir before using.

Makes 2 cups

Note: This may be frozen for up to 2 months. Thaw and stir before using.

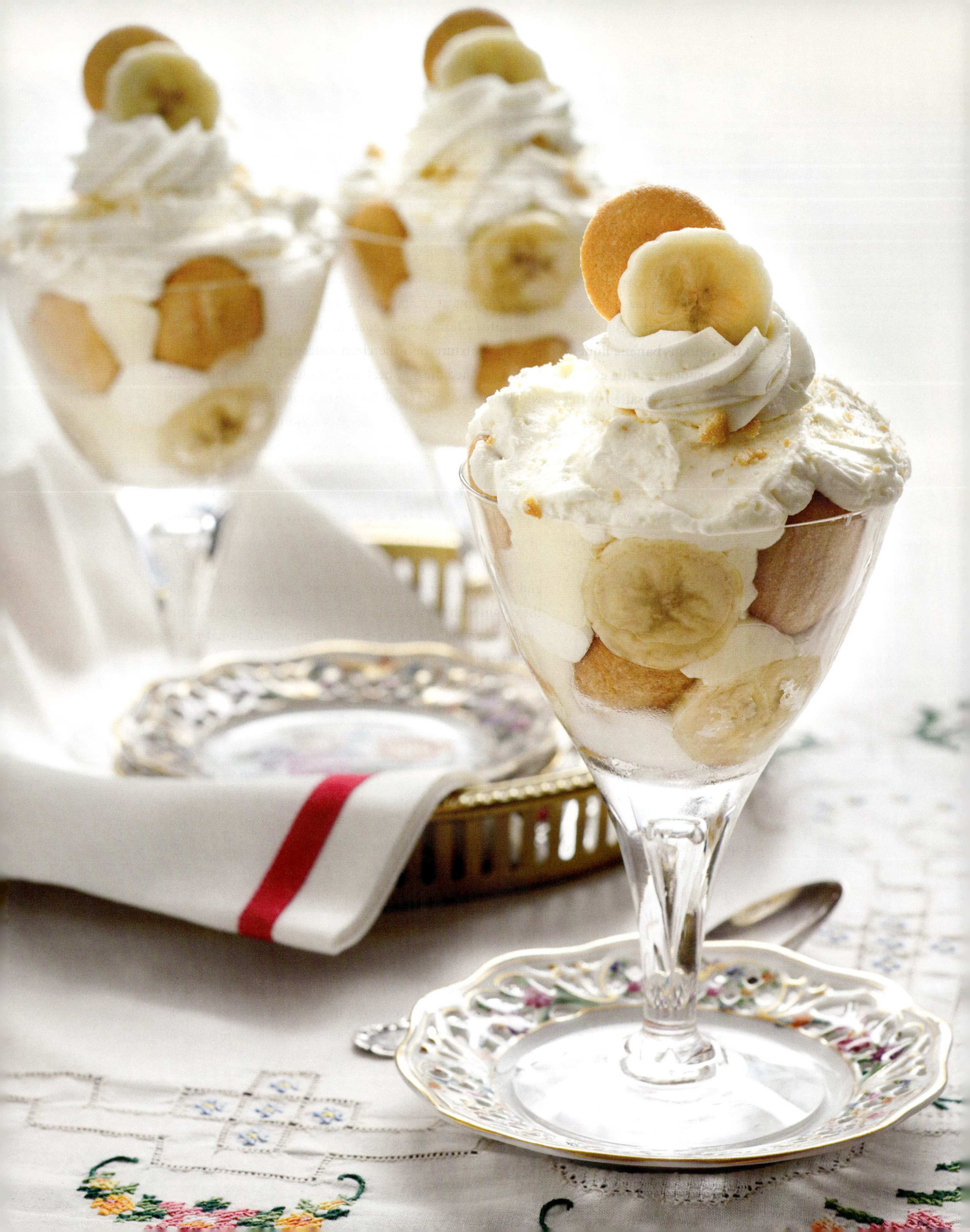

SWEETS & DESSERTS

Southern Banana Pudding Parfait

5 egg yolks
1/2 cup granulated sugar
1/4 cup cornstarch
1/4 teaspoon salt
2 cups whole milk
3 tablespoons banana liqueur
2 teaspoons vanilla extract
2 tablespoons unsalted butter
2 ripe bananas
24 to 30 vanilla wafers
2 cups heavy (36%) cream
1 tablespoon confectioners' sugar
6 whole vanilla wafers
or vanilla wafer crumbs

Whisk the egg yolks, granulated sugar, cornstarch and salt together in a medium bowl; set aside. Bring the milk to a boil in a medium saucepan; remove from the heat. Add a small amount at a time to the egg yolk mixture, whisking constantly. Clean the saucepan to prevent sticking. Pour the egg yolk mixture into the clean saucepan. Add the liqueur. Cook over medium-low heat for 2 minutes or until thickened, whisking constantly. Cook for 1 1/2 to 2 minutes longer or until the pudding is thick and glossy, whisking constantly. Pour into a bowl. Add the vanilla and butter. Whisk gently until incorporated. Press a sheet of plastic wrap over the pudding surface. Chill for 4 hours. Cut the bananas in half crosswise and then lengthwise to make each into 4 quarters. Cut each quarter into slices. Divide among 6 custard cups or martini glasses. Whisk the pudding for about 30 seconds or until soft and smooth. Layer with vanilla wafers over the bananas. Whip the cream with the confectioners' sugar until soft peaks form. Spoon over the top. Garnish each with an additional whole vanilla wafer or vanilla wafer crumbs.

Makes 6 servings

Blueberry Pudding

2 cups blueberries
1 tablespoon fresh lemon juice
Pinch of cinnamon
1/4 cup (1/2 stick) butter, softened
2/3 cup sugar
1 1/4 cups all-purpose flour
1 1/2 teaspoons baking powder
Pinch of salt
1/2 cup milk
1 cup boiling water

Combine the blueberries, lemon juice and cinnamon in a bowl and toss to mix. Spoon into an 8-cup soufflé dish and set aside. Beat the butter and sugar in a mixing bowl at medium speed for 5 minutes or until light and fluffy. Mix the flour, baking powder and salt together. Add to the butter mixture and beat at medium speed for 30 seconds or until crumbly. Add the milk and beat for 1 minute or until smooth, scraping the side of the bowl as needed. Dollop the batter by heaping spoonfuls over the blueberries in the soufflé dish. Pour the boiling water carefully over the batter and place the soufflé dish on a baking sheet. Bake at 350 degrees for 1 hour or until bubbly and the crust is golden brown, rotating the dish after 30 minutes of baking. Remove to a wire rack to cool slightly. Serve warm.

Serves 8

SWEETS & DESSERTS

Aunt Marty's Lemon Chess Tarts

My aunt, a graduate of Saint Mary's School, was a cheerful lady who shared many recipes benefitting the Joel Lane House and Haywood Hall House and Gardens.

Combine the butter, eggs, sugar, lemon juice, zest and flour in a blender. Mix well. Pour into the shells. Place the shells on a baking sheet. Bake at 350 degrees for 25 minutes.

1 stick butter, finely chopped
4 eggs
2 cups sugar
Juice of 2 lemons
$\frac{1}{2}$ teaspoon grated lemon zest
1 tablespoon all-purpose flour
16 unbaked tart shells

Lemon Pie

Whisk the lemon zest, lemon juice, sweetened condensed milk and egg yolks in a bowl until thick. Pour into the pie shell. Beat the egg whites and cream of tartar in a mixing bowl until foamy. Beat in the sugar gradually and beat until stiff peaks form. Spread the meringue over the filling, sealing to the edge. Bake at 400 degrees for 5 minutes or until golden brown. Remove to a wire rack to cool.

Serves 6 to 8

Note: If you are concerned about using raw egg yolks, use eggs pasteurized in their shells, which are sold at some specialty food stores.

$\frac{1}{2}$ teaspoon grated lemon zest
Juice of 2 lemons
1 (14-ounce) can sweetened condensed milk
2 egg yolks
1 (9-inch) graham cracker pie shell
3 egg whites
Dash of cream of tartar
3 tablespoons sugar

This silver gravy boat (ca. 1772–1773) and silver platter (ca. 1773–1774) were pieces in a collection once owned by Richard Quince, a merchant and political activist in the lower Cape Fear region. Sympathetic to the American cause, Quince organized the Sons of Liberty in Brunswick Town following passage of the Stamp Act in 1765 and contributed to the organization and funding of revolutionary activities against the British government. After the Boston Tea Party (December 16, 1773), he helped organize other branches of the Sons of Liberty and many Cape Fear–area merchants and planters to furnish aid to the northern port.

SWEETS & DESSERTS

Chocolate Seduction Pie

1 unbaked (10-inch) deep-dish pie shell
1 cup (2 sticks) butter
4 ounces unsweetened chocolate
2¹⁄₂ cups sugar
¹⁄₂ cup half-and-half
4 eggs, at room temperature
1¹⁄₂ teaspoons vanilla extract

Bake the pie shell at 425 degrees for 5 minutes. Remove to a wire rack. Melt the butter and chocolate in the top of a double boiler over gently simmering water, stirring frequently. Add the sugar and half-and-half and cook until the sugar is dissolved and the mixture is smooth, stirring frequently. Remove from over the water. Beat the eggs in a bowl. Add the chocolate mixture gradually, stirring until smooth. Stir in the vanilla and pour into the pie shell. Bake at 350 degrees for 35 minutes or until set.

Serves 8

Peanut Butter Pie

Chocolate Crust
3 cups ground chocolate wafer cookies (about 12 ounces)
¹⁄₄ cup sugar
¹⁄₄ cup (¹⁄₂ stick) butter, melted

Pie
16 ounces cream cheese, softened
2 cups creamy peanut butter
1 cup sugar
2 teaspoons vanilla extract
2 eggs, lightly beaten
1 cup heavy cream
¹⁄₂ to ³⁄₄ cup chopped Bertie County salted peanuts

Thick Fudge Sauce
2 (14-ounce) cans sweetened condensed milk
16 ounces semisweet chocolate, finely chopped
2 teaspoons vanilla extract

To make the crust, mix the cookie crumbs and sugar in a bowl. Add the melted butter and mix well. Press onto the bottom and up the side of a 9-inch springform pan. Bake at 375 degrees for 5 minutes. Remove to a wire rack to cool completely.

To make the pie, beat the cream cheese, peanut butter and sugar with the paddle attachment in a mixing bowl until smooth. Beat in the eggs and cream. Pour into the chocolate crust. Bake at 350 degrees for 45 minutes or until almost set in the center. Remove to a wire rack to cool completely. Chill, covered, overnight. Place on a serving plate. Run a sharp knife around the edge of the pie and remove the side of the pan. Cover the top of the pie with Thick Fudge Sauce and sprinkle with chopped peanuts.

To make the fudge sauce, heat the sweetened condensed milk to a simmer in a saucepan. Add the chocolate and cook until the chocolate is melted, stirring constantly. Simmer for 2 minutes. Remove from the heat and stir in the vanilla.

Serves 10 to 12

Variation: Add 2 tablespoons Kahlúa to 1¹⁄₂ cups of the Fudge Sauce to make a wonderful adult ice cream topping.

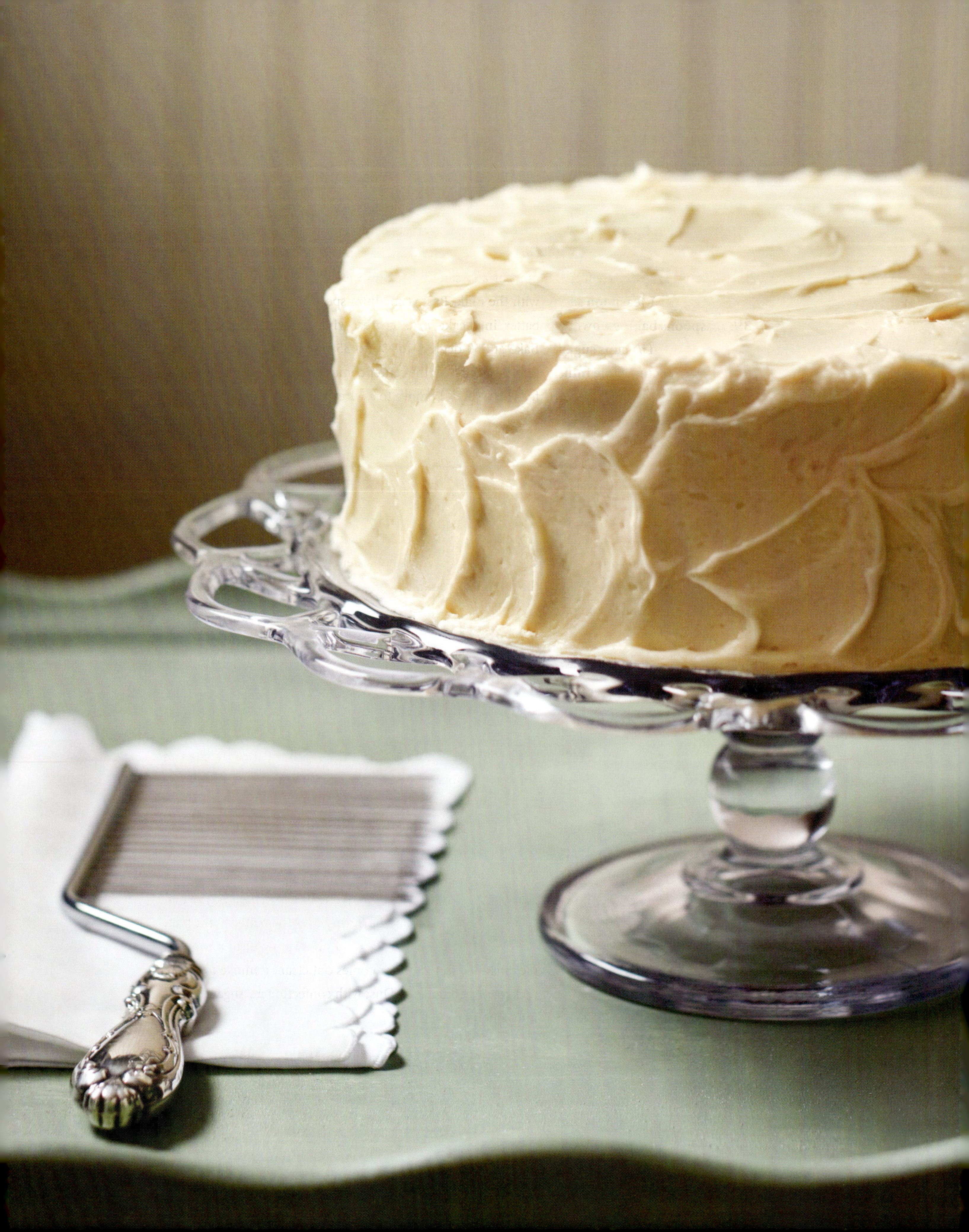

SWEETS & DESSERTS

Minnie's Caramel Cake

²/₃ cup shortening
1²/₃ cups sugar
2¹/₂ cups sifted all-purpose flour
1 teaspoon salt
3¹/₂ teaspoons baking powder
1²/₃ cups sugar
³/₄ cup whole milk
3 eggs
1 teaspoon vanilla extract

Caramel Icing
2 tablespoons butter or margarine
¹/₃ cup (or more) heavy cream
²/₃ cup packed brown sugar
¹/₈ teaspoon salt
Few drops of vanilla extract
1 to 2 cups sifted confectioners' sugar

Cream the shortening and sugar in a mixing bowl. Beat in the eggs one at a time. Stir in the vanilla. Combine the flour, baking powder and salt and add to the creamed mixture alternately with the milk. Beat at medium speed for 2 minutes. Pour the batter into cake pans coated with nonstick cooking spray. Bake at 350 degrees for 30 to 35 minutes or until a wooden pick inserted near the center comes out clean. Cool in the pans for 10 minutes. Remove to a wire rack to cool completely.

Makes 2 (8-inch) layers

Melt the butter in a saucepan over medium heat. Stir in the cream and brown sugar. Boil vigorously for 1 minute. Remove from the heat. Beat in ¹/₂ cup confectioners' sugar. Let cool slightly. Beat in the vanilla and remaining ¹/₂ cup confectioners' sugar unil of spreading consistency. Add more heavy cream if the mixture is too thick.

Jill's Crumb Cake

1¹/₂ cups cake flour
¹/₄ teaspoon baking soda
¹/₄ teaspoon salt
¹/₂ cup (1 stick) butter, softened
¹/₂ cup granulated sugar
1 egg
2 teaspoons vanilla extract
¹/₂ cup buttermilk
Confectioners' sugar for dusting

Topping
2 cups cake flour
¹/₂ cup granulated sugar
¹/₂ cup packed dark brown sugar
1 teaspoon cinnamon
¹/₂ cup (1 stick) butter, melted and cooled

To make the batter, mix the flour, baking soda and salt together. Beat the butter and granulated sugar in a mixing bowl at medium speed until light and fluffy. Beat in the egg and vanilla. Beat in the dry ingredients alternately with the buttermilk, beginning and ending with the dry ingredients. Spoon into a greased 8×8-inch baking pan.

To make the topping, mix the flour, granulated sugar, brown sugar and cinnamon in a bowl. Stir in the melted butter and set aside. Spoon the topping evenly over the batter in the pan. Bake at 325 degrees for 30 to 35 minutes or until a wooden pick inserted in the center comes out clean. Remove to a wire rack to cool completely. Dust with confectioners' sugar and cut into squares.

Serves 6 to 8

SWEETS & DESSERTS

Orange Date Nut Cake

Mix 3 cups flour, baking powder and baking soda together. Combine the dates, pecans and 1 cup flour in a bowl and toss to coat. Beat the margarine and 2 cups granulated sugar in a mixing bowl until light and fluffy. Add the eggs, one at a time, beating well after each addition. Beat in the dry ingredients alternately with the buttermilk. Stir in the date mixture and orange zest. Pour into a greased and floured bundt or tube pan. Bake at 300 degrees for $1^1/_2$ hours or until the cake tests done. Remove to a wire rack. Bring the orange juice and $1^1/_2$ cups granulated sugar to a boil in a saucepan, stirring frequently. Pour evenly over the hot cake in the pan. Let cool completely. Invert the cake onto a serving plate and dust with confectioners' sugar.

Serves 16

- 3 cups sifted all-purpose flour
- 1 teaspoon baking powder
- 1 teaspoon baking soda
- 1 (6-ounce) package dates, chopped
- 1 cup chopped pecans
- 1 cup sifted all-purpose flour
- 2 cups (4 sticks) margarine, softened
- 2 cups granulated sugar
- 4 eggs
- $1^1/_2$ cups buttermilk
- 2 tablespoons grated orange zest
- 1 cup orange juice
- $1^1/_2$ cups granulated sugar
- Confectioners' sugar

Pear and Dried Cherry Frangipane Cake

Coat an 8-inch springform pan with nonstick cooking spray. Line the bottom of the pan with baking parchment paper and coat the parchment paper with nonstick cooking spray. Beat 2 eggs, $^2/_3$ cup granulated sugar, olive oil, milk and vanilla in a mixing bowl until smooth. Add $1^1/_2$ cups flour and beat just until combined. Stir in the pears and cherries. Pour into the prepared pan. Crumble the almond paste into a mixing bowl. Add the cinnamon, 1 egg, 2 tablespoons granulated sugar and 1 tablespoon flour and beat just until mixed. Spoon evenly over the batter in the pan. Bake at 350 degrees for 1 hour and 20 minutes or until a wooden pick inserted in the center comes out with a few moist crumbs. Remove to a wire rack to cool completely. Run a sharp knife around the edge of the cake and remove the side of the pan. Remove the parchment paper and place the cake on a serving plate. Dust with confectioners' sugar before serving.

Serves 8 to 10

Note: This cake can be made 1 day ahead. It also freezes well for up to 2 weeks.

- 2 eggs
- $^2/_3$ cup granulated sugar
- $^1/_2$ cup extra-light olive oil
- $^1/_3$ cup whole milk
- 1 teaspoon vanilla extract
- $1^1/_2$ cups self-rising flour
- 2 large pears, peeled and cut into $^1/_2$-inch cubes
- $1^1/_3$ cups dried tart cherries, or 1 cup pitted fresh cherries plus $^1/_3$ cup dried cherries
- 1 (7-ounce) can almond paste
- 1 teaspoon cinnamon
- 1 egg
- 2 tablespoons granulated sugar
- 1 tablespoon self-rising flour
- Confectioners' sugar for dusting

SWEETS & DESSERTS

Mark's Cheesecake

2 cups graham cracker crumbs
⅓ cup sugar
½ cup (1 stick) butter or margarine, melted
32 ounces cream cheese, softened
1⅓ cups sugar
1 tablespoon vanilla extract
4 eggs
1⅓ cups sour cream
Grated zest of 1 orange

Mix the graham cracker crumbs and ⅓ cup sugar in a bowl. Add the melted butter and mix well. Press onto the bottom and 2½ inches up the side of an 8" or 9" springform pan and set aside. Beat the cream cheese, 1⅓ cups sugar and vanilla in a mixing bowl at high speed until smooth and creamy. Add the eggs, one at a time, beating well after each addition. Beat in the sour cream and orange zest at low speed just until blended. Pour into the prepared shell. Bake at 350 degrees for 60 to 70 minutes or until the center is set. Turn off the heat and leave the oven door slightly ajar. Do not remove the cheesecake from the oven for 1 hour. Remove to a wire rack to cool. Serve slightly warm or chill thoroughly. Serve topped with fruit.

Serves 10

Lady Margaret's Chocolate Mousse

4 ounces semi-sweet chocolate
4 egg yolks
1¼ cup (½ stick) butter, softened
Dash of salt
1 teaspoon vanilla extract
Dash of peppermint extract (optional)
4 egg whites
6 tablespoons sugar

This was my grandmother's recipe. My grandfather was Governor Angus Wilson McLean (1925–1929). Whether in the Governor's Mansion or at home in Lumberton at Duart House, she was well known for her entertaining. "Lady Margaret," as she was fondly called, "…planned every menu, ordered all food and sometimes even oversaw the cooking of meals." (From The First Ladies of North Carolina*)*

Combine the chocolate with 2 inches of very hot water in a saucepan. Let stand, covered, for 5 minutes or until the chocolate is very soft but melted. Drain off as much water as possible. Whisk in the egg yolks. Cook over very low heat until thickened, stirring occasionally. Remove from the heat. Stir in the butter, salt, vanilla and peppermint. Let cook to room temperature. Beat the egg whites in a mixing bowl until stiff. Beat in the sugar gradually. Fold a small amount of the egg whites into the chocolate mixture. Fold in the remaining egg whites. Spoon into a compote or individual serving dishes. Chill thoroughly before serving.

Serves 6

Note: Rosetta, my grandmother's cook, would pour a raspberry liqueur over the mousse and garnish with a sprig of mint on top.

INDEX

ACCOMPANIMENTS
Alicia's Cantaloupe Garnish, 103
Cindy's Apple Butter, 117
Frances' Green Tomato Pickle Relish, 74
Kay's Sweet Fig Pickles, 167
Lemon Curd, 179
Mulberry Hill Inn Chutney, 167
Pickled Red Onion, 49

APPETIZERS. *See also Dips/Spreads*
Artichoke Squares, 139
Black-Eyed Susan, 60
Carol's Peach and Brie Quesadillas with Lime Honey Dipping Sauce, 109
Cheese Pecan Crisps, 57
Duck Appetizer with Asian Sauce, 15
Edwina's Scallop Skewers, 137
Grandmother's Cheese Straws, 132
Jennie's Eggplant Appetizer, 134
Jon's Parched Peanuts, 21
Lou's Christmas Grapefruit Starter, 63
Manchego Stuffed Dates, 139
Martha's Pickled Shrimp, 31
Neese's Sausage Pinwheels, 115
Oh, So Good, 135
Remember Me Olive Puffs, 109
Stuffed Celery, 138
Those Oysters Dick Fixes, 137
Toasted Bleu Cheese Rounds, 131
White Bean Croustades with Pickled Red Onion, 49

APPLES
Apple Butter Pork Tenderloin, 117
Apple Sausage Bake, 90
Apple Walnut Cake, 105
Cindy's Apple Butter, 117
Fruit Salad with Honey Citrus Dressing, 73
Hot Apple Soup, 115
Jill's Mashed Sweet Potatoes with Apple Streusel, 171
Mary's Apple Chess Pie, 105
Miss Duncan's Hot Apple Toddy, 63
Mulberry Hill Inn Chutney, 167

Turkey, Brie, and Cranberry Apple Panini, 126

ARTICHOKES
Artichoke Squares, 139
Hearts of Palm, Artichoke and Belgian Endive Salad, 79

ASPARAGUS
Ann's Roasted Asparagus, 18
Asparagus Soup, 141
Creamed Asparagus Parmesan, 165
Garden Club Sugar Snap Pea Salad, 52
Mama Sally's Marinated Asparagus, 32
Sesame Chicken and Asparagus Salad, 159

BACON
Brunswick Stew Customized, 156
Brussels Sprouts with Bacon, 103
Day Ahead Green Salad, 143
Grilled Corn with Bacon and Vidalia Onion, 37
Grilled Potato Salad, 45
Hearts of Palm, Artichoke and Belgian Endive Salad, 79
Julia's Eggy Muffins, 75
Oh, So Good, 135
Those Oysters Dick Fixes, 137
Til's Corn Bread Salad, 147
Wedge Salad, 144

BEANS
Anne's Edamame Salad, 45
Annette's Three Bean Chili, 157
Bateman Brunswick Stew, 156
Brunswick Stew Customized, 156
Green Bean Bundles, 65
Green Bean Sauté, 165
Julie's Summer Succotash, 51
King K Dip, 134
Marcia's Election Night Dip, 133
Marinated Vegetable Salad, 60
White Bean Croustades with Pickled Red Onion, 49
Winnie's Baked Beans, 165

BEEF *See also Ground Beef*
Beef Stew, 149
Chemistry Roast, 150
Roasted Beef Tenderloin, 66
Steak Diane, 149

BEVERAGES
Beer 'Garitas, 57
Bloody Marys, 130
Cherry Bounce, 129
Hot Buttered Rum Batter, 115
Iced Cinnamon Coffee, 87
Magnolias, 73
Mary Powell's Cosmo, 107
Mint Julep, 79
Miss Duncan's Hot Apple Toddy, 63

BEVERAGES, PUNCH
Cheerwine Punch, 129
Coffee Punch, 21
Jean's Old Fashioned Milk Punch, 21
Rum Punch, 35

BEVERAGES, TEA
Margaret's Perfect Southern Sweet Tea, 29
Minted Iced Tea, 129
Minted Orange Iced Tea, 43
Salem College Iced Tea, 93

BISCUITS
Chaney's Herb Cheddar Biscuits, 74
Mama Jo's Man-Catcher Biscuits, 82
Sweet Potato Biscuits, 82

BLUEBERRIES
Betsy's Farm House Pie, 39
Blueberry Pancakes, 89
Blueberry Pudding, 181
Duck Breast Salad, 15
Fruit Salad with Honey Citrus Dressing, 73
Grace's Blueberry Tea Cakes, 83
Salad for All Seasons, 93

BREADS *See also Biscuits; Coffee Cakes*
Best Pie Crust, 19
Cheese Camellias, 131
Corn Light Bread, 119
Cranberry Orange Scones, 91
Evelyn's Spoon Bread, 173
Janie's Blueberry Muffins with Lemon Glaze, 89
Jill's Date Nut Bread, 24
Julia's Eggy Muffins, 75
June's Cornmeal Muffins, 52
Sour Cream Muffins, 18

White Bean Croustades with Pickled Red Onion, 49

BREAKFAST/BRUNCH
Anne's Eggs Bel Mar, 75
Apple Sausage Bake, 90
Blueberry Pancakes, 89

CAKES
Applesauce Cake, 119
Apple Walnut Cake, 105
Grace's Blueberry Tea Cakes, 83
Mary Elizabeth's Favorite Pound Cake with Buttercream Frosting, 47
Minnie's Caramel Cake, 185
Ocracoke Fig Cake with Buttermilk Glaze, 25
Orange Date Nut Cake, 186
Pear and Dried Cherry Frangipane Cake, 186
Pumpkin Roll, 127

CANDY
Billy's Family Fudge, 68
Mary Ruth's Candied Grapefruit Strips, 68
Old Fashioned Peanut Brittle, 177

CHEESECAKES
Kay's Rum Raisin Cheesecake with Myers's Rum Sauce, 33
Mark's Cheesecake, 187

CHERRIES
Big Kay's Holiday Fruit Bars, 175
Cherry Bounce, 129
Cherry Pecan Brie, 121
Cherry Sauce, 67
Pear and Dried Cherry Frangipane Cake, 186
Salad for All Seasons, 93
Susan's Rice Pudding Supreme with Cherry Sauce, 67

CHICKEN
Alexa's Simple Pasta with Basil, 94
Anne's Oven Fried Chicken, 59
Annette's Three Bean Chili, 157
Bateman Brunswick Stew, 156
Brunswick Stew Customized, 156
Chicken Chili, 157
Chicken Pot Pie, 94

Chicken Salad Tea Sandwiches, 23
Cold Lemon Chicken Salad, 143
Cindy's Barbecued Chicken, 161
Hot Chicken Salad, 160
Lou's New Old Fashioned Chicken Pastry, 160
Robin's Buffalo Wing Dip, 133
Sara's Chicken Salad Soufflé, 162
Sesame Chicken and Asparagus Salad, 159

CHOCOLATE
Best Brownies Ever, 69
Billy's Family Fudge, 68
Caramel Nut Fudgies, 61
Chocolate Seduction Pie, 183
Jenny's Hot Fudge Sauce, 68
Lady Margaret's Chocolate Mousse, 187
Thick Fudge Sauce, 183
White Chocolate Fresh Raspberry Miniature Tarts, 111

CLAMS
Jesse Boy Clam Chowder Down East, 142
Sarah's Down East Clam Chowder, 141

COFFEE CAKES
Coffee Cake, 91
Jill's Crumb Cake, 185

COLLARDS
Bo's Uptown Collards, 118
Southern Collards, 118

COOKIES
Best Brownies Ever, 69
Big Kay's Holiday Fruit Bars, 175
Caramel Nut Fudgies, 61
Cheese Cookies, 132
Fig Nut Roll Cookies, 53
Jeanne's Cornmeal Pecan Sandies, 97
Imogene's Date Nut Bar Cookies, 47
Marguerite's Brown Edge Cookies, 24
Mrs. Broughton's Russian Rocks, 177
Olzie's Sugar Cookies, 61
Scottish Shortbread, 77
Sour Lemon Bars, 111

188

INDEX

CORN
Anne's Edamame Salad, 45
Bateman Brunswick Stew, 156
Brunswick Stew Customized, 156
Corn and Basil Tart, 169
Corn Pudding, 32
Frances' Corn Dip, 133
Grilled Corn with Bacon and Vidalia Onion, 37
Julie's Summer Succotash, 51
King K Dip, 134
Marinated Vegetable Salad, 60

CRAB MEAT
Classic Crab Cakes, 31
Cream of Crab Soup, 142
Gert's Crab Cakes, 152
Julie's Crab Tarts, 110
Melissa's Hot Crab Spread, 137

CRANBERRIES
Cranberry Orange Scones, 91
Robin's Cranberry Salad, 124

CUCUMBERS
Cold Cucumber Soup, 101
Cucumber Cheese Dip, 109
Turkey, Brie and Cranberry-Apple Panini, 126

DATES
Black-Eyed Susan, 60
Imogene's Date Nut Bar Cookies, 47
Jill's Date Nut Bread, 24
Kathy's Kale Salad, 147
Manchego Stuffed Dates, 139
Orange Date Nut Cake, 186

DESSERTS *See also Cakes; Candy; Cheesecakes; Cookies; Ice Cream; Pies, Sweet; Puddings*
Angel Food Cake Dessert, 179
Charlie's Peach Cobbler, 77
Cold Strawberry Soufflé, 178
Grand Marnier Soufflé, 178

DIPS/SPREADS
Cathy's Shrimp Spread, 135
Charlie's Easy Guacamole, 35
Cherry Pecan Brie, 121
Cream Cheese and Olive Spread, 24
Cucumber Cheese Dip, 109
Curry Dip for Fresh Vegetables, 57
Frances' Corn Dip, 133
Hester's Sausage Dip, 139
Jalapeño Meat Dip, 134
Jalapeño Popper Dip, 135
Jessica's Bleu Cheese Soufflé, 168
King K Dip, 134
Linda's Shrimp Dip, 138
Marcia's Election Night Dip, 133
Martha's Vidalia Onion Soufflé, 168
Melissa's Hot Crab Spread, 137
Mushroom Spread, 132
Pimento Cheese, 60
Robin's Buffalo Wing Dip, 133
Zesty Pickled Shrimp, 138

DOVE
Dove and Sausage Gumbo, 43

DUCK
Duck Appetizer with Asian Sauce, 15
Duck Breast Salad, 15

FIGS
Fig Nut Roll Cookies, 53
Fresh Fig and Warm Goat Cheese Salad with Fig Vinaigrette, 104
Kay's Sweet Fig Pickles, 167
Ocracoke Fig Cake with Buttermilk Glaze, 25

FISH *See also Salmon*
Alicia's Macadamia Encrusted Grouper, 151
Anne's Baked Shad Exquisite, 17
Café Atlantic Baked Fish with Parmesan Crust, 31
Hatteras Rockfish Stew, 155
Lime Basil Grilled Trout Fillets with Alicia's Cantaloupe Garnish, 103
Roasted Red Snapper with Garlic Butter, 95
Sarah Ellen's Fish Stew, 154

FROSTINGS/GLAZES/ICINGS
Brown Sugar Boiled Icing, 119
Buttercream Frosting, 47
Buttermilk Glaze, 25
Caramel Icing, 185
Lemon Glaze, 89

FRUIT *See also Apples; Blueberries; Cherries; Cranberries; Dates; Figs; Grapefruit; Lemon; Orange; Peaches; Pineapple; Raspberries; Salads, Fruit; Strawberries; Watermelon*
Fruit Salad with Honey Citrus Dressing, 73
Lime Basil Grilled Trout Fillets with Alicia's Cantaloupe Garnish, 103
Southern Banana Pudding Parfait, 181

GRAPEFRUIT
Lou's Christmas Grapefruit Starter, 63
Mary Ruth's Candied Grapefruit Strips, 68

GROUND BEEF
Bateman Brunswick Stew, 156
Jalapeño Meat Dip, 134

HAM
Country Ham with Bourbon Cream Sauce, 82
Ham and Cheese Rolls, 59
Liz's Ham and Swiss Quiche, 81

ICE CREAM
Peach Ice Cream, 77
Peppermint Stick Ice Cream, 69

LAMB
Jill's Lamb and Butternut Squash Stew, 150

LEMON
Anne's Lemon Chess Pie, 19
Aunt Mary's Lemon Chess Tarts, 182
Lemon Curd, 179
Lemon Pie, 182
Lemony Ice Cream Pie, 19
Sour Lemon Bars, 111

MAIN DISHES
Alicia's Macadamia Encrusted Grouper, 151
Anne's Baked Shad Exquisite, 17
Anne's Oven Fried Chicken, 59
Apple Butter Pork Tenderloin, 117
Butterball Turkey with Giblet Gravy, 123
Café Atlantic Baked Fish with Parmesan Crust, 31
Chemistry Roast, 150
Classic Crab Cakes, 31
Cindy Barbecued Chicken, 161
Gert's Crab Cakes, 152
Ham and Cheese Rolls, 59
Hap's Cold Pork Tenderloin, 107
Hot Panned Oysters, 153
Joe's Barbecued Shrimp, 38
Lime Basil Grilled Trout Fillets with Alicia's Cantaloupe Garnish, 103
Perfect Ribs, 46
Pork Tenderloin with Glazed Onions, 151
Roasted Beef Tenderloin, 66
Salmon in Ginger Sauce, 17
Sara's Chicken Salad Soufflé, 162
Shrimp with Rémoulade Sauce, 107
Steak Diane, 149
Tony's Shrimp Creole, 38

MAIN DISHES, MEATLESS
Cheese Pastry Casserole, 163
Helen's Egg and Mushroom Casserole, 163

MUSHROOMS
Helen's Egg and Mushroom Casserole, 163
Melissa's Wild Mushroom and Onion Tartlets, 110
Mushroom Spread, 132

OLIVE
Cream Cheese and Olive Spread, 24
Remember Me Olive Puffs, 109

ONIONS
Anne's Edamame Salad, 45
Brunswick Stew Customized, 156
Grilled Corn with Bacon and Vidalia Onion, 37
Martha's Vidalia Onion Soufflé, 168
Melissa's Wild Mushroom and Onion Tartlets, 110
Multigrain Bread, Onion, Pecan and Golden Raisin Stuffing, 124
Pork Tenderloin with Glazed Onions, 151
Sarah Ellen's Fish Stew, 154
White Bean Croustades with Pickled Red Onion, 49

ORANGE
Cranberry Orange Scones, 91
Duck Breast Salad, 15
Fruit Salad with Honey Citrus Dressing, 73
Minted Iced Tea, 129
Minted Orange Iced Tea, 43
Orange Braised Carrots and Parsnips, 95
Orange Date Nut Cake, 186

OYSTERS
Hot Panned Oysters, 153
Kay's Oyster Stew, 63
Thanksgiving Oysters, 121
Those Oysters Dick Fixes, 137

PASTA
Alexa's Simple Pasta with Basil, 94
Sesame Chicken and Asparagus Salad, 159
Vodka Shrimp, 155

PEACHES
Carol's Peach and Brie Quesadillas with Lime, Honey Dipping Sauce, 109
Charlie's Peach Cobbler, 77
Peach Ice Cream, 77

PEAS
Cold Curried Rice with English Peas, 18
Day Ahead Green Salad, 143
Garden Club Sugar Snap Pea Salad, 52
Marinated Vegetable Salad, 60

PIES, SAVORY
Betty Anne's Seafood Quiche, 153
Cathy's Tomato Pie, 81
Chicken Pot Pie, 94
Corn and Basil Tart, 169
Julie's Crab Tarts, 110
Liz's Ham and Swiss Quiche, 81
Melissa's Wild Mushroom and Onion Tartlets, 110

INDEX

PIES, SWEET
Alma's Vinegar Pie, 32
Anne's Lemon Chess Pie, 19
Aunt Mary's Lemon Chess Tarts, 182
Balentine's Buttermilk Pie, 53
Betsy's Farm House Pie, 39
Chocolate Seduction Pie, 183
Jim's Bourbon Pecan Pie, 127
Lemon Pie, 182
Lemony Ice Cream Pie, 19
Mary's Apple Chess Pie, 105
Peanut Butter Pie, 183
Sandra's Strawberry Pie, 39
White Chocolate Fresh Raspberry Miniature Tarts, 111

PINEAPPLE
Big Kay's Holiday Fruit Bars, 175
Ruth's Baked Pineapple, 167

PORK See also Bacon; Ham; Sausage
Apple Butter Pork Tenderloin, 117
Hap's Cold Pork Tenderloin, 107
Perfect Ribs, 46
Pork Tenderloin with Glazed Onions, 151

POTATOES
Bateman Brunswick Stew, 156
Flo's Stuffed Potatoes, 169
Grilled Potato Salad, 45
Holiday Mashed Potatoes, 66
Sarah Ellen's Fish Stew, 154
Vichyssoise, 101

PUDDINGS
Blueberry Pudding, 181
Lady Margaret's Chocolate Mousse, 187
Old Salem Moravian Sugar Cake Bread Pudding, 97
Southern Banana Pudding Parfait, 181
Susan's Rice Pudding Supreme with Cherry Sauce, 67

QUAIL
Quail, 162

RASPBERRIES
Betsy's Farm House Pie, 39

Fruit Salad with Honey Citrus Dressing, 73
White Chocolate Fresh Raspberry Miniature Tarts, 111

SALAD DRESSINGS
Bleu Cheese Salad Dressing, 144
Fig Vinaigrette, 104
Fruit Salad Dressing, 87
Ginger Salad Dressing, 145
Honey Citrus Dressing, 73
White Balsamic Vinaigrette, 145

SALADS, FRUIT
Arugula and Watermelon Salad, 145
Fruit Salad with Honey Citrus Dressing, 73
Robin's Cranberry Salad, 124
Salad for All Seasons, 93

SALADS, MAIN DISH
Cold Lemon Chicken Salad, 143
Curried Salmon Salad, 17
Duck Breast Salad, 15
Hot Chicken Salad, 160
Sesame Chicken and Asparagus Salad, 159

SALADS, PASTA
Turkey Ranch Pasta Salad, 126

SALADS, VEGETABLE
Anne's Edamame Salad, 45
Bertie's Bleu Cheese Coleslaw, 37
Day Ahead Green Salad, 143
Garden Club Sugar Snap Pea Salad, 52
Grilled Potato Salad, 45
Hearts of Palm, Artichoke and Belgian Endive Salad, 79
Kathy's Kale Salad, 147
Marge's German Slaw, 173
Marinated Vegetable Salad, 60
Roasted Beet Salad, 51
Til's Corn Bread Salad, 147
Wedge Salad, 144

SALMON
Curried Salmon Salad, 17
Salmon in Ginger Sauce, 17

SANDWICHES
Chicken Salad Tea Sandwiches, 23
Cream Cheese and Olive Spread, 24

Egg Salad Tea Sandwiches, 23
Tomato Basil Tea Sandwiches, 23
Turkey, Brie and Cranberry, Apple Panini, 126

SAUCES, SAVORY
Asian Sauce, 15
Bourbon Cream Sauce, 82
Garlic Butter, 95
Giblet Gravy, 123
Horseradish Cream Sauce, 66
Jim Bane Sauce, 46
Tomato Sauce, 172

SAUCES, SWEET
Cherry Sauce, 67
Jenny's Hot Fudge Sauce, 68
Lime Honey Dipping Sauce, 109
Thick Fudge Sauce, 183

SAUSAGE
Apple Sausage Bake, 90
Bateman Brunswick Stew, 156
Dove and Sausage Gumbo, 43
Hester's Sausage Dip, 139
Jalapeño Meat Dip, 134
Neese's Sausage Pinwheels, 115

SEAFOOD See also Clams; Crab Meat; Fish; Oysters; Shrimp
Edwina's Scallop Skewers, 137

SHRIMP
Alexa's Simple Pasta with Basil, 94
Betty Anne's Seafood Quiche, 153
Cathy's Shrimp Spread, 135
Joe's Barbecued Shrimp, 38
Linda's Shrimp Dip, 138
Martha's Pickled Shrimp, 31
Shrimp and Grits à la Edwina, 154
Shrimp with Rémoulade Sauce, 107
Tony's Shrimp Creole, 38
Vodka Shrimp, 155
Zesty Pickled Shrimp, 138

SIDE DISHES See also Accompaniments
Cold Curried Rice with English Peas, 18
Multigrain Bread, Onion, Pecan and Golden Raisin Stuffing, 124
Ruth's Baked Pineapple, 167
Thanksgiving Oysters, 121

SOUPS, COLD
Cold Cucumber Soup, 101
Hatteras Rockfish Stew, 155
Vichyssoise, 101
Watermelon Gazpacho, 29

SOUPS/STEWS
Annette's Three Bean Chili, 157
Asparagus Soup, 141
Bateman Brunswick Stew, 156
Beef Stew, 149
Brunswick Stew Customized, 156
Chicken Chili, 157
Cream of Crab Soup, 142
Cream of Fresh Tomato Soup, 49
Dove and Sausage Gumbo, 43
Hot Apple Soup, 115
Jesse Boy Clam Chowder Down East, 142
Jill's Lamb and Butternut Squash Stew, 150
Kay's Oyster Stew, 63
Lou's New Old Fashioned Chicken Pastry, 160
Sarah Ellen's Fish Stew, 154
Sarah's Down East Clam Chowder, 141

SQUASH
Jill's Butternut Squash with Pecans and Bleu Cheese, 65
Jill's Lamb and Butternut Squash Stew, 150
Julie's Summer Succotash, 51
Zucchini Rounds with Tomato Sauce, 172

STRAWBERRIES
Betsy's Farm House Pie, 39
Cold Strawberry Soufflé, 178
Fruit Salad with Honey-Citrus Dressing, 73
Sandra's Strawberry Pie, 39

SWEET POTATOES
Jill's Mashed Sweet Potatoes with Apple Streusel, 171
Stag's Sweet Potato Pudding, 171
Sweet Potato Balls, 173
Sweet Potato Biscuits, 82
Sweet Potato Casserole, 125

TOMATOES
Anne's Edamame Salad, 45
Bateman Brunswick Stew, 156
Brunswick Stew Customized, 156
Cathy's Tomato Pie, 81

Cream of Fresh Tomato Soup, 49
Frances' Green Tomato Pickle Relish, 74
Jalapeño Meat Dip, 134
Julie's Summer Succotash, 51
Tomato Basil Tea Sandwiches, 23
Watermelon Gazpacho, 29

TURKEY
Butterball Turkey with Giblet Gravy, 123
Turkey, Brie and Cranberry, Apple Panini, 126
Turkey Ranch Pasta Salad, 126

VEGETABLES See also Artichokes; Asparagus; Corn; Cucumbers; Mushrooms; Onions; Peas; Potatoes; Salads, Vegetable; Squash; Sweet Potatoes; Tomatoes
Brussels Sprouts with Bacon, 103
Jennie's Eggplant Appetizer, 134
Orange Braised Carrots and Parsnips, 95
Roasted Broccoli with Parmesan Cheese, 125
Spinach Supreme, 172
Stuffed Celery, 138

WATERMELON
Arugula and Watermelon Salad, 145
Watermelon Gazpacho, 29

COOKBOOK CONTRIBUTORS

Anna Akins
Alicia Alford
Anne Allen
Annette Anderson
Sarah Ellen W. Archie
Dena Aretakis-Horn
Michael Ausbon
Kay Baldridge
Johnny Balentine
Margaret Barclay
Joseph Barnes
Katherine Beery
Michael Bertics
Dorothea Bitler
Derry Blackwell
Neal Blinken
Lynda Blount
Karen Boone
Mattie Moye Bridgers
Lynn Brower
Jane Brown
Senator Jim Broyhill
Louise Broyhill
Michael Bryan*
James Lee Burney
Maurice M. Bursey
Butterball LLC
Cathryn Carlisle
Dawn Carter
Rick Carter
Janet Chesson
Rosemary Chiariello
Sylvia Johnson Churchwell
Nicole Connolly
Elizabeth Cook
Bet Isabell Cooper
Morgan Corbett
Sally Long Pierce Corpening
Barbara Bitler Coughlin
Deborah Cox
Evelyn Cox
Betty Crisp
Pam Critoria
Liz Crute*
Carol Dabbs
Anne Daniel
Julia Daniels

Marion Dees
Sarah Downing
Chuck Duncan*
Rufus Edmisten
Juanita Efird
Sandra Elam
Robert Elder
Anne Ellis
Julie Ewing
Hughlene Frank
Grace Fishel
Anne Flowers
Wortley Forbes
Bob Franks
Michael E. Gery
Julie Gilbert
Diane Godbold
Jim Graham
Linda Graves
Sara T. Graves
Kathy Greeley
Myra Greene*
Marcia Griffin
Carol Grossi*
Neil Gustafson
Sharon Gustafson
Debbie Haile
Caroline Haley
Charlotte Harris
Edna Harvey
Karen Hatcher
Anna Hathaway
Jennie Jarrell Hayman
Til Herring
Margaret B. Hill
Patricia Hines
Cindy Hobbs
Karen Hodgin
Pat Holder
Imogene Holmes
Nancy Walker House
Charles Hudson
Jane Worley Hunt
Betsy Hutchinson
Elizabeth Sue Hyde
Ann B. Jennings
James Jennings
Louise Johanson

Betsy Joyner
Luann Joyner*
Chancy Kapp
Betty Minton Kapp
Katherine Keinbach
Sally Brooks Pullen Kelly
Dave Kempf
Mary Kepley
Nan Kester
Hester Anne Kidd
Jean Kilgore
Betsy King
Ginny Kirkland*
Frances Kunstling
Diane Land
Mark Langford*
Sydney Langford*
Judy Beck Lasseigne
Dick Leach
Katirie Leach
Rebecca Warren Leary
Karen Lee
Katherine Leinbach
Betty Anne Lennon*
Donna Levy
Curtis Lewis
Lucinda Lucas
Judy Mann*
Nancy Marlowe
Mae Marshall
Martha Marshall*
Carolyn McCall
Betsy McDonald
Hal McKinney
Dale McVickers
Tommy McVickers
Kathryn Meares
Ann H. Milan
Ann Milam
Georgia B. Mixon
Susan Moffat Thomas
Patti Mordecai
Perry Morrison
Sydney Langford*
Jill Moye*
Tish Murray
Katie Kapp Muto
Rene Myers

Greg Nathan
Andrea Neese
Nancy Nelson
Carol Newcomb
Bill Nicholson
Anne Osborne
Kathy Oschwald
Betty Parker*
Chuck Parker*
Sara Jane Pate
Anne Peden
Laura Pendleton
Cheryl W. Perry
Sandra Peyser
Jane Pfister
Kay Phillips
Tricia Phoenix*
Brenda Pollard
Jon Powell
Sydnor Presnell
Penny Prichard
Wren Rehm
Judith H. Rhodes
Evelyn Horton Rickert
Alice Risko
Jeanne Robbins
Bert Rosefield
Donna Rosefield
Ted Sain
Jill Santa Lucia
Kay Schoellhorn*
John B. Scott, Jr.
Pat Sevier
Lois Sharpe
Edwina Hardy Shaw*
Charlie Silver*
Dena Silver
Maiya Silver*
Ann C. Sloan
Cindy Smith
Cindy Turner Smith
Kay Snow
Eleanor Cox Sojka
Melanie Soles
Debbie Souza*
Catherine Spangler
Beth Steed*
Margaret Steed*

Sarah J. Strange
Janet Stenersen
George Stevenson*
Jean Olive Stubbs
Caitlin Nugent
The Tavern in Old Salem
Carol Taylor
Lianda Taylor*
Melissa Tillman
Ruth Toth
Sunburst Trout
Lyn Lewis Troxler
Jo Anna Tudor
Ann Turlington
Alda Minton Turner
Martha Underwood
Angela Urquhart
Jane Van Hoven
Patti Vargas*
Nancy Vassey
Joan Vess*
Laura Anne Vick
Anne Wagoner
Jessica Wahler
Cathy Ward*
Bethany Weathersby
Lee Webster
James Weld
Florence B. Werden
Mary Powell White
Mal Whitmore*
Mary Lillie Talton Wilkins
Peggy Wilson
Charles Winston
Jenny Winston
Flo Winston*
Janie S. Wood
Sarah Woodard
Joe Ann Wright
Mary Brent Wright
Kakie Yelverton
Robin Zevenhuizen*

*Served on Testing Committee.

NORTH CAROLINA
An Appetizing State

menus | recipes | traditions

©2014 by North Carolina Museum of History Associates, Inc.
5 East Edenton Street
Raleigh, North Carolina 27601

Published by

Favorite Recipes® Press

An imprint of

SOUTHWESTERN Publishing Group

Post Office Box 305142
Nashville, Tennessee 37230
1-800-358-0560

This cookbook is a collection of favorite recipes, which are not necessarily original recipes. All rights reserved. No part of this publication may be reproduced in any form or by any means, electronic or mechanical, including photocopying and recording, or by any information storage or retrieval systems, without prior written permission from the North Carolina Museum of History Associates, Inc.

Library of Congress Control Number: 2014954887

ISBN: 978-0-87197-634-5

Executive Editor: Billy Wilson
Editorial Director: Mary Cummings
Book Design: Sheri Ferguson Swisher

Manufactured in the United States of America
First Printing: 2014   5,000 copies

ACKNOWLEDGMENTS

Foreword: Van Eure

Region Photography: Emily Chaplin
Introduction and Region Copy: Warren Bingham
Introduction and Region Copy Editing:
    Frances Kunstling

Artifact Caption Copy: Megan Lybrand
Artifact Caption Copy Editing: Stephen Evans
Editing Assistant: Anna Capel

Recipe Coordination: Anne Lennon
Recipe and Menu Coordination: Carol Grossi
Recipe Editing: Mary Cummings

Food Photography: Tony Pearce
Food Photography Retouching: Natalia Weedy
Food Photography Food Stylist: Jill Santa Lucia
Food Photography Prop Stylist: Billy Wilson

Map: State Archives of North Carolina
    The map of North Carolina is from Sidney E. Morse,
    A New Universal Atlas of the World, engraved by
    Nathaniel and Simeon S. Jocelyn in 1825.
Illustrations: ClipArtETC, Florida Center for
    Instructional Technology

Page 2: John Wheeler House, Murfreesboro
    (murfreesboronc.org/wheeler)
Page 12: Chicamacomico Life-Saving Station, Rodanthe
    (www.chicamacomico.net)
Page 26: Tryon Palace, New Bern (tryonpalace.org)
Page 40: Roadside Stands and Farmers Markets
    (ncfarmfresh.com)
Page 54: State Capitol, Raleigh
    (nchistoricsites.org/capitol)
Page 70: Sandhills Horticultural Gardens, Pinehurst
    (sandhillshorticulturalgardens.com)
Page 84: Vineyards and Winery's (www.ncwine.org)
Page 98: Winkler Bakery at Old Salem Museums and
    Gardens, Winston-Salem (www.oldsalem.org)
Page 112: Biltmore House, Asheville
    (www.biltmore.com)

Cover Painting : "Tea Time" by Mike Hoyt